cier

b

END

QUEL'THALAS

Silvermoon

The Plaguelands

LORDAERON

ROM

Ironforge

KHAZ MODAN

Stormwind

The
Broken Isles

Hiji

AZEROTH

WARCRAFT

THE ROLEPLAYING GAME

SWORD & SORCERY

Check out upcoming Sword and Sorcery Studio products online at:

http://www.swordsorcery.com

Distributed for Sword and Sorcery Studio by White Wolf Publishing, Inc.

Credits

Authors:

Christopher Aylott, Zach Bush, Jeff Grubb, Luke Johnson, Seth Johnson, Mur Lafferty, and Greg Netcher

Creative and Rules Design Assistance and Additional Material:

Chris Metzen and Bob Fitch

Developer:

E. Deirdre Brooks with Andrew Bates

Editor:

Mike Johnstone

Managing Editor:

Andrew Bates

Art Director:

Richard Thomas

Layout and Typesetting:

Ron Thompson

Cover Artist:

Samwise Didier

Interior Artists:

Ted Beargeon, David Berggren, Samwise Didier, David Griffiths, Jeff Holt, Roman Kenney, Chris Metzen, Bill Petras, Richard Thomas and Ru Weerasuriya

Front & Back Cover Design:

Ron Thompson

Special Thanks

To the dynamic duo at Blizzard Entertainment: Chris Metzen and Bob Fitch deserve an extra round of thanks in addition to the credits above. They were a *huge* help every single step of the way and did it all with humor and enthusiasm.

To the other incredible people at Blizzard Entertainment who gave us an amazing level of assistance and support at every turn: Paul Sams, Elaine Di Iorio, Neal Hubbard, and Lisa Bucek.

To the folks at Wizards of the Coast who started the ball rolling: James Jacobs, Paul Peterson, Cindi Rice, Lezlie Samuel, Mike Selinker, and Anthony Valterra.

To those fans who never get tired of clicking on units, and to those fans who never get tired of confirming that crit!

Contents

Tables

The two armies collided in the waning light of a dying sun. From her vantage point at the forest's edge, Oakwidow knelt, gripping her bow. She had spent most of the afternoon watching the two armies gather and form up along the edges of the shallow valley. Now, beneath a red and heavy sun low on the horizon, they finally surged forward.

How easy it was, the night elf thought, for a conflagration to light from a single spark. A fragment of a rumor: a gold strike could be found within this wasted valley. Alliance and Horde adventurers rushed in, each eager to claim the place for their people, only to stumble across one another. Then they stood back as nature took its course — distrust turning rivals into bitter enemies, small bands into organized armies, and a deserted vale into a battlefield.

From her right came the orcs, thick-shouldered grunt soldiers surging down the valley wall like a green-fleshed tide. They swirled around great shamans who drew magical energies into themselves to shape bolts of power. Bull-headed tauren snorted and bellowed, towering among the shorter orcs. Mighty kodo beasts lumbered forward, drooling and lowing, while from their backs orcs thundered on their oversized war drums, driving the other warriors of the Horde into a frenzy of battle lust.

On Oakwidow's left, the humans surged forward to meet the orcs, the sunset gleaming off their armor like blood. The swordsmen slogged forward through the dry grass while a great battle shout leapt from their lips. Armored knights astride powerful destriers led the assault, and behind them came a rabble of peasants armed with whatever tools could be turned into serviceable weapons. Behind all, Alliance sorceresses ripped the air with waves of magical power. Finally, there, just cresting the hill to the rear, clattering siege engines chugged forward in a fog of foul black mist.

Three weeks previous, neither side cared anything for this dry, windswept valley. Now both human Alliance and orc Horde were willing to die for this land. Their previous union during the Battle of Mount Hyjal meant nothing here as the armies hurled themselves down the slopes.

Oakwidow allowed herself a humorless smile, the grin tugging at the scar that ran from her forehead over a now-empty eye socket and down her cheek. These groups' rivalries were deep pools indeed, so very easily brought to a boil. Even now they would seize the last rays of the day to battle one another rather than suffer a single night with enemies in close proximity.

The two armies slammed against one other in waves of steel and green flesh. The ground shook from the impact of their blows. The cries of battle became shouts of pain as sword bit into flesh, as mace crushed bone, and as eldritch spell energy flensed the living skin from its targets.

An explosion erupted from the rear of the Alliance army's ranks as one of the siege engines fell to enemy spellcasting. Shards of hot metal rained down, and the surrounding forces responded with screams of pain and cries of dismay.

Screams now from the orc side as well — a shaman's bodyguard was stripped away, and waves of arrows streaked at the shaman like a hundred deadly insects. Bristling like thistledown, the spellcaster pitched forward and was lost to view.

Back in the valley center, the neat battle lines degenerated into a myriad of deadly melees. A tauren warrior unhorsed a mounted knight. A wedge of armed peasants followed a paladin warrior as he drove deeply into the Horde, only to disappear screaming beneath a wave of green muscle and bloodied swords. Along the top of the Alliance's ridgeline, dull, flat thunderings told Oakwidow that dwarven mortars were in position. Confusion and death fell upon the orc forces. Maddened by the smoke, noise, and pain, one of the kodo beasts went berserk, drums and drummer falling beneath its heavy gallop as it left a path of smashed allies and enemies to flee the field of battle.

Oakwidow watched with her one good eye as Alliance and Horde ripped at one another. The night elves cared little enough for mining gold, but they did not avoid this vale due to lack of interest. A great demon was felled here. Its corruption left an abiding taint, stirring thoughts of bloodlust in any who entered the valley.

Oakwidow had warned of this. Her people were ostensibly aligned with the humans. Yet the young race was brash and did not listen to wisdom. Now, they clashed with the orcs in an orgy of violence.

Two of the combatants, each bloodied by earlier fights, fought dangerously near the night elf's vantage point. The human had lost his helmet and crimson was smeared across his forehead. A dark river ran thick from a shoulder wound down the green flesh of the orc's arm. Human and orc spun, locked blade, parted, charged at each other again. The human brought his longsword in a wide sweep, and the orc blocked it with the thick, notched haft of his axe. In response, the orc lunged with a heavy overhand chop, which the human beat aside with a powerful blow of his own blade.

The two were locked in a deadly dance, exchanging a battery of blows, then retreating again. Once, twice, three times, each time weakening the other but expending energy as well. Though death stalked the shallow vale around them, this battle seemed a draw.

Then they noticed Oakwidow. First the orc shot her a glance, his thick forehead drawn in puzzlement. The human caught the look and spared a moment to see what drew his foe's gaze.

The smile faded from Oakwidow's face. She rose to her feet at the edge of the forest, bow still in hand. She was the only unwounded thing on the battlefield and as such was immediately suspect.

...human offering a grim nod as they came to an unspoken, silent agreement. Battle cries burst from their throats as they leapt toward the night elf.

Although the orc was more muscular, even clad in plates of hammered steel the human was faster. Oakwidow concentrated on him first. She touched an amulet, and vines and roots erupted around the human in a thick tangle. The human cursed as the undergrowth clutched at him, making each step more difficult than the last. Oakwidow turned her attention to the orc, though she would not forget the human. The man was delayed, but he was not yet out of the fight.

The orc found caution, turning his charge to a flanking maneuver. Oakwidow smiled; the orc had played to her strengths. With a short prayer to Elune, the moon goddess, Oakwidow raised her bow and loosed an arrow, then a second and a third. The prayer empowered each shot, and the arrows burst into flame in a series of miniature fireballs. Cursing, the orc lunged to one side. The first arrow streaked past him in a trail of acrid smoke, but the second and third found their mark. The orc warrior howled as the mystic flame, blessed by the moon goddess herself, spread over his form as if he were coated with oil. Dropping his axe and beating his arms wildly in a vain attempt to still the blaze, the orc fell just moments later. The sharp stench of burning meat joined the tang of spent gunpowder and steam that hung over the battlefield.

The human was still cursing and surging against the tangling undergrowth, undeterred by the orc's death. Oakwidow nodded toward him in respect, making no move to finish him. She could feel the seductive whisper of the demon bloodlust, but she would not be its victim. Night elves were made of sterner stuff.

She glanced beyond the vine-held human toward the shallow vale. The sun was all but gone, a mere sliver of blood against a darkening sky. Smoke rose from numerous locations, and cries of pain declared that the battle was over for many. Still, the sound of steel against steel rang from the growing shadows, announcing that the fight was not yet finished for all.

With a slight bow to the struggling human, Oakwidow stepped back into the darkened foliage. In an instant, she was gone, melded with the shadows. When the soldier finally fought his way free and rushed to the edge of the woods, all he found was the faint sound of Oakwidow's mocking laughter on the wind.

Welcome to the world of the **Dungeons & Dragons Warcraft Roleplaying Game**!

This is a world in which feral night elf priestesses ride great cats into battle, in which dwarves carry rifles capable of piercing dragon hide, in which orcs wield ancient and potent shamanistic powers, and in which humans battle with sword and spell to keep the world safe from demonic and undead forces.

It is a world whose history is built upon conflict and endless struggle, a world ravaged by invasion from demonic forces known as the Burning Legion. The demons were defeated, but not without great cost. Now, in the aftermath of this apocalypse, races and nations struggle to rebuild and the current peace could shatter into violence at any moment.

It is a world in which heroes can win glory against implacable foes and drive back the darkness!

What is the Warcraft RPG?

If you are reading this, you have probably either played the great *Warcraft* real-time strategy computer game series or a pen-and-paper fantasy roleplaying game — or perhaps even both. Here's the lowdown on just what the **Warcraft RPG** means to you:

If you play pen-and-paper fantasy roleplaying games but have never played the *Warcraft* real-time strategy games… you're ready to go! In this book, you will find rules for playing d20 campaigns set in the world of the best-selling *Warcraft* real-time strategy computer games. Source material includes new races, character classes, feats, spells, technology, and a whole lot more that you can add to your fantasy campaign.

If you play the *Warcraft* real-time strategy games but are new to traditional pen-and-paper roleplaying games… this book translates the RTS experience into an interactive roleplaying situation. The **Warcraft RPG** is based upon Blizzard's popular computer game series, but you make up your own heroes and the quests they go on!

The only complication is as the cover says: "Requires the use of the *Dungeons & Dragons Player's Handbook*, Edition 3.5, published by Wizards of the Coast." The *PHB* has the details on rolling dice, how your character grows in power, what this whole roleplaying thing is about, and so on. This book builds upon those core rules. So, if you are even a little familiar with the d20 System, you will do just fine. If not, get a copy of the *PHB* and you'll be up to speed in no time.

If you play pen-and-paper fantasy roleplaying games *and* the *Warcraft* real-time strategy games… then what are you waiting for? Get your pen-and-paper gaming group together and start a new campaign set in the **Warcraft** universe or integrate a **Warcraft** character into your existing game.

What's in this Book?

After you skip past this introduction, you will find all sorts of exciting details you can use to create a **Warcraft** hero or an entire campaign. Here's a run down by chapter:

Chapter One: A World at War gives you a brief history of the **Warcraft RPG** world and a general idea of what the place is like now so that you are ready for the rest of the book.

Chapter Two: Heroes is the largest — and meatiest — part of the book. It details the wide range of character races that you can play in the **Warcraft RPG**, along with new core classes and prestige classes, and the skills and feats available to them all.

Chapter Three: Adventuring discusses other details important to your character, from his affiliation to faiths to new equipment (including firearms!).

Chapter Four: Magic describes what magic is like in the **Warcraft** setting and includes a host of new spells for use in your d20 campaign.

Chapter Five: The World of Warcraft takes you on a tour of Kalimdor, the wild new continent that the various races are in the midst of exploring and colonizing, with additional information on the rest of the world of Azeroth.

Chapter Six: Campaigning wraps things up with advice for players and Game Masters on how to run games in the **Warcraft** campaign setting.

More Warcraft!

The **Dungeons & Dragons Warcraft Roleplaying Game** is the first in a series of sourcebooks for the **Warcraft** campaign setting. The upcoming **Manual of Monsters** covers the creatures that populate the world of Azeroth — and the things that lurk in the darkness beyond. **Alliance & Horde Compendium** builds further on what you find in this book, including more character races, prestige classes, and even rules on **Warcraft** technology and mass combat. And that's just the beginning!

The Warcraft RPG and Other Worlds

Although this book is intended to help you run a d20 campaign set in the world of the popular *Warcraft* computer games, there is no reason why you can't use some or even all of this material in a campaign set in another game world. Certain races, prestige classes, or spells might strike your fancy, and you can certainly make them available to your players. Every effort has been made to keep the rules compatible and balanced with the revised 3rd Edition rules.

One consideration to keep in mind, though, is that certain things in this book have similar names as to what you might find in the *PHB* — classes such as the elven ranger or the druid of the wild, or the Azeroth version of orcs, goblins, harpies, and centaurs. If you choose to incorporate these elements into your existing game, you must decide whether they replace similar existing versions. If you decide to have *both* versions in your game, you should track each carefully or change the name of one or the other to avoid confusion.

Ultimately, how you use the information in this book is entirely up to you. The **Warcraft RPG** is *your* game!

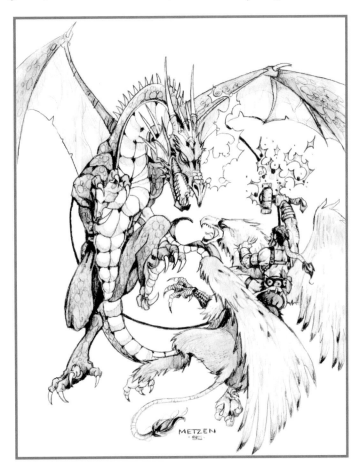

Gennet had been fleeing through the night, a headlong rush through the moon-dark forest. Branches tore at him, roots tripped him, and his face and bare arms were lacerated by scratches and deadened by bruises. Twice he stopped, out of breath, his chest heaving in pain, convinced he could run no further. Yet what lay behind him outweighed any peril that might lie ahead. He pressed on through dark woods.

His bedroll and jacket were lost in his flight, along with his longsword and rations. His shirt and pants were torn and ragged, and his boots were tearing away at the seams. His only weapon was a long knife that swung from his belt as he ran.

Gennet spotted a light ahead, a hint of red flickering through the undergrowth. Steering by that distant warmth, he found the underbrush diminishing and then disappearing entirely into low rolling hillocks covered by moss and ferns. The trees thinned as well, and at last Gennet stepped into a clearing, a small plaza at the base of what was once some ancient temple to a forgotten god. Though heartened by the light, Gennet was cautious. He had no idea who had built the fire and whether they were friendly to humans or to strangers in general. He was not, however, prepared for the beings he saw gathered in the firelight.

They were a motley group, a veritable menagerie of thinking beings. A hulking, great-horned tauren sprawled on one of the rune-carved blocks of the temple. The massive creature raised himself on one elbow to regard the new arrival. Two elves, one blonde and fair, the other with purplish flesh that seemed to blend into the darkness, broke off a heated conversation and likewise stared at Gennet. A wiry, green-skinned goblin tending the fire raised his eyebrows at the sight of the tattered visitor at the edge of the firelight. Lastly, a dwarf reclining across from the elves gave Gennet a nod while placing his hand on the long rifle resting in the grass nearby.

The goblin looked at the others and spoke a few words, too low for Gennet to hear from across the plaza. Then the short humanoid ambled forward.

"Hey, human. What'choo you doin' way out 'ere?" the goblin asked, presenting both palms upward, showing itself weaponless. Gennet glanced at the others, noting that the dwarf held his rifle with practiced nonchalance.

"I am a traveler," Gennet stammered. "No, a caravan guard, really. Five wagons, five drivers, ten guards. We were attacked by demons. I think they were demons. Big, winged beasts with red skin and flaming eyes. They were...." He gestured back at the darkness — how far had he fled? "They were back there a ways."

The goblin nodded. "Demons, sure. Lots around 'ere — left over from Kil'jaeden and Sargeras and all da rest. Bad times, y'know? Ain't safe t'be alone. You hate 'em, right? Fight the demons if ya could?"

Gennet thought of his allies, locked in combat with the creatures as he fled. His face felt hot with embarrassment, but he said, "I hate the demonspawn, yes."

The goblin nodded again, regarding him with small, bright eyes. "Me an' my friends, 'ere, we fight 'em. When we gotta. We dig 'round the dark places for dere treasure, too; secrets, power, alls dat. I'm da leader — don't serve nobody, but I speak for all da rest of 'em. So, what'cha think? Wanna join up?"

Gennet regarded the group again and for the first time considered his situation — alone, lost, lacking supplies, and practically weaponless. A great cat snarled, distressingly near in the surrounding darkness.

Gennet returned his attention to the goblin. "I would be honored to join you." He spoke loud enough for the others at the campfire to hear.

"Great! Always good t' have anudder set o' hands t' help out," the goblin said with a huge grin. The dwarf set his weapon aside as casually as he had picked it up, the tauren sprawled back on the great altar stone, and the elves resumed their conversation, nattering on in tones that suggested it was a long-running argument.

A rustle came from one side of the plaza. An orc stumbled forth, his thick arms piled high with firewood. At the sight of Gennet, his eyes grew fierce, his brow lowered, and his fanged lower jaw jutted out in a challenge.

"Hey! This fella's agreed to join up wit' us," the goblin announced.

"Yeah?" the orc growled in a voice like a rockslide. His small dark eyes took Gennet's measure. "Good. Let him get the firewood next time."

CHAPTER ONE:
A WORLD AT WAR

Azeroth, the world in which the **Warcraft** campaign setting is set, has been beset by conflict for countless ages. Years of strife have torn through the fabric of society. From afar came terrifying demons with dark agendas. Though defeated, their legacy lingers on in the shattered ruins of ancient civilizations and the wary survivors who struggle to build a future.

In this time of conflict, heroes — your characters — are needed to lead their people to a brighter tomorrow and to battle those who would deny this destiny.

History of the World

Life on Azeroth is nasty, brutish, and short. Yet the world was not always torn by war and scarred by conflict. There was a time in which the world teemed with life and vitality. People lived in peace and balance with their surroundings, and wondrous magical beasts roamed the wilds and skies uncontested. It was a time before the arrival of the Burning Legion.

Ten thousand years before the orcs and humans clashed in their First War, the world of Azeroth had only one massive continent — surrounded by the infinite, raging seas. That landmass was home to a number of disparate races and creatures, all vying for survival among the savage elements of the waking world. At the continent's center was a mysterious lake of incandescent energies. The lake, which would later be called the Well of Eternity, was the true heart of the world's magic and natural power. Drawing its energies from the infinite Great Dark Beyond, the Well acted as a mystical fount, sending its potent energies across the world to nourish life in all its wondrous forms.

The shimmering power drew the greatest tribe in the land, a race called the Kaldorei. These ancient people named the great land Kalimdor and settled near the vortex of cosmic energy. After several ages spent in peace and learning, the Kaldorei grew in power and wisdom so that they soon outstripped the other humanoid races of Azeroth.

The Well of Eternity was key to the Kaldorei's advancement. This connection did not come without a price, ultimately both beneficial and malevolent. In studying the Well's energies, the Kaldorei were infused with its power, becoming immortal and gleaning mastery over the creatures of the land. In time, they learned to manipulate the powerful energies directly. Thus did the study of arcane magic begin.

Some Kaldorei believed that abusing the Well's arcane energies could only lead to ill, but their words of caution were ignored as their brethren flew headlong into the study of magic. Their greatest wizards and sorcerers built beautiful cities, crafted amazing magical devices, and reshaped their world to better suit their needs. One of the greatest of their sorcerers was Azshara, a gifted woman who seemed to know more about magic than anyone alive even though she never studied a single treatise on the subject — as if she understood magic at its most primal level. Before long, Azshara was crowned the Sorceress-Queen of Kalimdor. She gathered about her the Highborne, those Kaldorei of the upper classes who most reveled in magic. The Highborne soon acted as Azshara's chosen sect and venerated her as a goddess.

The Coming of the Burning Legion

The mighty Highborne became haughty and decadent as they grew in power. Unknown to them, their abuse of and obsession with the Well's otherworldly energies attracted the attention of a terrible race of creatures that fed upon magic. These beings, demons of the Burning Legion, dwelled in an extraplanar reality called the Twisting Nether. Sensing the sudden bloom of magical energies on Azeroth, these demons were drawn to Kalimdor like flies to a corpse. The barrier between realities kept the demons from feeding directly upon the Well's energy. Not to be denied, Sargeras, the dark titan and lord of the Burning Legion, exerted an unholy influence upon the nobles of Kalimdor. As Sargeras began his subtle manipulations, his lieutenants Archimonde the Defiler and Mannoroth the Destructor prepared the infernal minions to strike.

Queen Azshara and her Highborne servitors, overwhelmed by the terrible ecstasy of magic, fell victim to Sargeras's undeniable power. To show their allegiance, the Highborne aided their queen in opening a portal within the depths of the Well of Eternity. Though insufficient to allow Sargeras entry, it was enough for the Burning Legion to begin its assault.

The warrior-demons stormed through the Well of Eternity and laid siege to the night elves' sleeping cities. Led by Archimonde and Mannoroth, the Legion swarmed over the lands of Kalimdor, leaving only ash and sorrow in its wake. The demon warlocks called down the searing Infernals that crashed like hellish meteors into the graceful spires of Kalimdor's temples. A band of burning, blood-letting killers called the Doomguard marched across Kalimdor's fields, slaughtering everyone in their path. Even packs of wild, demonic fel stalkers ravaged unopposed across the countryside.

Nature rose up in shock and anger against this violent intrusion from beyond. The seas roiled as demonfire rained from the skies. The Kaldorei were shaken enough from their arcane haze to recognize the severity of this threat. They did what they could, but the Burning Legion was the manifestation of destruction. Cities were blown apart like fallen leaves, and the night elves were pushed back as the demons savaged their once idyllic realm.

The War of the Ancients

It fell to a young Kaldorei scholar, Malfurion Stormrage, to find salvation for his people. Malfurion had long felt incensed by the growing corruption among the upper class. His own brother, Illidan, practiced the Highborne's magics, but Malfurion convinced him to forsake his dangerous obsession and help battle the invaders. The young priestess Tyrande Whisperwind agreed to accompany the brothers.

The three heroes met with the reclusive demigod Cenarius, who brought the aid of the powerful dragons. Led by the great red leviathan Alextrasza, the dragonflights agreed to engage the demons while Malfurion looked for a way to banish them from the world.

Malfurion was convinced that the Well of Eternity was the demons' umbilical link to the physical world and insisted that it should be destroyed. As the Well was also the source of the night elves' immortality and powers, his companions were shocked by the rash notion. Yet Tyrande saw the wisdom of Malfurion's theory and helped convince Cenarius and their dragon comrades to storm Azshara's temple.

Illidan was unnerved at the thought of never again wielding magic… and resentful that Tyrande had chosen romance with his brother rather than himself. Fear and jealousy curdled as Illidan vowed to protect the Well's power by any means necessary.

Malfurion found his brother missing, but assumed only that he could not face the thought of destroying the Well. Though heartbroken by Illidan's departure, Malfurion was committed to his course. The Highborne were in the midst of summoning Sargeras when Malfurion's forces struck, but they were far from surprised. Illidan had already whispered to Azshara of the plan, and she unleashed her mighty powers upon the attackers. Tyrande fell even as she made to strike the mad queen, sending Malfurion into a murderous rage. The battle between Malfurion and Azshara threw the Highborne's carefully crafted spellwork into chaos. The vortex within the Well's depths spun out of control and the Well of Eternity collapsed upon itself.

With its link to the Well severed, the Burning Legion was flung back into the primal chaos from whence it came. In the ages that followed, they would become the stuff of legend.

The Sundering of the World

The seas rushed in to fill the gaping wound left by the Well's implosion. Kalimdor was sundered into a handful of separate continents surrounding the new, raging sea. At the center of the new sea, where the Well of Eternity once stood, was a tumultuous storm of tidal fury and chaotic energies that came to be called the Maelstrom. It stood throughout the passing centuries as a chilling testament to the terrible cataclysm that forever shattered the utopia once enjoyed by the night elves.

A handful of night elves survived the explosion — including Malfurion, Tyrande, and Cenarius, miraculously enough. They sailed upon crude rafts to the only landmass in sight: the holy mountain Hyjal. Azshara and her acolytes were smashed to the bottom of the raging sea, but other Highborne survived the sundering. Though Malfurion mistrusted them, he was satisfied that they could cause no real mischief without the Well's energies.

The night elves climbed the slopes of Hyjal to the wooded bowl nestled between the mountain's enormous peaks. A small, tranquil lake awaited them, but, to their horror, the lake's waters were fouled by magic.

Malfurion did not know at the time, but Illidan was present at the fight against the Highborne. He hid in the shadows, taking advantage of the confusion of battle to fill seven vials with the Well's shimmering waters. Having survived the Sundering, Illidan fled to Mount Hyjal and poured one of the vial's contents into the mountain lake. The Well's potent energies quickly ignited and coalesced into a new Well of Eternity. Illidan intended it as a gift to future generations, but Malfurion was outraged. Arcane power was innately chaotic, and use of the Well's energies would lead to a repeat of the horrors just endured by the night elves. Illidan denied his brother's accusations and refused to relinquish his magical powers.

With Cenarius's help, Malfurion sealed his own brother within a vast underground chamber. The Well was not so easily handled. Fearing that its destruction would unleash another catastrophe, the night elves looked for a way to protect it. The three great dragons — Alextrasza, Ysera, and Nozdormu — helped them create Nordrassil, the World Tree. Sustained by the Well's magic, but divine rather than arcane in origin, Nordrassil obscured the existence of the Well of Eternity and protected the world against any future threats from the Burning Legion.

Seclusion of the Night Elves

In the aftermath of the Burning Legion's first assault on the world of Azeroth, the surviving Kaldorei on Mount Hyjal vowed never again to tamper with arcane magic. They set about building a new empire, one at peace with the world and with nature. Over the next several thousand years, the Kaldorei became masters of manipulating the gentler and more divine magic of nature.

Yet some Highborne who survived the Sundering still felt that arcane magic was not inherently dangerous, if used with proper control and moderation. Like Illidan before them, they fell victim to the withdrawal that came from the loss of their coveted magics. They were tempted, once more, to tap the energies of the Well of Eternity. Malfurion and the druids warned the Highborne that any use of arcane magic would be punishable by death. In turn, the Highborne unleashed a terrible magical storm in an ill-fated attempt to convince the druids to rescind their law. Unable to bring themselves to slaughter so many of their kin, the druids instead exiled the reckless Highborne from their lands. The Highborne — or Quel'dorei, as Azshara had named them in ages past — were glad to be rid of their conservative cousins. Though none knew what awaited them, they eagerly boarded ships and braved the waters of the Maelstrom.

As the Quel'dorei departed, the Kaldorei wove a powerful druidic spell to close their borders within an eternal mist. There they remained for thousands of years, hidden by the mist and by the swirling seas of the Maelstrom, untouched by time and the creatures of the waking world.

Settlement of Lordaeron

The Highborne braved the dangers of the Maelstrom and came upon the land that humanity would someday call Lordaeron. There, they set to establishing their own magical kingdom — Quel'Thalas — and rejected the night elves' precepts of moon worship and nocturnal activity. Forever after, they would be known only as the "high elves."

As part of their new start, the Quel'dorei created a new mystic well from which they would draw their arcane power. This font was born of one of the vials that Illidan had drawn from the first Well of Eternity and that was taken by the Highborne after his imprisonment. In keeping with the high elves' casting aside of night culture, they called this new font the Sunwell. Though potent indeed, the Sunwell lacked the full power of the Well of Eternity. Mighty though the Quel'dorei magic was, it did not bestow the immortality their cousins enjoyed. Combined with their day-oriented culture, high elf society soon grew significantly different from what they once knew on Kalimdor.

Some of the elves, wary of the Kaldorei's warnings, felt that their use of magic might draw the attention of the banished Burning Legion. They decided to mask their lands within a protective barrier that would prevent anyone from sensing magic within their borders while not restricting their use of it. They constructed huge, monolithic runestones at various points around Quel'Thalas that marked the boundaries of the magic barrier. In addition to the runestones, the Convocation of Silvermoon was founded. This group of seven of the greatest high elf lords vowed to watch over and protect their new homeland.

As their empire grew, the high elves skirmished constantly with the savage forest trolls of Zul'Aman. The green-skinned humanoids were disorganized and primitive, but their cunning

METZEN·15

earned them a place as the most dangerous enemy the high elves faced for many, many years. The high elves also learned that they shared their new continent with humans, but left them to their own crude culture for some time.

The Rise of Humans

The humans lived a nomadic life for many years until the rise of the Arathi. This tribe saw the potential in uniting the individual human tribes, particularly when faced with the increasing danger of troll warbands. The Arathi brought other human tribes under their rule over the next few years, eventually establishing the nation of Arathor with the massive fortified city of Strom as its capital.

Word of the new nation reached the high elves, who were increasingly hard pressed to keep the trolls at bay. The high elves made contact with the humans, beseeching them for aid. The humans agreed to an alliance with the elves in exchange for being taught how to use magic. The united forces of humans and high elves defeated the trolls so decisively that the troll race never again approached the dominance it once enjoyed.

The growth of Arathor also brought humans in contact with dwarves, who had long lived in underground realms. High elf and dwarf cultures were so different that little trust was shared between the two, but the humans formed a bond with the dwarf race. In time, the humans settled so much of Lordaeron that the single empire of Arathor eventually fragmented into different kingdoms, each developing its own beliefs, governments, and lifestyles.

The Guardians of Tirisfal

As the human and elven cultures mingled, humans displayed an astounding natural affinity for magic — indeed, many human wizards eventually outstripped the skill of their high elf teachers. These human mages were greedy and careless, however. Each new generation became more obsessed with mystic power and grew conceited and aloof.

Once more, the abuse of magic attracted the Burning Legion.

The first demons who slipped back onto Azeroth were relatively weak and easily defeated, but rumors soon spread throughout the human and high elf lands. The descendents of the original Quel'dorei remembered the tales of their ancestors, and the Council of Silvermoon entered into a pact with the Magocrat lords of Arathor. They formed a secret order called the Guardians of Tirisfal, after the secret forested glade in which the wizards first met. The Guardians kept quiet the true threat of the Burning Legion to prevent mass panic and revolution.

The Guardians carried on as a unified, though largely secret force even as the human kingdoms fragmented. Some time later, the foremost Guardian, a human woman named Aegwynn, learned that a number of demons had settled on the northern continent of Northrend. The demons hunted dragons to drain the mighty creatures of their magic. With the aid of the dragons, Aegwynn destroyed the demon forces. Even as the last demon fell, the mighty Sargeras appeared before Aegwynn to warn her that the Burning Legion would return. Enraged and overconfident, Aegwynn destroyed Sargeras's physical form with ease. Fearing that his spirit would linger, she sealed the ruined carcass in one of the ancient vaults of Kalimdor deep beneath the sea.

Alas, when Aegwynn unleashed her power, Sargeras infected her with a portion of his own spirit. This taint passed on to her child Medivh years later. As ignorant of the infection as his mother was, Medivh gained renown for his magical prowess even as a youth. His childhood in the southern kingdom of Stormwind was innocuous enough otherwise — that is, until he turned 14. Then his inherent arcane power clashed with the dormant spirit of Sargeras. Medivh fell into a coma for many years. When he awakened, so did the soul of Sargeras. The demon began to pervert Medivh's mind and soul to his own foul ends.

The World of Draenor

Azeroth was not the only world subjected to the depredations of the Burning Legion. Elsewhere in the Great Dark Beyond was Draenor, a lush world home to a shamanistic, clan-based society of orcs and another race, the peaceful draenei. Sargeras's second in command, the demon Kil'jaeden, discovered Draenor some time after the Sundering upon Azeroth. This new world offered a great opportunity for the Burning Legion if cultivated properly.

Of the two races, Kil'jaeden saw that the orcs were more suitable for corruption. He seduced the orc shaman Ner'zhul in much the same way that Sargeras brought Azshara under his control. Using the brute as his conduit for corruption, the demon spread battle lust and savagery throughout the orc clans. Before long, a spiritual race was transformed into a bloodthirsty people.

Kil'jaeden then urged Ner'zhul to take his people the last step, to give themselves over entirely to the Burning Legion. Yet the mighty shaman somehow resisted the demon's command — there were some lines even a battle-enraged orc would not cross. Kil'jaeden needed a mortal to open a gateway to Azeroth and settled on a talented novice named Gul'dan. The young orc became an avid student of demonic magic and grew to be a powerful warlock.

He taught other young orcs the arcane arts, and soon the last of the orcs' shamanistic traditions were replaced with a terrible new magic that reeked of doom.

The warlocks quickly ran things in the form of a Shadow Council that acted as "advisors" to the clans' chieftains. Kil'jaeden knew his orcs were almost ready, but he wanted to be certain. He had the warlocks summon Mannoroth — the living vessel of destruction and rage — and perform a ceremony in which the clan chieftains drank of the pit lord's blood. Consumed with the curse of bloodlust, the orc clans united in a single Horde and wiped out the draenei.

The First War

With the only opponents of any significance eradicated and the warlocks' energy twisting and blackening the once fertile lands of Draenor, Gul'dan grew nervous. With no foes to face, the orcs would soon turn on one another. Gul'dan's power, however, was sufficient to reach across the barrier of worlds and look for a way out.

On Azeroth, Medivh had been resisting Sargeras's corruption as best he could. Medivh's lifelong friends sensed the change in him, but their growing awareness could not stop Medivh's descent into madness. Finally, Medivh fell victim to Sargeras's power. Not long after, Gul'dan's consciousness touched that of Medivh — now possessed by Sargeras. The two made a bargain to lead the Horde to Azeroth.

The mortal orcs would be far easier to bring onto Azeroth than the demons of the Legion. Once there, the Horde would soften up any resistance and generate the arcane power necessary to bring the Legion through. With the warlocks working on Draenor and Medivh on Azeroth, the gateway was opened between the worlds. The Horde came through near the human kingdom of Stormwind and launched the first strike of what proved to be a devastating war. During the struggle that followed, Lord Anduin Lothar, a friend of Medivh's since youth, foresaw the destruction of the world if he did not take a drastic step. With the aid of Medivh's own apprentice, Khadgar, Lothar slew his old friend, destroying Sargeras's spirit and freeing Medivh's at last.

Led by the cunning Warchief Orgrim Doomhammer, the orcs carried on relentlessly against the human forces, crushing all resistance in the southern kingdom of Stormwind. Lothar rallied the remnants of his armies and launched a massive exodus across the sea to the northern kingdom of Lordaeron.

The Second War

Lothar met with the leaders of the seven nations of Lordaeron. They agreed that the orcs would eventually wipe out all of humanity if left unchecked. The Alliance of Lordaeron was formed, a union of human nations with support from high elves and dwarves. Lord Lothar was appointed as the Supreme Commander of the Alliance forces.

In the south, the orcs brought ogre allies from their home world and conscripted the native forest trolls of Azeroth. They launched a new campaign that ended up raging across the conti-

nents of Lordaeron, Khaz Modan, and Stormwind. The battles of the Second War ranged from traditional land wars to naval conflicts and even to massive aerial dogfights. Despite the Horde's relentless savagery, the Alliance managed to push the Horde armies back into Stormwind, the first kingdom to fall at the Horde's hands.

Though the Alliance was heartened by its success, the Horde's defeat hinged on the warlock Gul'dan. A mighty orc warrior named Durotan warned Warchief Orgrim Doomhammer of Gul'dan's ties to the demon Kil'jaeden and the warlock's plans for godhood. Aware of the degree of corruption that lay within his people, Orgrim realized that Gul'dan must be stopped or he would destroy orcs and humans alike.

Gul'dan sought out the legendary Tomb of Sargeras, believing the power of godhood awaited him there. The warlock used his infernal powers to raise the tomb from the sea floor — creating a new, volatile island chain in the process. Doomhammer sent much of his army after the traitorous warlock. Gul'dan entered the raised tomb nevertheless, but he did not find the power he sought. Rather, he unwittingly released a swarm of demons that tore the warlock and much of the Horde forces to shreds. Then the Alliance struck, pushing the shattered Horde back to the very threshold of the Dark Portal.

Though the Alliance defeated demon and orc alike, victory was bittersweet: mighty Lothar had fallen in battle.

The Destruction of Draenor

The grieving Alliance rebuilt its shattered homeland, and surviving orcs were hunted down and herded into internment camps. Khadgar, Medivh's former apprentice, was ordered to watch over the ruins of the Dark Portal.

Some orcs who escaped back to Draenor began plotting revenge. The shaman Ner'zhul, however, held no interest in revenge or the schemes of demons. He decided to open a new Portal to a world where his people could rebuild their society. To do so without the aid of demons (thereby breaking the pact he had made with Kil'jaeden that began the corruption of the orc race), he needed several magical artifacts from Azeroth.

Ner'zhul re-opened the Dark Portal and sent several warriors to recover the relics. Khadgar's men failed to stop the orcs, and the warriors returned to Draenor with the relics in hand. Thinking the orcs were preparing a new attack, the Alliance ordered Khadgar and his troops through the Portal to stop the Horde once and for all.

Unaware of the Alliance's plans, Ner'zhul opened a number of new Portals that would lead to uncorrupted worlds. To Ner'zhul's shock, the existence of two Portals on a single world began to tear Draenor apart. Great earthquakes and storms shook Draenor to its core. Khadgar's forces fled back to Azeroth and destroyed the Dark Portal as Ner'zhul led his orcs through the second Portal. As the last orc fled through the Portal, the potent magic at last overwhelmed the ravaged world of Draenor in a final catastrophic explosion.

The New Horde

In the aftermath of the First War, a human soldier named Blackmoore found an orc infant alone on the battlefield. The child, the son of Durotan, was the sole orc survivor. Blackmoore named the infant Thrall and took him home to Durnholde. The human raised the orc as a favored slave, intending to train him as a powerful but educated warrior. Blackmoore desired to use Thrall to make orcs tractable to human rule, but Thrall escaped before his training had finished.

Thrall searched out his people and was dismayed to find them lethargic and directionless on their reservations. He decided to track down

the last free chieftain, Grom Hellscream, who continued to lead his Warsong clan in an underground war. Thrall located Hellscream and learned from him of another clan far to the north that could teach him something of his heritage. Thrall ventured north, where he encountered the Frostwolf clan. From them, he discovered his heritage as the son of Durotan and the clan's rightful leader.

Thrall was taught the ways of the shaman and showed a natural affinity for the spirit magic. In the course of his training, Thrall also discovered that the orcs' lethargy was caused by a racial "addiction" to the demon magics. With the warlocks slain during the Second War, the orcs were suffering a kind of withdrawal from the demons' arcane influence. He came to realize that his people must restore their spiritual ties or they would waste away to nothing. Soon after, Thrall left the Frostwolf clan to free the other captive clans, restore their heritage, and ensure their future survival.

Upon his return south, Thrall encountered the aged warchief Orgrim Doomhammer, who had lived as a hermit since the end of the Second War. Doomhammer sensed Thrall's power and honor and wasted no time naming him the new Warchief of the Horde. Thrall set about freeing his people, his forces swelling with each new clan released from the prisons and reservations.

Perhaps even more significantly, Thrall's heroism and mystic power reawakened the orcs' spiritual heritage. Those who joined Thrall cast aside the last taint of demonic influence and embraced their shamanistic roots once more.

Rise of the Lich King

Shortly before Draenor tore apart, Kil'jaeden captured the shaman Ner'zhul and his followers as they attempted to escape from the dying world. The vengeful demon was not about to let the orc get away with breaking their pact. He tortured Ner'zhul, slowly tearing his body to pieces, but keeping the shaman's spirit intact. Ner'zhul pled for mercy more than once, but Kil'jaeden reminded the orc of their blood pact. He still had a use for the willful shaman.

The orcs' failure to conquer Azeroth forced Kil'jaeden to create a new army. This new force could not be allowed to fall prey to the same petty rivalries and infighting that had plagued the Horde. It would need to be merciless and single-minded in its mission.

Kil'jaeden offered the tortured spirit of Ner'zhul one last chance to serve the Legion… or suffer eternal torment. Driven near to madness with agony already, Ner'zhul agreed.

His spirit was placed within a specially crafted block of diamond-hard ice gathered from the far reaches of the Twisting Nether. Encased within the frozen cask and warped by Kil'jaeden's chaotic powers, Ner'zhul became a spectral being of unfathomable power. At that moment, the orc known as Ner'zhul was shattered forever… and the Lich King was born.

Ner'zhul's loyal death knights and warlock followers were also transformed, the wicked spellcasters ripped apart and remade as skeletal liches. Kil'jaeden insured that even in death, Ner'zhul's followers would serve him unquestioningly.

Remade in undeath, Ner'zhul was commanded to spread a plague of death and terror across Azeroth that would snuff out human civilization forever. All those who died from the dreaded plague would arise as the undead… and their spirits would be bound to Ner'zhul's iron will forever. Kil'jaeden promised that if Ner'zhul accomplished his dark mission of scouring humanity from the world, he would be freed from his curse and granted a new, healthy body to inhabit.

Though Ner'zhul appeared agreeable, Kil'jaeden remained skeptical of his pawn's loyalties. Keeping the Lich King bodiless and trapped within the crystal cask assured his good conduct for the short term, but he required a constant, watchful eye. Kil'jaeden called upon his elite demon guard, the vampiric Dreadlords, to police Ner'zhul. Tichondrius, the most powerful and cunning of the Dreadlords, warmed to the challenge.

Kil'jaeden cast Ner'zhul's icy cask back into Azeroth, followed by his minions. The hardened crystal streaked across the night sky and smashed into the arctic continent of Northrend and buried itself deep in the Icecrown glacier. The frozen crystal, warped and scarred by its violent descent, resembled a throne… and Ner'zhul's vengeful spirit stirred within it.

From the confines of the Frozen Throne, Ner'zhul reached out with his vast consciousness and touched the minds

METZEN-96

of Northrend's inhabitants. He enslaved the minds of many with ease — among them ice trolls and the fierce wendigo — and drew their evil brethren into his growing shadow. Ner'zhul quickly devastated the mortal population of Northrend with his plague, and with each fatality his undead armies grew.

A handful of powerful individuals heard the Lich King's mental summons, most notably the archmage Kel'Thuzad of the magical nation of Dalaran. Kel'Thuzad abandoned the ways of his people to pledge his soul to the Lich King before the Frozen Throne. Kel'Thuzad's first mission was to found a new religion that would worship the Lich King as a god.

To help the archmage accomplish his mission, Ner'zhul left Kel'Thuzad's humanity intact. Under disguise, the wizard used illusion and persuasion to lull the downtrodden, disenfranchised masses of Lordaeron and establish the Cult of the Damned. Its members, many turned from the philosophy of the Holy Light, were promised eternal life in return for their obedience.

With Kel'Thuzad's success, the Lich King made the final preparations for his assault. Ner'zhul placed his energies into a number of portable artifacts and ordered Kel'Thuzad to distribute these plague-cauldrons among cult-controlled villages. The cauldrons would then act as plague-generators, sending the plague seeping out across the unsuspecting farmlands and cities of northern Lordaeron.

Many of Lordaeron's northern villages were contaminated almost immediately. Just as in Northrend, the citizens who contracted the plague died and arose as the Lich King's willing slaves. As the plague spread, Kel'Thuzad looked upon the Lich King's growing army and named it the Scourge — for it would soon march upon the gates of Lordaeron and scour humanity from the face of the world.

The Alliance first learned of this new trouble through fragments of rumors about "death cults," then increasing appearances of undead. Uther Lightbringer and the Knights of the Silver Hand, a brotherhood of holy paladin warriors, investigated the infected regions in hopes of finding a way to stop the plague. Despite the Knights' efforts, the plague continued to spread and threatened to tear the Alliance apart. Indeed, one of their number, Prince Arthas, so feared the threat of the undead that he took increasingly extreme steps to conquer them. This fear and resolve proved his ultimate defeat. He tracked the plague's source to

Northrend, intending to end the threat. Instead, Prince Arthas fell to the Lich King's tremendous power — his soul stolen by the cursed blade Frostmourne — and became the greatest of his death knights. Arthas then led the undead Scourge on a rampage throughout the continent of Lordaeron.

Return of the Burning Legion

After crushing the majority of Alliance forces, Arthas and Kel'Thuzad (now a lich) led the Scourge to Dalaran. Even the wizards of Kirin Tor lacked sufficient power to stop the undead from stealing the spellbook of Medivh from the city. With this artifact, Kel'Thuzad had all he needed to summon forth the Burning Legion. The mighty demon Archimonde and his host emerged at last upon the world of Azeroth. Yet Dalaran was not their final destination. Instead, they would head for Kalimdor and Nordrassil, the World Tree.

In the midst of this chaos, a lone prophet had appeared to lend the mortal races guidance. This prophet proved to be none other than Medivh, the last Guardian, miraculously returned from the Beyond to redeem

himself for past sins. He told the Horde and the Alliance of the dangers they faced and urged them to band together. Orcs and humans would have none of it, so Medivh dealt with each separately, using prophecy and trickery when necessary to guide them across the sea, past the dangers of the Maelstrom, and to the legendary land of Kalimdor.

The forces soon encountered the long-hidden Kaldorei civilization. The night elves reacted to the news of demonic invasion with grim determination. The Burning Legion had never ceased in its desire for the Well of Eternity, long the source of strength for the World Tree and itself the heart of the night elf kingdom. If successful, the demons would literally tear the world apart.

Even as the mortal races understood the full import of the threat, the Burning Legion followed the undead Scourge to Kalimdor. The continent was no longer hidden from detection, and the demons did not hesitate to lay siege to the World Tree that grew over the Well of Eternity.

The Battle of Mount Hyjal

Under Medivh's guidance, Jaina Proudmoore and Thrall, leaders of the human and orc forces respectively, realized that they must put aside their differences. Similarly, the night elves, led by Malfurion Stormrage and Tyrande Whisperwind, agreed that they must unite against the demons if they hoped to succeed in defending the World Tree.

Unified in purpose, the races of Azeroth worked together to strengthen the World Tree's energies to the utmost. Empowered by tremendous spiritual energies, Nordrassil held the power to destroy Archimonde and sever the Legion's anchor to the Well of Eternity. The final battle shook the continent of Kalimdor to the roots. Unable to draw power from the sundered Well, the Burning Legion crumbled under the combined might of the mortal armies.

The Aftermath... and the Future

Though victory was theirs, the mortal races found themselves in a world shattered by war. The Scourge and the Burning Legion had all but destroyed the civilizations of Lordaeron — and had almost finished the job in Kalimdor.

The orcs, led by Warchief Thrall, have found a new homeland on the continent of Kalimdor and spirit brothers in the race of tauren who lent their aid in the climactic battle. The once unstoppable juggernaut of the Horde became a loose coalition of orcs, tauren, and others dedicated to survival and prosperity rather than conquest. Their peace was short lived, regrettably, when new Alliance forces arrived from Lordaeron some months later. The fleet was under the command of Grand Admiral Daelin Proudmoore — father of Jaina Proudmoore, a hero of the Second War, and a staunch enemy of the Horde.

With little enough to return to, and a perilous crossing required to reach Lordaeron, the majority of Alliance forces remained in the new land of Kalimdor. In the year after the Third War ended, they established a stronghold on the island of Theramore. Though Jaina Proudmoore held the orcs in high regard in the wake of the recent war, the truce established between the Alliance and the Horde soon suffered strain when her father arrived. Unlike his daughter, Daelin Proudmoore believed the orcs incapable of reform. He quickly launched assaults upon Durotar, determined to eradicate the orc presence and make Kalimdor suitable for human colonization. In turn, the orcs and their Horde allies mobilized to secure defenses throughout Kalimdor and struck back at the Grand Admiral's forces.

Once Jaina realized she could not dissuade the Grand Admiral from his mission, she saw only one course of action that might forestall the return to rampant genocide that gripped both Alliance and Horde in the past. With a heavy heart, Jaina Proudmoore aided Thrall in shattering the Grand Admiral's forces. She acted to save both Durotar and Theramore and paid the price with her father's death in the battle. Grand Admiral Proudmoore's forces were repelled, and Jaina and Thrall signed a non-aggression pact to keep their two lands safe.

The high elves on Kalimdor face problems of their own. Their proud home of Quel'Thalas was razed in the war, and very few came with Jaina Proudmoore's army to settle in Theramore. They have begun acting even haughtier and more withdrawn than ever before and spend much of their time venturing into Kalimdor — hunting down the remaining undead and demons who destroyed their home, they say. More surreptitiously, they also look for new sources of arcane magic to replace what they lost with the destruction of Quel'Thalas.

Ironforge dwarves were stranded upon Kalimdor like the rest of the Alliance forces. To their surprise, they discovered tantalizing information about a progenitor race they call the titans, ancient beings who may have created dwarves. Fueled by curiosity, the inquisitive dwarves have left but a token force in Theramore while the rest of their kind roam Kalimdor in search of their mysterious origins. Indeed, many have resettled on Bael Modan, "Red Mountain," a site of some titan ruins located in the southern part of the Barrens.

The night elves still have their homeland and much of their population. They lost much of their solitude, however, and must deal with the lingering effects of the Legions' corruption. Furthermore, they sacrificed much of their spiritual energy to empower Nordrassil in the Battle of Mount Hyjal, resulting in a loss of their immortality. Once protected and alone, they now must deal with numerous races and peoples — including an offshoot of their race that hungers still for arcane power.

Table 1–1 Timeline of Events

–14,000	Night elves establish the first great civilization by the Well of Eternity in Kalimdor. Investigating the Well releases magic upon the world.
–10,000	The Burning Legion invades Azeroth to drain the world of its innate magic. The demons are vanquished, but vow to return.
–4,000	After centuries of wandering in exile, the high elves establish the kingdom of Quel'Thalas in northern Lordaeron.
–2,800	Humans establish the Empire of Arathor in Lordaeron. High elves teach humans the ways of magic.
–1,200	The Empire of Arathor fragments into seven autonomous nations.
–40	The Burning Legion corrupts orcs on the world of Draenor. The once noble, shamanistic orc clans unite and become the rampaging Horde.
1	The Dark Portal is opened and the Horde begins its invasion of Azeroth.
4	The Horde conquers the kingdom of Stormwind. The seven human nations of Lordaeron unite against the Horde, with assistance from high elves and dwarves. The Alliance of Lordaeron is founded under the command of Lord Anduin Lothar.
6	The Horde invades Lordaeron and destroys much of Quel'Thalas. Alliance forces push back, but Lord Lothar is killed. Spurred by Lothar's death, the Alliance armies crush the Horde and destroy the Dark Portal. The Alliance places Horde survivors into internment camps.
7	The shaman Ner'zhul reopens the Dark Portal between Draenor and Azeroth, sending orcs to steal artifacts to open multiple Portals on Draenor. Alliance forces venture through the Dark Portal to stop Ner'zhul. The shaman opens his new Portals, but their energies spiral out of control. The Alliance forces destroy the Dark Portal so that Azeroth is not consumed by the raging energies. The blasted world of Draenor tears itself apart.
23	The orc Thrall, raised as a slave by humans, sets out on a quest to find his lost heritage. He reunites a number of renegade orc clans and leads them in revolt against the Alliance.
24	Thrall becomes the new Warchief of the Horde and reintroduces his people to their abandoned shamanic culture.
25	The Horde captures Alliance ships and makes a dangerous journey past the Maelstrom to the unexplored lands of Kalimdor. A mysterious plague of undeath sweeps across the northern realm of Northrend on Lordaeron; the Knights of the Silver Hand investigate.
	Prince Arthas, a Knight of the Silver Hand, becomes corrupted in overzealous pursuit to destroy the undead Scourge. He is transformed into a death knight and leads the Scourge in a rampage across Lordaeron. The destruction heralds the return of the Burning Legion; Alliance forces flee to Kalimdor in hopes of finding the means to defeat the demons.
	Horde and Alliance forces unite against the Burning Legion. They empower the World Tree to destroy the demon Archimonde and defeat the Burning Legion. The surviving mortal forces establish new colonies on Kalimdor.
26	Present time. One year after the Battle of Mount Hyjal, mortal races explore and settle the wild continent of Kalimdor. Increasing encounters with demons and undead suggest that the long years of battle are not over....

Blademaster Redjaw cursed the undead. He cursed the uneasy graves from which they rose and the hellish spells that empowered them. He cursed the fell wizards who held the demonic knowledge of twisting corpses into unliving pawns. He cursed the terror that the mindless hordes unleashed on the world.

He also cursed the one-eyed night elf who had told him of this town, and he cursed himself for listening.

The story sounded too good to be true. A dwarf village with more gold than the stunted folk could pull out of the ground, looking for heroes to guard their treasure as they put together a caravan for the lowlands. Good work, and they didn't care if you were man, orc, or tauren. That was what the night elf said, and Redjaw, like a damned fool, had listened to her.

Ten of them entered the town near nightfall, their orc ears keenly aware of oppressive silence, their noses filled with the faint scent of decay. Of the inhabitants there was no sign.

They reached the center of the town where a great white fountain stood, now dry and lined with leaves. They shouted for the inhabitants, for anyone.

In response, skeletons spilled out of buildings and rose from sewer grates. They were of all sizes — sturdy human frames, delicate elven forms, and many, many stocky dwarven skeletons. Their bare-boned feet scraped along the cobblestones like hollow wooden reeds, and their jaws clacked together as they came to greet their orc visitors.

Two of Redjaw's comrades fell in the first moments, caught by surprise and dragged down by the tide of bones. Two more disappeared when the paving stones beneath their feet gave way, undermined by something beneath the street itself. Another died as the remaining orcs formed up within the dried fountain, their backs to the center as they faced the encroaching undead.

The things surged forward once, twice, and then a third time. Each assault was beaten back by a flurry of blades, and the dry fountain filled with splinters of bone. The orcs held their own, but they could last only so long against the undead onslaught.

One of his fellow orcs shouted, and Redjaw followed his gesture. A battle-worn female dwarf called out to them from the temple balcony, then raised what looked like a flowerpot with a burning taper. As Redjaw watched, the dwarf tossed the device into the midst of the undead.

Redjaw and his fellows crouched reflexively, using the thin lip of the fountain for cover as the makeshift bomb detonated. Smoke, dust, and bone flew in all directions. The blast deafened Redjaw for the moment, but he motioned for his followers to use the confusion

and smoke to escape. He dashed through the twitching wreckage of half-shattered skeletons as he led the rush for the temple.

The undead legions had despoiled the temple, and some still remained inside. Apparently, their dwarf rescuer was busy with her own problems to dispatch the creatures. Three dwarven ghouls — red-eyed, ashen-faced parodies of the living — lurched down a temple staircase toward Redjaw. Fresh blood dripped from their mouths, evidence of recent feasting upon their former townsfolk. Inhuman bellows burst from undead throats as the ghouls leapt at Redjaw and his fellows.

Redjaw met them with steel, slicing the first one cleanly and bringing his blade back to cut deeply into chest of the second. Both collapsed, their momentum sending their remains cascading down behind him. One of his two remaining comrades traded blows with the third ghoul, but that fight ended when Redjaw smashed the creature's skull with a backhanded blow. The three orcs then dashed up the stairs.

Redjaw found the dwarf collapsed by the gallery railing, her healer's robes tattered and her face pale from loss of blood and magical energy. He saw at once that she was wounded beyond even her own ability to heal.

"Fool," the healer gurgled. "You should have run when you had the chance."

"You helped us, I help you," Redjaw said. "I'm not afraid of the dead."

The dwarf gave a blood-choked laugh. "What I fear," she said, "is when they don't stay dead."

Redjaw cursed again as he heard the sound of shattered bones reassembling, of skeletal feet moving across paving stones, and of the baying of resurrected ghouls.

The **Dungeons & Dragons Warcraft Roleplaying Game** is all about the heroes — the people who lead the armies, defeat the rampaging monsters, and save the world. Player characters (PCs) are necessarily of heroic stature, even if they need time and experience to grow into their roles.

Races of Warcraft

Humans are the dominant (as in, "most obvious") intelligent species on Azeroth, but they are by no means alone. Elves, dwarves, tauren, imports such as orcs, and so on all share the world with humanity. In some cases, such races have proven far more influential than humanity over the long term.

Of the races detailed in the *PHB*, only humans, elves, dwarves, half-elves, and half-orcs are available in the **Warcraft RPG**. Halflings do not exist in the **Warcraft** universe, and gnomes are nowhere to be found upon Kalimdor.

These races own a few differences from the descriptions and stats provided in the *PHB*. The world of **Warcraft** is nasty and brutal; magic and the supernatural influence the land and the people in ways distinct from other settings. As such, while there are general similarities between the races in the *PHB* and this rulebook, the racial descriptions for races in the **Warcraft RPG** campaign setting take precedence over the descriptions in the *PHB*.

In addition to the above races, the **Warcraft RPG** adds four new PC races: the entrepreneurial goblins, the reclusive night elves, the warlike orcs, and the shamanistic tauren.

Race Descriptions

Each race receives a brief account of how it exists in the **Warcraft RPG**:

Description: General details on the race as a whole, focusing on the race's society and culture.

Appearance: Details of size, build, complexion, and the like common to the race.

Region: The general types of areas in which the race is found, geographically speaking.

Affiliation: Whether the majority of that race is affiliated with the Alliance or Horde or is neutral. This also includes some notes on how the race gets along (or not) with other races.

Racial Traits: Abilities specific to the race. These abilities likely have differences from what you might find in the *PHB*.

Starting Characters and Level Adjustment

Azeroth is a brutal world in which only the strong survive. As such, *newly created heroes start at 2nd level*, with all of the skills, feats, equipment, and other benefits that come with advancement from 1st level.

Some races available in the **Warcraft RPG** campaign setting are inherently more powerful than other common races, however. To maintain the balance of power, the **Warcraft RPG** applies a level adjustment of +1 to the more powerful character races. PCs of such races begin play with greater natural power but gain levels more slowly than races that have no level adjustment.

A hero from a race with a level adjustment *starts at 1st level* for the purposes of skills, feat, Hit Dice, and class abilities. The PC, however, has an effective character level (ECL) of 2 for the purposes of advancement and starting equipment. A hero's ECL is determined as follows:

$$ECL = level\ adjustment + character\ level$$

Thus, a high elf character (level adjustment +1) with 4 levels in wizard (Wiz4) and 2 in rogue (Rog2) has ECL 7.

Human

Description: Humans are among the youngest races on Azeroth, but they make up for it by being the most populous. With life spans generally shorter than the other races, humans seem to strive all the harder to achieve great heights in empire building, exploration, and magical study. This aggressive and inquisitive nature leads the various human nations to become quite active and influential in the world.

At least, such was the case prior to the invasion of the Burning Legion. Human kingdoms have suffered greatly in the course of the three wars against the demonic hordes. A large number fell in the latest confrontation, leaving behind battered yet unbowed survivors of the Alliance Expedition under the command of the sorceress Jaina Proudmoore. This group has begun settlement of the wild continent of Kalimdor.

Humans value virtue and honor, though they also pursue interests in power and wealth. After battling the forces of darkness for generations, humans tend to use a warrior's approach to diplomacy — attack first, ask questions later. Aided by belief in the mystical philosophy of the Holy Light, they have fought the hardest and endured the most during the wars against the Horde and the Burning Legion.

Despite all their tragedy, humans remain hardy and brave — thoroughly committed to building a strong society in the harsh lands of Kalimdor. Though they lament the passing of their former kingdom of Lordaeron, they look toward a bright future unscarred by the rigors of war and battle.

Appearance: Humans come from a variety of backgrounds. Their appearance and stature are equivalent to that described for humans in the *PHB*.

Region: After the end of the Third War, Alliance forces under Jaina Proudmoore's command pulled to the south of Kalimdor. They founded a stronghold called Theramore, a small, walled city on a rocky isle just east of Dustwallow Marsh. Theramore Isle and the nearby mainland fall under human control and border Durotar, the orcs' new homeland to the north. Humans and orcs maintain a tentative peace along their borders, but clashes are by no means uncommon. Since most of the mighty human warriors and mages lost their lives during the war against the Burning Legion, only a handful of veteran (or, high-level) mages and paladin warriors remain in Theramore. While Ironforge dwarves and some high elves also occupy the small island city, humans hold the seats of greatest power. Goblin vendors and traders are a common enough sight in and around the rocky isle.

METZEN

Affiliation: Alliance. Humans and orcs banded together to face the menace of the Burning Legion, but old habits returned once they dispatched the demonic threat. Although Thrall (the orc warchief) and Jaina Proudmoore bear a healthy respect for one another, the old racial hatreds boil still within the hearts of their troops. Humans also look upon tauren with suspicion, thanks to ties the tauren have to orcs. Humans and dwarves have long enjoyed a good relationship, a bond only strengthened since the dwarves have been re-energized by their desire for exploration. Elves are, by turns, a source of mystery and frustration — especially the exotic night elves.

Human Racial Traits

- *Medium:* As Medium creatures, humans have no special bonuses or penalties due to their size.
- Human base land speed is 30 feet.
- 1 extra feat at 1st level. Humans are quick to master specialized tasks.
- 4 extra skill points at 1st level and 1 extra skill point at each additional level. Humans are versatile and capable.
- +2 racial bonus on saves against fear-related spells or effects. Humans are known for their courage, no matter what the circumstances.
- +2 racial bonus on Diplomacy, Gather Information, and Knowledge (nobility and royalty) checks. Humans are a gregarious bunch. These skills are also considered class skills for all human characters.
- +1 racial bonus on attack rolls against orcs. Humans and orcs have a long history of enmity.
- *Automatic Language:* Common.
- *Bonus Languages:* Any unrestricted.
- *Favored Class:* Any. When determining whether a multiclass human takes an XP penalty, his highest-level class does not count (see *PHB*, Chapter 3: Classes, "Multiclass Characters," *XP for Multiclass Characters*).

Dwarf, Ironforge

Description: Ironforge dwarves are stoic and tough, similar to dwarves in the *PHB*. They thrill to the prospects of battle and storytelling alike. Originally from Ironforge in Khaz Modan on the continent of Lordaeron, they came to Kalimdor as part of the human Alliance to battle the Burning Legion. In the aftermath of that struggle, the dwarves learned that they might well have been created by an ancient race called the titans. Legends claim that these beings helped shape the world itself in its earliest days and were eternal enemies to the demons of the Burning Legion.

This revelation has triggered a major transformation in dwarven attitude and interests. Where once Ironforge dwarves lived only to mine precious minerals and craft halls of stone, they now revel in exploration and digging for insights into the ancient world their ancestors helped to craft. Ironforge dwarves are obsessed with investigating the relics and locations of titan holdings throughout Kalimdor.

In addition to awakening a thirst for discovery, this newfound knowledge also unlocked enchanted energies of their heritage, enabling Ironforge dwarves to perform spectacular feats such as turning their skin to stone for limited periods of time.

Dwarves are as interested in invention as they are exploration. They have virtually perfected the use of firearms such as blunderbusses and cannons. Members of any race can learn to use these mechanical devices, but Ironforge dwarves own an uncanny knack for constructing and using them.

Appearance: The stature and appearance of Ironforge dwarves are equivalent to that described for dwarves in the *PHB*.

Region: Ironforge dwarves retain contact with the Alliance forces on Theramore Isle. They typically go there only to resupply and catch up on sporadic news from distant Lordaeron; they otherwise spend much of their time roaming Kalimdor with archaeological fervor. They have established a few different dig sites, including one major site: the ancient ruins they have named Bael Modan (Red Mountain), located in the southern region of the Barrens.

Affiliation: Alliance. Ironforge dwarves respect the orcs' fighting prowess, but too long a history of bad blood prevents any meaningful relations. While they share an affiliation with high elves, the dwarves have never experienced good relations with that race. The secrecy inherent to night elves virtually guarantees that Ironforge dwarves spare them little kindness as well. Ironforge dwarves are noncommittal toward tauren, though they do exercise caution due to that race's Horde affiliation. This situation makes exploration of Kalimdor more difficult than it might be otherwise, since the night elves and tauren races are more familiar with the land than the newly arrived Ironforge dwarves.

Ironforge Dwarf Racial Traits

• +2 Constitution, –2 Charisma. Ironforge dwarves are a tough lot, though their blunt demeanor makes them none too appealing to delicate sensibilities.

• *Medium:* As Medium creatures, Ironforge dwarves have no special bonuses or penalties due to their size.

• Ironforge dwarves' base land speed is 20 feet.

• *Darkvision:* Ironforge dwarves can see in the dark up to 60 feet. Darkvision is black and white only, but it is otherwise like normal sight.

Ironforge dwarves can function just fine with no light at all.

• *Stability:* Ironforge dwarves are exceptionally stable on their feet, gaining a +4 bonus on ability checks made to resist being bull rushed or tripped when standing on the ground (but not when climbing, flying, riding, or otherwise not standing firmly on the ground).

• *Stonecunning:* Stonecunning grants Ironforge dwarves a +2 racial bonus on checks to notice unusual stonework such as sliding walls, stonework traps, new construction (even when built to match the old), unsafe stone surfaces, shaky stone ceilings, and the like. Something that is not stone but that is disguised as stone also counts as unusual stonework. An Ironforge dwarf who merely comes within 10 feet of unusual stonework can make a Search check as if he were actively searching, and an Ironforge dwarf can use the Search skill to find stonework traps as a rogue can. An Ironforge dwarf can also intuit depth, sensing his approximate depth underground as naturally as a human can sense which way is up. Dwarves have a sixth sense about stonework, an innate ability that they get plenty of opportunity to practice and hone in their underground homes.

• *Stone Flesh (Su):* Once per day as a free action, Ironforge dwarves may transform their very flesh into stone. This grants a +2 natural armor bonus for a number of rounds equal to their Constitution modifier + character level. This bonus increases by 1 at 6th level and at every 6 character levels thereafter (+3 at 6th, +4 at 12th, and +5 at 18th level).

• *Weapon Familiarity:* Dwarves may treat blunderbusses, long rifles, flintlock pistols, dwarven urgroshes, and dwarven waraxes as martial weapons, rather than exotic weapons.

• +2 racial bonus on saving throws against poison. Ironforge dwarves are hardy and resistant to toxins.

• +1 racial bonus to attack rolls against giants.

• +2 racial bonus on Appraise checks related to stone or metal items, Craft checks related to stone or metal, and Craft checks related to gunsmithing. These are also considered class skills for all Ironforge dwarf characters.

- *Automatic Languages:* Common and Dwarven.
- *Bonus Languages:* Gnome, Goblin, Orc, and Thalassian.
- *Favored Class:* Fighter. A multiclass Ironforge dwarf's fighter class does not count when determining whether he suffers an XP penalty for multiclassing (see *PHB*, Chapter 3: Classes, "Multiclass Characters," *XP for Multiclass Characters*).

Elf, High

Description: High elves were born long ago when a band of night elves were exiled from their homeland for continuing to abuse arcane magic. This abuse eventually transformed the exiled night elves into high elves — or the Quel'dorei, as they came to call themselves. In the course of their exile, the high elves founded the nation of Quel'Thalas on the continent of Lordaeron and used their magic to protect themselves from the indigenous peoples. In time, they constructed many amazing cities. The high elves rarely interacted with the other races, which they viewed as "lesser"; only in times of great danger did high elves seek out aid from dwarves and humans. The Horde posed just such a threat, leading the high elves to join the Alliance. Alas, their wondrous lands were ultimately destroyed for their troubles.

The few high elves who traveled with the Alliance forces to Kalimdor in the course of the Third War learned to their horror that Quel'Thalas had fallen to the undead Scourge. Left with no homeland to return to and gripped with a burning desire for vengeance, these high elves decided to remain in Kalimdor. In fact, on the infrequent occasions that ships brave the treacherous seas, other high elves have joined them from the ruins of Lordaeron. This aloof and brooding lot spends much of its time hunting down the remaining undead that plague Kalimdor's wilds.

The high elves are interested in Kalimdor for another reason. It is home to the wondrous World Tree, long in the care of their cousins the night elves. As well, a series of hidden moon wells — receptacles of mystic energy — also dot this land. With Quel'Thalas gone, the possibili-

ties that such places offer draw the high elves. This interest is more than academic: the high elves have used magic for countless generations, falling prey to its addictive allure. Even non-spellcasting high elves cannot operate or even think clearly without replenishing their energies daily.

Appearance: The willowy high elves stand a few inches taller than humans, ranging over 6 feet tall on average. They are typically slimmer than the more muscular humans, however, with an average weight of 100 to 175 pounds. They have fair hair and skin, with brilliantly colored eyes. They reach adulthood at 110 years of age, but can live up to 2,000 years before dying of old age.

Region: Theramore Isle serves as the high elves' home base on Kalimdor. They are not the most social of beings, however. Those who live in Theramore keep to themselves, distrustful of the other races, who they secretly believe are trying to steal their magical artifacts and power.

High elves are known to roam the continent of Kalimdor, but with no clear pattern or area of focus. Relations with their cousins are not good, though, so high elves steer clear of Ashenvale and other night elf controlled lands.

Affiliation: Alliance. Overcome with grief for their dead nation and burdened with magical dependency, high elves have withdrawn from their human and dwarven allies to the point of virtually ostracizing themselves. Though humans still accept the high elves' aid, Ironforge dwarves deal with high elves only when necessary — sensing, perhaps, how far the elves might go to feed their secret racial addiction.

As for the high elves' relations with night elves… well, they are not strong. The two races split in ancient times due to the high elves' lust for arcane magic, and matters have apparently not changed much. Similarly, there is no love lost between high elves and orcs. Tauren are dismissed as uncultured savages.

High Elf Racial Traits

- +2 Dexterity, +2 Intelligence, −2 Constitution. High elves are a magically adept race, but their slight frames make them rather frail.

• *Medium:* As Medium creatures, high elves have no special bonuses or penalties due to their size.

• High elf base land speed is 30 feet.

• +2 racial bonus on saving throws against all mind-affecting spells or effects.

• *Low-Light Vision:* High elves can see twice as far as humans in starlight, moonlight, torchlight, and similar conditions of poor illumination. They retain the ability to distinguish color and detail under these conditions.

• *Arcane Ability:* High elves with Intelligence scores of 10 or higher have the racial ability to cast 4 0-level spells (cantrips) each day, chosen from the sorcerer and wizard spell lists (see *PHB*, Chapter 11: Spells, "Sorcerer/ Wizard Spells"). They cast these spells as a 1st-level sorcerer in all respects: they need not prepare these spells in advance; they may cast them in any combination up to their spell limit; they are subject to any chances of arcane spell failure.

When casting these spells, a high elf functions as a 1st-level caster for all spell effects dependent on level. This racial ability is handled separately from any spellcasting the high elf performs as part of any class ability.

• *Increased Caster Level:* Owing to their long and intimate study of arcane magic, high elves are considered to have an effective +1 caster level in all their arcane spellcasting classes. High elves do not receive spells earlier or obtain any other benefits for gaining a level in an arcane spellcasting class (such as bonus metamagic or item creation feats, class abilities, and so on). Rather, the spells that they normally cast are considered 1 level higher in terms of effects such as range, duration, damage, and so forth.

• *Empowered Magic:* Once per day, a high elf can apply the Empower Spell feat to any spell as it is being cast without incurring the normal spell slot penalty. This use must be declared before casting the spell, and it is lost if the spell cannot be completed (such as if the high elf fails a Concentration check).

• *Magic Addiction:* High elves are addicted to arcane energy. A high elf must spend time each morning resisting the distractions of addiction or suffer a –1 penalty to caster level for all spells and a –2 penalty on all saving throws against spells. Thus, a high elf can effectively be prevented from casting any spells at all while in the addiction's grip (i.e., reduced to caster level 0). This time is spent the same as if the high elf was preparing divine or arcane spells, although it is independent of any time actually spent in spell preparation. (This effectively doubles the time a high elf spellcaster must devote to spell preparation, although the two time periods need not be done in sequence.)

Devoting time to resisting the addiction is unnecessary if the high elf is within 50 feet of a moon well. In fact, even after leaving the well's vicinity, its lingering energies are sufficient to stave off the addiction for a number of days equal to the high elf's Wisdom modifier.

Night elves and tauren can sense the high elves' addiction on some mystical level. As such, high elves suffer a –2 circumstance penalty to all Charisma-based skill checks relating to night elves and tauren.

• *Weapon Proficiency:* High elves receive the Martial Weapon Proficiency feats for the longbow, composite longbow, and either the short sword or rapier (choose at character creation).

• +2 racial bonus to Concentration, Knowledge (arcana), and Spellcraft checks. These skills are also considered class skills for all high elf characters.

• *Automatic Languages:* Common and Thalassian.

• *Bonus Languages:* Darnassian, Dwarven, Goblin, Kalimdoran, Orc.

• *Favored Class:* Sorcerer or wizard. A multiclass high elf's sorcerer or wizard class does not count when determining whether she suffers an XP penalty for multiclassing (see *PHB*, Chapter 3: Classes, "Multiclass Characters," *XP for Multiclass Characters*). High elves are known for their heritage as masters of arcane spellcasting; some train their talent (becoming wizards) while others tap into their natural affinity (becoming sorcerers). The choice of sorcerer or wizard as a character's preferred class must be selected as soon as the character acquires a level in either the sorcerer or wizard class, and it cannot be changed thereafter.

• *Level Adjustment:* +1. Due to their arcane power, high elves are somewhat more powerful yet gain character levels more slowly than most of the other races common to Azeroth. See Starting Characters and Level Adjustment, above, for more details.

Elf, Night

Description: Night elves — or Kaldorei, as they call themselves — are a reclusive race based in the ancient land of Kalimdor. The Kaldorei were the first race to awaken in the world of the **Warcraft RPG**. They were also the first to study arcane magic and let it loose upon the world, ultimately ending in the first invasion by the Burning Legion. That catastrophic event caused the night elves to forsake arcane magic for fear that the demonic forces would return. The Kaldorei closed themselves off from the rest of the world and remained hidden atop the holy mountain of Hyjal for thousands of years.

Although they resisted the lure of arcane magic, night elves were closely linked to other power. Mount Hyjal was a source of great mystical energy; prolonged exposure to this magical essence gifted the Kaldorei with immortality and tremendous resistance to magic. Useful though these remarkable powers were through the centuries, the night elves gave them up to help repel the Burning Legion in the final confrontation at the Battle of Mount Hyjal.

Night elves are wild, passionate, and fervent in their defense of the land. They can be very superstitious about some issues, such as the right time of day for a battle, while being just as brutally pragmatic about other matters, such as accepting losses in the course of battle. While most Kaldorei long for the past when they were immortal, they do not regret the choices made in the course of defeating their ages-old enemies.

Night elves began worshipping nature deities and totem spirits in ancient times, after the first battles against the Burning Legion. The pantheon includes Elune, the moon goddess; Cenarius, the demigod of the Groves; and Malorne, the Waywatcher.

Appearance: Night elves stand an imposing 7 feet tall and typically weigh between 200 and 250 pounds. They are far more muscular than humans and high elves, though their forms are lithe and graceful rather than heavyset. In addition to their larger stature, they also appear somewhat more feral than their high elf cousins. Their skin runs in hues of violet to shadowy purple, and their hair can range from amber to deep blues and greens. Night elves' eyes have no pupils, and most glow silver especially in moonlight. A night elf's ears are even more pronounced than a high elf's, often tapering to a point up to a foot long. Their clothes reflect their ties to nature, usually being adorned with leaf or animal motifs. Night elves achieve adulthood at 110 years and, while no longer immortal, can live to see a second millennium.

Region: Much of the night elves' original home of Ashenvale Forest was either destroyed or corrupted during the Burning Legion's invasion of Kalimdor. That conflict raged across the face of Kalimdor, and though the demons were defeated, night elf society was left in tatters in the aftermath. Druids of the wild now strive to heal and restore the land, while sentinels keep their eternal watch for enemies both seen and unseen.

Night elves live in and around the village of Nighthaven, located within the sacred Moonglade on the slopes of Mount Hyjal. Surrounded by colossal trees, ancient ruins, and the holy moon wells, Nighthaven is one of the last remaining refuges of the night elf race.

Though night elves value their allegiance to the Alliance, few humans or dwarves are allowed into the heart of Nighthaven, nor are they ever shown the sacred moon wells. The distrusted high elves are *never* allowed near Nighthaven. Only deranged satyrs and the feral furbolgs offer any real threat to the night elves' otherwise tranquil abode.

Affiliation: Alliance. Night elves worked well with the orcs against the Burning Legion, but the night elves' native caution and the orcs' natural distrust have since soured those relations.

Night elves are not the life of the party among the Alliance races, either. Although honorable and just, their natural distrust of the other races, their wild — even feral — appearances, and their nocturnal habits and shadowy powers make integration with other cultures difficult. That night elves are hesitant to leave the shadowy beauty of the forests surrounding Mount Hyjal does not help. Still, many among them are wise — or curious — enough to believe that maintaining their friendship with the Alliance in Theramore and Bael Modan is imperative. They are fascinated by the younger races and thrill to the prospects of trade and exotic wares. These more adventurous spirits have journeyed into the southlands as explorers, merchants, and ambassadors.

This curiosity does not extend to the high elves. The night elves can almost smell their cousins' magic addiction. The Kaldorei remember banishing them long ago for their unrepentant dabbling in arcane magic and still view high elves as rabid dogs that are bound to bite someone sooner or later. If ever the necessity arose, night elves would feel no remorse at slaying their wayward cousins. They respect Jaina Proudmoore's call that the high elves are part of the Alliance, but spare them no love. Night elves work with high elves when necessary, but it takes time and effort for a high elf to overcome a night elf's dislike.

Of all the Alliance races, night elves show the highest incidence of going over to the Horde, mainly because their hatred of high elves overwhelms any dislike of orcs. Still, such defections remain uncommon.

Night Elf Racial Traits

• **+2 Wisdom, –2 Intelligence.** Night elves have very keen senses, but they often rely on instinct over intellect.

• *Medium:* As Medium creatures, night elves have no special bonuses or penalties due to their size.

• Night elf base land speed is 30 feet.

• *Superior Low-Light Vision:* Night elves can see 3 times farther than a human can in starlight, moonlight, torchlight, and similar conditions of poor illumination. They retain the ability to distinguish color and detail under these conditions.

• *Energy Resistance:* Night elves have cold and fire resistance 1. This trait represents but a lingering portion of the resistance that the race once enjoyed.

• *Shadowmeld:* A night elf may blend into the surrounding darkness. At night or in low-light environments, this extraordinary ability grants a +10 circumstance bonus to Hide checks when not moving.

• *Spell Resistance:* Night elves have spell resistance equal to 5 + character level. A spellcaster must make a caster level check (1d20 + caster level) at least equal to the night elf's spell resistance rating to affect the night elf. Spell resistance is constant and automatic; the night elf does not need to do anything special to use it. This extraordinary ability is but a lingering portion of the resistance that the race once enjoyed.

• *Weapon Familiarity:* Night elves may treat the moonglaive as a martial weapon, rather than an exotic weapon.

• +2 racial bonus on Knowledge (nature) and Survival checks. These skills are also considered class skills for all night elf characters.

• *Automatic Languages:* Common and Darnassian.

• *Bonus Languages:* Goblin, Low Common, Orc, Thalassian.

• *Favored Class:* Scout. A multiclass night elf's scout class does not count when determining whether he suffers an XP penalty for multiclassing (see *PHB*, Chapter 3: Classes, "Multiclass Characters," *XP for Multiclass Characters*).

• *Prohibited Classes:* Night elves foreswore the practice of arcane magic centuries ago and even built up great resistance against it. They can master arcane power, although doing so changes them forever. Once a night elf gains a level that grants the use of arcane spellcasting, he suffers a painful transformation that strips away his native night elf abilities and replaces them with high elf racial abilities. The complete change occurs in the space of one week and cannot be reversed once it has started.

• *Level Adjustment:* +1. Due to their mystic resistance, night elves are somewhat more powerful, yet they gain character levels more slowly than most of the other races common to Azeroth. See Starting Characters and Level Adjustment, above, for more details.

Goblin

Description: Goblins are crafty and shrewd small humanoids with an overwhelming interest in commerce and a strong curiosity about all things mechanical. Goblin society is a fragmented thing at best, defined chiefly by commerce and trade. The ultimate schemers and con artists, goblins are always in search of a better deal.

They do value technology as a useful aspect of commerce. Some say that their advantage — and their curse — is to be the primary users of technology in a world governed by magic. They employ vast teams of engineers who strive to expand on current technology for a wide array of applications. They constantly build and repair machines and work on new ideas. Unfortunately, their lack of discipline means that many creations end up half finished as something else catches their attention or that a machine explodes after its creator forgot to add a vital release valve.

They are quite envious of the Ironforge dwarves' invention of firearms — both from a commercial and a technological standpoint. Goblins recognize the potential such technology could have… and the profits that could be gained from bringing it to the world. The goblins will not master that aspect of technology for some time, at least, since many past experiments with gunpowder and explosives have ended more than a few goblins' curiosity.

A number of trade princes rule over the various goblin holdings around the world. Though the trade princes all live in the goblin island city of Undermine far from Kalimdor, they each control their own private armies and trade fleets. In turn, each controls vast rings of trade, mining, deforestation, slave rings, and poaching.

The trade princes are the most cunning of their race and will stop at nothing to amass their fortunes and power, whether through legitimate means or via black markets and treachery. Goblins encountered on Kalimdor are either privateers or agents of the various trade princes of Undermine.

Goblins are tenacious fighters. They attack from range with crossbows and use maces when the fighting gets in close. When attacked in their warrens, they fight with tools as well. They have a good grasp of tactics and strategy, and are masters of sieges. Their love of large machines makes them ideal for attacking fortifications.

They are tricksters and con artists to the extreme. Their mission in the world is to create incredible new inventions, accrue the resulting wealth, and cause as much subtle mischief as possible along the way.

Appearance: Goblins are slight and wiry, averaging 3 feet in height and weighing between 30 and 50 pounds. They have large noses and ears and green skin. Their long arms and fingers are very useful for reaching into the back of some machine they are currently working on. They tend to wear leather clothing, often cut into aprons to protect against caustic fluids.

Region: Goblins are a wily, cunning race of traders and tinkers typically encountered as part of a trading envoy… or when on a pirate raid. Goblin ships frequent the seas around Kalimdor, seeking riches, slaves, or exotic wares. The main goblin port in Kalimdor is Ratchet, a medium-sized harbor city located on the eastern shore of the Barrens directly between Durotar and Theramore.

Since goblins are essentially neutral to everyone, Ratchet entertains members of each race who come for the nightlife. All in all, Ratchet is a wild place, offering great bars, fight clubs, girls (and guys), and fast boats. The goblins run their operations around the clock, and boats are always pulling in and out of harbor carrying loads of precious goods and cargo. Goblin guardsmen patrol the streets, making sure that the various Horde and Alliance visitors play nice with each other. More than one drunken hooligan has laughed at being told to calm down by a pair of tiny goblin guardsmen… only to wake up in jail with bruises and singed clothing.

Affiliation: None. Constantly building and inventing requires massive amounts of resources, both for creating the machines themselves and to maintain the ones that actually work. Cannibalizing the old machines can only sustain this by so much, so goblins rely on trade with as many races and cultures as possible.

Their mechanical and mercantile pursuits are not always performed within the bounds of polite society. Though not evil, goblins are willing to embark on shady business ventures — slavery, deforestation, environmentally unsound oil drilling — to accomplish their goals. They are opportunists to the core and revel in bartering the better deal at every turn.

Goblin Racial Traits

• +2 Dexterity, –2 Strength. Goblins are quite clever, but not terribly strong.

• *Small:* As a Small creature, a goblin gains a +1 size bonus to Armor Class, a +1 size bonus on attack rolls, and a +4 size bonus on Hide checks. He must use smaller weapons than humans use, however, and his lifting and carrying limits are three-quarters of those of a Medium character.

• Goblin base land speed is 20 feet.

• *Low-Light Vision:* Goblins can see twice as far as humans can in starlight, moonlight, torchlight, and similar conditions of poor illumination. They retain the ability to distinguish color and detail under these conditions.

• +2 racial bonus on Appraise, Craft (alchemy), Diplomacy, and Listen checks. These skills are also considered class skills for all goblin characters.

• +4 racial bonus on Craft (mechanical objects) checks. Goblins are master craftsmen.

• *Weapon Familiarity:* Goblins may treat blunderbusses, flintlock pistols, and long rifles as martial weapons, rather than as exotic weapons.

• *Automatic Languages:* Common and Goblin.

• *Bonus Language:* Any unrestricted.

• *Favored Class:* Tinker. A multiclass goblin's tinker class does not count when determining whether he suffers an XP penalty for multiclassing (see *PHB*, Chapter 3: Classes, "Multiclass Characters," *XP for Multiclass Characters*).

Half-Elf

Description: Half-elves are a mix of human and high elf. High elves are not prolific to begin with, and coupling with another race is not looked upon with favor. As such, half-elves are rare in Kalimdor. Most came west with Jaina Proudmoore's army and settled in Theramore. Few spend much time among their high elf cousins, who look upon them with disdain.

Even among humans, half-elves do not receive much acceptance. Many humans are envious of the half-elves' extended life spans and mistrustful of the simple fact that they are *different*. Born of two cultures but fully accepted in neither, most half-elves develop a grim outlook on life. Some struggle against prejudice to gain acceptance among high elves and/or humans, while others spurn their heritage and strike out on their own.

Appearance: Half-elves have much the same build as humans. Like their high elf parents, they tend to have fair skin and hair and brilliantly (usually blue or green) colored eyes. They are more heavily built than purebred high elves, however. Though lacking his elven parent's longevity, a half-elf still enjoys a long life span, reaching maturity at 20 years of age and living for two or three centuries on average.

Region: Theramore serves as the home base for most half-elves, although few spend a great deal of time there. Lack of acceptance in human and high elf society leads many half-elves to wander Kalimdor. Several have become scouts simply to spend long periods of time away from other people.

Affiliation: Alliance. Half-elves try to socialize with humans more than with high elves —

the latter are known to snub these mixed breed offspring before a half-elf can even say hello. Humans do not always act much better, as attempts to fit in often fail to work out as well as the half-elves would like. Interestingly, half-elves find more acceptance among other races such as dwarves and goblins, who hold no strong opinions on human-elf mating. Half-elves likewise find kindred spirits in half-orcs, who are shunned in much the same way.

Faced with enough prejudice, some half-elves will discard their mixed heritage and side with the Horde.

Half-Elf Racial Traits

• *Medium:* As Medium creatures, half-elves have no special bonuses or penalties due to their size.

• Half-elf base land speed is 30 feet.

• *Low-Light Vision:* Half-elves can see twice as far as humans in starlight, moonlight, torchlight, and similar conditions of poor illumination. They retain the ability to distinguish color and detail under these conditions.

• *Elven Blood:* For all special abilities and effects, a half-elf is considered a high elf (as appropriate).

• +1 racial bonus on saving throws against spells or spell-like effects. A half-elf does not enjoy a full high elven legacy that would otherwise bestow Arcane Ability (and the corresponding addiction); however, a half-elf's blood does carry enough mystical heritage to offer some resistance to magic.

• +2 racial bonus on Gather Information and Sense Motive checks. Half-elves have learned to be wary of deception and the possibility of persecution. These skills are also considered class skills for all half-elf characters.

• *Automatic Languages:* Common and Thalassian.

• *Bonus Languages:* Any unrestricted.

• *Favored Class:* Any. When determining whether a multiclass half-elf takes an XP penalty, his highest-level class does not count (see *PHB*, Chapter 3: Classes, "Multiclass Characters," *XP for Multiclass Characters*).

Half-Night Elves

Only a year has passed since the Horde and Alliance joined forces with the night elves to repel the attack upon Nordrassil. As such, night elves and humans have not found sufficient time to mingle and produce any adult offspring. This does not mean they cannot exist, though they would be far rarer than the typical breed of half-elf.

If a player simply *must* play a half-elf of night elven descent, the only rules difference is that the half-elf looks more like a night elf and is treated as a night elf for all special abilities and effects (as appropriate). Instead of Thalassian, the half-elf has Darnassian as an automatic language.

Half-Orc

Description: The existence of half-orcs is something both humans and orcs would prefer to ignore. In fact, the parent races commonly ignore half-orcs whenever they have the opportunity.

Unlike half-elves, who prefer to become loners rather than face prejudice, half-orcs often become highly visible and vocal members of their parent society. Almost by necessity, they present their half-breed circumstance as a defiant badge of honor. They are proud and fearless — indeed, they will take risks that other races would consider too dangerous (or downright suicidal) in an effort to prove themselves the equal of the "pure" races.

This behavior is seldom entirely successful. The parent cultures will take advantage of a half-orc's fearless nature and encourage him to pursue all manner of foolhardy tasks — "for the sake of his people," of course. No great loss ensues if the half-orc dies in the attempt, and some other suicide mission is always waiting if the half-orc somehow beats the odds on the last one.

Along similar lines, many in the parent cultures are not above goading a half-orc into performing ridiculous dares — stealing a guard's helm, mooning a ruler during a formal affair,

eating spoiled meat, and so on. A half-orc desperate for acceptance may take on such stupid challenges, but they can also backfire if a half-orc has enough and turns on those who provoke him. An enraged half-orc should not be taken lightly.

Appearance: Half-orcs stand 6 1/2 feet in height on average and weigh from 200 to 250 pounds. Males are noticeably taller and heavier than females. Their skin ranges from light green to grayish brown, and their hair is coarse like an orc's, ranging from brown to black in color. The orc lineage is unmistakable, but not as pronounced as a purebred orc — the ears are not quite as large, the nose not as piggish, and the tusks jut far less. Half-orcs are longer lived than their orc parents, with life spans equivalent to a human's.

Region: Refer to the human and orc racial entries. If raised by humans, a half-orc most likely makes Theramore his home. If raised by orcs, he probably comes from the city of Orgrimmar in Durotar.

Affiliation: Either. Half-orcs are Alliance or Horde depending primarily upon where they were raised. Still, half-orcs more often find a place within the Horde. Acceptance is grudging even among orcs, which is better than nothing. They have to work twice as hard to prove themselves, but at least they *can* prove themselves. Humans see half-orcs as barely civilized beasts, little better than orcs themselves.

Elves and dwarves tend to lump half-orcs in with the orc side of things, while tauren and goblins prove more tolerant. Half-orcs can find kindred spirits in half-elves, who are shunned in much the same way.

Half-Orc Racial Traits

• +2 Constitution, –2 Wisdom. Half-orcs are smarter than their orc parents, but are given to rash action to prove their honor and courage.

• *Medium:* As Medium creatures, half-orcs have no special bonuses or penalties due to their size.

• Half-orc base land speed is 30 feet.

• *Low-Light Vision:* Half-orcs can see twice as far as humans in starlight, moonlight, torchlight, and similar conditions of poor illumination. They retain the ability to distinguish color and detail under these conditions.

• *Orc Blood:* For all special abilities and effects, a half-orc is considered an orc.

• +1 racial bonus on saving throws against fear-related spells or effects. Debate continues over whether half-orcs are fearless due to some aspect of their human parentage or if this trait is simply another way in which they prove that they are the equal of any "pureblood" race.

• +2 racial bonus on Intimidate and Sense Motive checks. Half-orcs are as intimidating as their orc parents and have learned to look beyond surface appearances in order to survive. These skills are also considered class skills for all half-orcs.

• *Automatic Languages:* Common and Orc.

• *Bonus Languages:* Any unrestricted.

• *Favored Class:* Barbarian. A multiclass half-orc's barbarian class does not count when determining whether he suffers an XP penalty for multiclassing (see *PHB*, Chapter 3: Classes, "Multiclass Characters," *XP for Multiclass Characters*).

Orc

Description: Orcs once cultivated a shamanistic society upon the dying world of Draenor. Then the dark magics of the Burning Legion corrupted them, transforming the orc people into a voracious, unstoppable Horde. Lured to the world of Azeroth through a dimensional gateway, the Horde was manipulated into waging war against the human nations of Stormwind and Lordaeron. These struggles went on for generations.

Recently, under the visionary leadership of Thrall, the orcs stripped themselves of demonic influence. They now strive to recover their lost heritage and return to their ancient, shamanistic ways. Even as they rebuild their culture, the orcs do not forget recent events. They will stop at nothing to ensure that they are never used as pawns again.

Though they often appear to outsiders as a barbaric and brutal people, orcs are very proud and noble in their own way. They prize honor and skill above material wealth. Though brutal in combat, orcs fight with surprising grace and style. They do not throw their lives away recklessly, but neither do they avoid danger, trusting their honor and skill to carry them through most encounters.

They value honor above all and go to great lengths to prove themselves to those whom they respect. The easiest way to pick a fight with an orc is to insult his honor. Orcs distrust outsiders, but make strong friendships quickly when trust has been proven.

The concept of honor is seen in every level of orc society, even in their naming practices. An orc's first name is given early in life, often derived from a family name or the name of a great hero. The tribe bestows the second name after the orc reaches maturity, this name based upon some great deed. Such a practice gives rise to surnames such as Doomhammer, Elfkicker, Foe-ender, Skullsplitter, Thumper, and the like. This second name may be changed if a new one seems more appropriate. Many young orcs leave their tribe to seek their way in the world and bring honor to themselves and their family through great deeds. Adventuring provides a wide door to both honor and combat skill.

Orcs do not worship a set pantheon of gods. Instead, their shamans worship nature, the elements, and orc ancestors. The race boasts a long tradition of rulership by shamans. Orcs venerate their elders, especially those who accomplished great deeds in their lifetime. They express this veneration through oral tradition, passing the legends of great orcs through the generations in legend and song.

Appearance: Male orcs average almost 7 feet tall and weigh from 250 to 300 pounds, with women typically a half foot shorter and 50 to 100 pounds lighter. Their skin ranges from light green to grayish brown, and their hair is coarse and usually black or brown, graying with age. Large ears, flattened noses, and a large mouth full of sharp teeth with jutting lower canines comprise their most prominent features. Orcs wear a variety of clothing styles, from furs and hides in some clans to heavy metal armor in others. Orcs are a relatively short-lived people, reaching maturity

in about 18 years and rarely living longer than 75 years.

Region: The orcs came to Azeroth from another world entirely. What passed for a homeland in Lordaeron was lost. Yet under the guidance of Thrall, the orcs came to Kalimdor to establish a new home. In the aftermath of the vicious struggle against the Burning Legion, they have begun to do just that with the realm of Durotar. The harsh landscape is much like the orcs' original, blasted home world of Draenor.

The capital city of Orgrimmar, nestled within a jagged mountain valley, bustles with crude industry and trade. The orcs are fond of their tauren neighbors (whose homeland Mulgore lies west, across the Barrens) and delight in trading and hunting with them. Tauren are often found milling with their orc friends around Orgrimmar's sport arenas and taverns.

Though orcs hold no lingering interest in conquest or domination, they understandably remain wary of their human neighbors to the south. Orc patrols set out regularly to ensure that the agents of Theramore keep their distance from Durotar's borders.

Affiliation: Horde. Orc relations with most other races are shaky at best. The Alliance races can little forget invasions of years past and are loath to trust that the orcs now follow more peaceful ways — especially when many orc tribes have not left the warrior lifestyle. While affairs are less than calm with humans, dwarves, and elves, the orcs get along well with tauren. The two races enjoy many cultural similarities, making for a strong bond despite their disparate heritage. Goblins are looked upon with tolerance, as they often have interesting things worth trading for.

Orc Racial Traits

- **+2 Constitution, –2 Intelligence.** Orcs are tougher than humans, but they are not as refined.
- *Medium:* As Medium creatures, orcs have no special bonuses or penalties due to their size.
- Orc base land speed is 30 feet.
- *Low-Light Vision:* Orcs can see twice as far as humans in starlight, moonlight, torchlight, and similar conditions of poor illumination. They retain the ability to distinguish color and detail under these conditions.
- *Battle Rage:* An orc can channel his warrior fury to become truly fearsome in combat. This is considered a racial ability and works almost exactly like the barbarian's rage (*PHB*, Chapter 3: Classes, "Class Descriptions," *Barbarian*).

The only distinction is that the orc can normally fly into a rage once each day. If the orc is of a class that provides a similar rage ability (such as the barbarian class), the orc's racial battle rage allows him to rage one additional time that day. Regardless, an orc may rage only once per encounter.

- *Weapon Familiarity:* Orcs may treat orcish claws of attack as a martial weapon, rather than an exotic weapon.
- *Weapon Proficiency:* Orcs receive the Martial Weapon Proficiency feat for the battleaxe.
- +2 racial bonus on Handle Animal (wolf) and Intimidate checks. These skills are also considered class skills for all orc characters.
- +1 racial bonus on attack rolls against humans. Humans and orcs have a long history of enmity.
- *Automatic Language:* Common and Orc.
- *Bonus Languages:* Goblin, Low Common, Taur-ahe.
- *Favored Class:* Fighter. A multiclass orc's fighter class does not count when determining whether he suffers an XP penalty for multiclassing (see *PHB*, Chapter 3: Classes, "Multiclass Characters," *XP for Multiclass Characters*).

Tauren

Description: Tauren are a fierce race of nomads who long roamed the plains of Kalimdor. They are largely xenophobic toward other races, but do keep up trading relationships. Occasionally, an individual tauren will feel the need to leave his home and seek his fortune in the outside world, where his immense strength and combat ability are highly valued.

Tauren exemplify the strong, silent type. They rarely speak or laugh, especially among people whom they do not know well. They prefer to let their actions do the talking for them. Many an argument with a tauren has ended after the tauren squeezes a bench until it splinters. A tauren can take a long time to open up to his companions, but they will find him a great friend and staunch defender once he does.

Tauren bear little love for warfare or strife — but when riled, they are implacable enemies. Ferocious fighters, they rely on their tremendous strength to carry them through battle.

Moderation in all things and living in harmony with the world are attitudes that the tauren value greatly. Guarding the rugged beauty of the land and maintaining a sense of continuity between past and future generations, they live in careful balance with their environment. Indeed, they worship the spirits and elements of the plains on which they live, and they commune with the spirits of their ancestors for guidance.

They have a primitive goddess they call the Earth Mother, whom they worship above all else. She is the harmony of nature itself. Some conjecture that she may be a manifestation of the legendary Alextrasza, the red dragon Aspect of life.

While the tauren have a written language, based on pictoforms rather than an alphabet, their nomadic ancestry discouraged writing. As such, written documentation usually falls to the tribe's shamans and is done on the sides of huts, clothing, tools, or even rocks and other natural formations. Most history and lessons are passed down orally from one generation to the next.

Tauren have several names. They receive a name at birth and another during a ceremony to celebrate reaching adulthood. This adult name describes some event in their lives or some notable individual characteristic: for instance, Blackhide, Earthborn, Halfhorn, Hidemaker, Riverwatcher, Scar, Splithoof, Stormchaser, or

Windrunner. A tauren may also acquire a third name that he uses when dealing with outsiders.

Appearance: Tauren are very large and muscular. Males average 7 1/2 feet tall and typically weigh 350 pounds or more, most of which is muscle; females are a bit shorter and lighter than males. Tauren are terrifically strong, but they lack much fine coordination. Their bodies are covered in a shaggy coat of hair that varies greatly depending on the individual's family line. Hair can range in color from black to brown to white, with even some multicolored pelts. Their eyes are generally black or brown.

Tauren wear natural clothing such as animal hides and furs, partly from tradition but also because finding more refined clothes or armor that fits proves difficult. They prize jewelry of all kinds and often twine gems into their coats or wrap bracelets around their horns. Tauren have relatively short life spans, reaching adulthood around age 15 and rarely living for longer than 100 years.

Region: After living as nomads for generations, the peace-loving tauren followed their aged chief Cairne Bloodhoof to a new home atop a flat mesa-like peak called Thunder Bluff. Nestled in the lightly wooded foothills of Mulgore, Thunder Bluff stands as a peaceful agrarian refuge for the mighty hunter race. The tauren revel in their new city and enjoy the peace and security of a standing military.

Contact with outsiders is usually limited to those who seek out the fine hides and furs the tauren provide from the herd animals their hunters track and the high-quality grains that the tauren now cultivate. In exchange, tauren usually get luxury items they cannot produce for themselves, such as jewelry and forged steel tools and weapons.

Tauren encountered outside of their lands are generally mercenaries, herdsmen, or laborers. Many find work as bodyguards to the wealthy, as few wish to tangle with a 7-foot pile of muscle.

Affiliation: Horde. Tauren welcome the orcs of Durotar as spiritual brethren. Though the tauren bear no direct hatred of humans or dwarves, they feel that the aggressive newcomers could be trouble for their land. The tauren spare no trust for high elves, sensing the taint of their magic addiction. In contrast, tauren hold night elves in awe, remembering both the greatness and recklessness achieved by the Kaldorei in ancient times… and the resultant cataclysm wrought by their pride.

Tauren Racial Traits

• +4 Strength, +2 Constitution, –2 Dexterity. Tauren are some of the most powerful creatures on two legs, but this strength comes at a cost to their agility.

• *Large (tall):* As Large (tall) creatures, tauren have a –1 size penalty to Armor Class, a –1 size penalty to attack rolls, and a –4 size penalty to

Hide checks. Tauren have lifting and carrying limits twice those of a Medium character, and have a space of 10 feet and a natural reach of 10 feet.

- Tauren base land speed is 30 feet.
- *Tauren Charge:* On a charge, a tauren may lower his head to spear a target with his mighty horns. In addition to the normal benefits and hazards of a charge, this ability allows the tauren to make a single gore attack that deals 1d8 points of damage, plus 1 1/2 times his Strength modifier.

A tauren may also use a ready action to lower his head and set his horns against a charge, dealing the same damage as above if he scores a hit against the charging opponent.

- *Weapon Familiarity:* Tauren may treat tauren halberds and tauren totems as martial weapons, rather than exotic weapons.
- *Weapon Proficiency:* Tauren receive the Martial Weapon Proficiency feat for longspears and shortspears. Tauren are skilled nomadic hunters.
- +2 racial bonus on Handle Animal and Survival checks. These skills are also considered class skills for all tauren characters.
- +1 racial bonus on attack rolls with longspears and shortspears.
- *Automatic Languages:* Common and Taurahe.
- *Bonus Languages:* Goblin, Low Common, Orc.
- *Favored Class:* Fighter. A multiclass tauren's fighter class does not count when determining whether he suffers an XP penalty for multiclassing (see *PHB*, Chapter 3: Classes, "Multiclass Characters," *XP for Multiclass Characters*).
- *Level Adjustment:* +1. Due to their physical might, tauren are somewhat more powerful yet gain character levels more slowly than most of the other races common to Azeroth. See Starting Characters and Level Adjustment, above, for more details.

Classes of Warcraft

The world of **Warcraft** is a distinct fantasy realm that adjusts — or simply dismisses — certain staples of the genre. The character classes available in the game perhaps most clearly demonstrate this distinction. As you will see below, some of the standard *PHB* and *DMG* classes are adjusted, while new core and prestige classes are introduced. Most notably, the following core and prestige classes from the *PHB* and *DMG* do not exist in the **Warcraft RPG**:

Core classes: Bard, cleric, druid, monk, paladin, ranger.

Prestige classes: Arcane archer, arcane trickster, assassin, blackguard, dragon disciple, dwarven defender, eldritch knight, hierophant, horizon walker, loremaster, mystic theurge, red wizard, shadowdancer, thaumaturgist.

Some classes, such as the bard and monk, are simply not relevant to the **Warcraft** game world. Others, such as the druid and paladin, are different enough in the **Warcraft RPG** that they receive entirely new descriptions as prestige classes.

All of the NPC classes detailed in the *DMG* (adept, aristocrat, commoner, expert, warrior) exist in the world of **Warcraft**.

Classes and Spells

The sources of arcane and divine energies have a significant relationship to the rest of the **Warcraft** universe. As such, the spells and the spellcasting classes in the **Warcraft RPG** differ in key ways from what you find in the *PHB*.

Some spells function differently than what is described in the *PHB*, and there are new spells unique to **Warcraft**. See Chapter Four: Magic for changes to *PHB* spells and for any new spell descriptions.

New spells on class spell lists (see below) are marked with an asterisk (*); see Chapter Four: Magic for their descriptions.

Divine Spellcasters

Divine spellcasters in the **Warcraft RPG** gain their divine powers and spells by adhering to detailed philosophies or by petitioning nature spirits, rather than through worship of actual deities.

Human, dwarf, high elf, and half-elf priests follow the teachings of the Holy Light, which claim that all life is united beyond the physical world in one great spiritual union (see "Faiths" in Chapter Three: Adventuring).

Night elf divine spellcasters (and any rare half-elves born of human-night elf unions) most often follow a path of druidism and gain their spells from the power of nature. Night elf priests worship the moon goddess Elune.

Orc and tauren divine spellcasters follow shamanistic beliefs that focus heavily on spirit and ancestor worship.

As well, isolated cults of demon worshipers pray to the Burning Legion and gain their divine spells and powers from unknown dark forces.

Divine spellcasters do not choose domains as such, although they are restricted from using certain ones depending on their class.

Note: No core class in the **Warcraft RPG** receives the "turn or rebuke undead" class feature. Prestige classes such as the necromancer, paladin warrior, and priest receive special abilities for dealing with the undead (for the necromancer, see the forthcoming supplement **Alliance & Horde Compendium**; for the paladin warrior and priest, see "Prestige Classes," below).

Existing Core Classes

This section lists the core classes from Chapter 3: Classes in the *PHB* that are available to starting **Warcraft RPG** characters: barbarian, fighter, rogue, sorcerer, and wizard.

Barbarian

Description: Barbarians in the **Warcraft** setting typically come from orc and tauren tribes, although some humans and half-orcs may have adopted a barbaric lifestyle on Kalimdor. A few night elves choose this path also, harnessing the wildness within.

Affiliation: Any.

Altered Class Features

Orc barbarians can rage one extra time per day, from their battle rage racial ability. All barbarians gain Knowledge (military tactics) (Int) as a class skill.

This class is otherwise unchanged from the *PHB*.

Fighter

Description: Fighters are very common in the violent world of Azeroth. They can be found among all the races, from human foot soldiers to night elf archers.

Affiliation: Any.

Altered Class Features

Fighters gain Knowledge (military tactics) (Int) as a class skill.

Fighters also have more options to choose from for their bonus feats. Add the following feats to the fighter bonus feats indicated on Table 5–1: Feats in the *PHB*: Bash, Battle Language, Close Shot, Defend, Expert Rider, Lightning Reload, Mounted Sharpshooter, Pistol Whip, Storm Bolt, Sunder Armor, and Trick Shot. (See "Feats," below, for descriptions of these new feats.)

This class is otherwise unchanged from the *PHB*.

Rogue

Description: Rogues can be found among all races on Azeroth. Whether they are diplomats, spies, thieves, scoundrels, entertainers, or simply adventurers, you can find them plying just about any trade from Mount Hyjal to Ratchet.

Affiliation: Any.

Altered Class Features

Rogues gain Use Technological Device (Int) as a class skill.

This class is otherwise unchanged from the *PHB*.

Sorcerer

Description: Sorcerers own great talent for arcane spellcasting, but they have not harnessed it through the intensive training that wizards pursue. Most people do not make a distinction between sorcerers and wizards, although the latter may often refer to the former as "hedge-wizards" or some other pejorative term.

Night elves bear a particular dislike for sorcerers, seeing them as vessels of demonic power. Wizards, at least, attempt to manipulate arcane power through controlled processes, rather than letting their own bodies act as conduits.

Affiliation: Any.

Races: Any. A night elf who takes this class is stripped of her racial heritage. She effectively transforms into a high elf, although her physical attributes do not change (see "Elf, Night" in Races of Warcraft, above).

Altered Class Features

Due to **Warcraft** cosmology, many conjuration and necromancy spells are unavailable to sorcerers. Instead, they are the purview of the necromancer and warlock prestige classes (for the necromancer, see the forthcoming supplement **Alliance & Horde Compendium**; for the warlock, see "Prestige Classes," below). The following spells are excluded from the sorcerer/wizard spell lists:

- All *monster summoning (I-IX)* spells.
- All *planar binding* spells.
- The following necromancy spells: *animate dead, chill touch, circle of death, command undead, control undead, create greater undead, create undead, disrupt undead, energy drain, enervation, gentle repose, ghoul touch, halt undead, horrid wilting, soul bind*, and *undeath to death*.

Other arcane spells may be different, as noted under "Classes and Spells," above. The sorcerer is otherwise unchanged from the *PHB*.

Wizard

Description: Wizards are arcane spellcasters who have undertaken intensive study of magic in places such as the Violet Citadel of Dalaran or the Academies of Silvermoon in Quel'Thalas.

They do not channel arcane power, but instead use their vast knowledge of otherworldly forces to harness the energies to their will.

Race: Any. A night elf who takes this class is stripped of her racial heritage and effectively transforms into a high elf (see "Elf, Night" in Races of Warcraft, above). Orcs and tauren are unlikely to take this class, since they lack wizards available to train anyone and have a bias against arcane spellcasting to begin with.

Altered Class Features

Due to **Warcraft** cosmology, many conjuration and necromancy spells are unavailable to wizards. Instead, they are the purview of the necromancer and warlock prestige classes (for the necromancer, see the forthcoming supplement **Alliance & Horde Compendium**; for the warlock, see "Prestige Classes," below). The following spells are excluded from the sorcerer/wizard spell lists:

- All *monster summoning (I-IX)* spells.
- All *planar binding* spells.
- The following necromancy spells: *animate dead, chill touch, circle of death, command undead, control undead, create greater undead, create undead, disrupt undead, energy drain, enervation, gentle repose, ghoul touch, halt undead, horrid wilting, soul bind*, and *undeath to death*.

Other arcane spells may be different, as noted under "Classes and Spells," above. The wizard is otherwise unchanged from the *PHB*.

New Core Classes

This section lists three new core classes available to starting **Warcraft RPG** characters: healer, scout, and tinker.

Healer

Description: Healers are the heart of a community — and of an adventuring party. They use their powers to heal the wounded and bolster the spirits of those around them. Healers form the core of all the divine spellcasting organizations in Kalimdor, from priests of the Holy Light to druids of the wild to shamans.

Races: Any.

Alignment: Any.

Affiliation: Any.

Abilities: Wisdom is most important, though Charisma sees a fair amount of use.

Hit Die: d8.

Class Skills: The healer's class skills (and the key ability for each skill) are Bluff (Cha), Concentration (Con), Craft (Int), Diplomacy (Cha), Gather Information (Cha), Handle Animal (Cha), Heal (Wis), Knowledge (arcana) (Int), Knowledge (religion) (Int), Listen (Wis), Profession (Wis), Sense Motive (Wis), Speak Language, Spellcraft (Int), and Spot (Wis). See Chapter 4: Skills in the *PHB* for skill descriptions.

Skill Points at 1st Level: (4 + Int modifier) x 4.

Skill Points at Each Additional Level: 4 + Int modifier.

Class Features

Weapon and Armor Proficiency: Healers are proficient with all simple weapons. They are proficient with light armor only.

Spells: A healer casts divine spells. He may prepare and cast any spell from the healer spell list, provided that he can cast spells of that level, but he must choose and prepare his spells in advance during his daily meditation (see below).

To prepare or cast a spell, a healer must have a Wisdom score equal to at least 10 + the spell level (Wis 10 for 0-level spells, Wis 11 for 1st-level spells, and so on). The Difficulty Class for a saving throw against a healer's spells is 10 + the spell's level + the healer's Wisdom modifier.

Like other spellcasters, a healer can cast only a certain number of spells of each spell level per day. His base daily spell allotment is given on Table 2–1: The Healer (Hlr). In addition, he receives bonus spells per day if he has a high Wisdom score (see Table 1–1: Ability Modifiers and Bonus Spells in the *PHB*).

Table 2–1: The Healer (Hlr)

Class Level	Base Attack Bonus	Fort Save	Ref Save	Will Save	Special
1st	+0	+2	+0	+2	Brew Potion
2nd	+1	+3	+0	+3	—
3rd	+2	+3	+1	+3	—
4th	+3	+4	+1	+4	—
5th	+3	+4	+1	+4	Bonus feat
6th	+4	+5	+2	+5	—
7th	+5	+5	+2	+5	—
8th	+6/+1	+6	+2	+6	—
9th	+6/+1	+6	+3	+6	—
10th	+7/+2	+7	+3	+7	Bonus feat
11th	+8/+3	+7	+3	+7	—
12th	+9/+4	+8	+4	+8	—
13th	+9/+4	+8	+4	+8	—
14th	+10/+5	+9	+4	+9	—
15th	+11/+6/+1	+9	+5	+9	Bonus feat
16th	+12/+7/+2	+10	+5	+10	—
17th	+12/+7/+2	+10	+5	+10	—
18th	+13/+8/+3	+11	+6	+11	—
19th	+14/+9/+4	+11	+6	+11	—
20th	+15/+10/+5	+12	+6	+12	Bonus feat

Spells per Day

Level	0	1	2	3	4	5	6	7	8	9
1st	3	1	—	—	—	—	—	—	—	—
2nd	4	2	—	—	—	—	—	—	—	—
3rd	4	2	1	—	—	—	—	—	—	—
4th	5	3	2	—	—	—	—	—	—	—
5th	5	3	2	1	—	—	—	—	—	—
6th	5	3	3	2	—	—	—	—	—	—
7th	6	4	3	2	1	—	—	—	—	—
8th	6	4	3	3	2	—	—	—	—	—
9th	6	4	4	3	2	1	—	—	—	—
10th	6	4	4	3	3	2	—	—	—	—
11th	6	5	4	4	3	2	1	—	—	—
12th	6	5	4	4	3	3	2	—	—	—
13th	6	5	5	4	4	3	2	1	—	—
14th	6	5	5	4	4	3	3	2	—	—
15th	6	5	5	5	4	4	3	2	1	—
16th	6	5	5	5	4	4	3	3	2	—
17th	6	5	5	5	5	4	4	3	3	1
18th	6	5	5	5	5	4	4	4	3	2
19th	6	5	5	5	5	5	4	4	3	3
20th	6	5	5	5	5	5	4	4	4	4

A healer must choose a time each day during which he must spend 1 hour in quiet contemplation to regain his daily allotment of spells. This contemplation is not handled through worship *per se*, but is rather a meditative state in which the healer contemplates the teachings of the Holy Light or of Elune or communes with nature spirits (depending upon religion).

Since a healer does not gain his spells as divine gifts, he does not get access to domain spells in addition to his standard spells per day. Time spent resting has no effect on whether the healer can prepare spells.

Spontaneous Casting: Good healers can channel stored spell energy into healing spells that they have not prepared ahead of time. The healer can "lose" a prepared spell in order to cast any *cure* spell of the same level or lower (a *cure* spell is any spell with "cure" in its name).

An evil healer, on the other hand, converts prepared spells to *inflict* spells instead (an *inflict* spell is one with "inflict" in the title).

A healer who is neither good nor evil can convert spells either to *cure* spells or to *inflict* spells (player's choice), depending on whether the cleric is more proficient at wielding positive or negative energy. Once the player makes this choice, it cannot be reversed.

Healing Touch or Evil Touch: A good-aligned healer begins play with access to the Healing domain and can cast spells of that domain at +1 caster level. An evil-aligned healer begins play with access to the Evil domain and can cast spells of that domain at +1 caster level. A neutral-aligned healer begins play with one or the other (player's choice). Once the player makes this choice, it cannot be reversed. The healer does not cast an extra domain spell each day like *PHB* clerics; rather he simply has the ability to prepare spells of the stated domains at +1 caster level.

Brew Potion: Any healer, regardless of alignment, begins play with the Brew Potion item creation feat.

Bonus Feats: At 5th level, and every 5 levels thereafter, a healer gains a bonus feat chosen from the following types: item creation, metamagic, or Spell Focus.

Healer Spell List

A healer lacks mastery over primal forces such as nature, death, or the elements. Command of such forces comes with training as a druid of the wild, necromancer, or shaman (for the necromancer, see the forthcoming supplement **Alliance & Horde Compendium**; for the druid of the wild and the shaman, see "Prestige Classes," below). A healer may nonetheless wield powerful energies to protect his flock.

0 level — *create water, cure minor wounds, detect magic, detect poison, guidance, inflict minor wounds, light, mending, purify food and drink, read magic, resistance, virtue.*

1st level — *bane, bless, bless water, cause fear, command, comprehend languages, cure light wounds, curse water, deathwatch, divine favor, doom, entropic shield, inflict light wounds, remove fear, sanctuary, shield of faith.*

2nd level — *aid, augury, bear's endurance, bull's strength, calm emotions, consecrate, cure moderate wounds, darkness, delay poison, enthrall, find traps, gentle repose, hold person, inflict moderate wounds, lesser death coil*, lesser restoration, make whole, moonglaive*, remove paralysis, shatter, shield other, silence, sound burst, spiritual weapon, zone of truth.*

3rd level — *bestow curse, blindness/deafness, contagion, continual flame, create food and water, cure serious wounds, daylight, death coil*, deeper darkness, dispel magic, entangling roots*, glyph of warding, helping hand, inflict serious wounds, invisibility purge, locate object, magic vestment, obscure object, prayer, remove blindness/deafness, remove curse, remove disease.*

4th level — *cure critical wounds, death ward, dimensional anchor, discern lies, divination, divine power, freedom of movement, greater death coil*, greater magic weapon, imbue with spell ability, inflict critical wounds, neutralize poison, poison, repel vermin, restoration, sending, spell immunity, status, tongues.*

5th level — *flame strike, greater command, hallow, healing rain*, lesser planar ally, mass cure light wounds, mass inflict light wounds, raise dead, rejuvenation*, righteous might, scrying, slay living, spell resistance, true seeing, unhallow.*

6th level — *blade barrier, find the path, geas/quest, greater dispel magic, greater glyph of warding, harm, heal, heroes' feast, mass bear's endurance, mass bull's strength, mass cure moderate wounds, mass inflict moderate wounds, word of recall.*

7th level — *destruction, greater restoration, greater scrying, mass cure serious wounds, mass inflict serious wounds, planar ally, refuge, regenerate, repulsion, resurrection.*

8th level — *antimagic field, discern location, greater spell immunity, holy aura, mass cure critical wounds, mass inflict critical wounds, unholy aura.*

9th level — *greater planar ally, implosion, mass heal, miracle, second soul*, soul bind, touch of life*, true resurrection.*

Scout

Description: The scout excels in wilderness survival and is skilled in combat. She can track a days-old trail and snipe from the treetops with equal facility. Scouts often serve as guides for adventurers, if they are not out adventuring themselves.

Though the scout is at home in the wild, she is more of a guerilla fighter than a defender of nature (for that, see the elven ranger prestige class).

Races: Any.

Alignment: Any.

Affiliation: Any.

Abilities: Scouts rely upon Dexterity and Wisdom to survive in the wilderness and to gain the most benefit from their reliance upon bows and light armor.

Hit Die: d8.

Class Skills: The scout's class skills (and the key ability for each skill) are Climb (Str), Craft (Int), Heal (Wis), Hide (Dex), Jump (Str), Knowledge (military tactics) (Int), Knowledge (nature) (Int), Listen (Wis), Move Silently (Dex), Profession (Wis), Search (Int), Spot (Wis), Survival (Wis), Swim (Str), and Use Rope (Dex). See Chapter 4: Skills in the *PHB* for skill descriptions.

Skill Points at 1st Level: (6 + Int modifier) x 4.

Skill Points at Each Additional Level: 6 + Int modifier.

Class Features

Weapon and Armor Proficiency: A scout is proficient with all simple and martial weapons, light armor, medium armor, and shields.

Track: A scout gains Track (*PHB*, Chapter 5: Feats) as a bonus feat.

Nature Sense (Ex): A scout begins play with a +2 bonus to Knowledge (nature) and Survival checks.

Wild Healing (Ex): At 2nd level, a scout with 5 ranks in Survival can use natural materials found in the wilderness to heal wounds. The scout makes a DC 15 Survival check representing 1 hour of searching for and preparing roots, rare leaves, berries, and other such materials used for a natural brew or poultice. Once the subject ingests or applies the concoction (as appropriate), the scout makes a DC 10

Heal check. The subject recovers 1 hit point for every point that the roll exceeds 10. Wild healing affects a single subject per attempt, and the same subject benefits from the concoction only once per day.

In addition, the scout gains a +5 competence bonus to the Heal check at 6th level. This bonus applies only to Heal checks made for wild healing and increases by 5 for every 4 scout levels thereafter (+10 at 10th level, +15 at 14th level, +20 at 18th level).

Woodland Stride (Ex): At 3rd level, a scout may move through any sort of undergrowth (such as natural thorns, briars, overgrown areas, and similar terrain) at her normal speed and without taking damage or suffering any other impairment. Thorns, briars, and overgrown areas that are enchanted or magically manipulated to impede motion still affect her, however.

Trackless Step (Ex): At 4th level, a scout leaves no trail in natural surroundings and cannot be tracked. She may choose to leave a trail if so desired.

Uncanny Dodge (Ex): Starting at 4th level, a scout retains her Dexterity bonus to AC (if any) even if she is caught flat-footed or struck by an invisible attacker. She still loses her Dexterity bonus to AC if immobilized, however.

If a scout already has uncanny dodge from a different class (a scout with at least 2 levels of barbarian, for example), she automatically gains improved uncanny dodge instead (see below).

Trap Sense (Ex): At 5th level, a scout gains an intuitive sense that alerts him to danger from traps, giving him a +1 bonus on Reflex saves made to avoid traps and a +1 dodge bonus to AC against attacks made by traps. This bonus increases by 1 for every 3 scout levels thereafter (+2 at 8th, +3 at 11th, +4 at 14th, +5 at 17th, and +6 at 20th).

Locate Object (Sp): At 6th level, the scout can cast *locate object* once per day as a spell-like ability, as if he was a divine spellcaster of his class level.

Improved Uncanny Dodge (Ex): Starting at 7th level, the scout can no longer be flanked; he can react to opponents on opposite sides of him

as easily as he can react to a single attacker. This defense denies a rogue the ability to sneak attack the scout by flanking him, unless the attacker has at least 4 more rogue levels than the target has scout levels.

If a character already has uncanny dodge (see above) from a second class, the character automatically gains improved uncanny dodge instead, and the levels from the classes that grant uncanny dodge stack to determine the minimum rogue level required to flank the character.

Swift Tracker (Ex): Beginning at 8th level, a scout can move at his normal speed while following tracks without taking the standard –5 penalty. He takes only a –10 penalty (instead of the normal –20) when moving up to twice normal speed while tracking.

Venom Immunity (Su): At 9th level, a scout gains immunity to all organic poisons, including monster poisons but not mineral poisons or poison gas.

Locate Creature (Sp): At 11th level, the scout can cast *locate creature* once per day as a spell-like ability, as if he was a divine spellcaster of his class level.

Evasion (Ex): At 12th level, a scout can avoid even magical and unusual attacks with great agility. If he makes a successful Reflex saving throw against an attack that normally deals half damage on a successful save (such as a *fireball*), he instead takes no damage. Evasion can be used only if the scout is wearing light armor or no armor. A helpless scout (such as one who is unconscious or paralyzed) does not gain the benefit of evasion.

Commune with Nature (Sp): At 13th level, a scout can cast *commune with nature* once per day as a spell-like ability, as if he was a divine spellcaster of his class level.

Find the Path (Sp): At 16th level, a scout can cast *find the path* once per day as a spell-like ability, as if he was a divine spellcaster of his class level.

Wind Walk (Sp): At 20th level, a scout can cast *wind walk* once per day as a spell-like ability, as if he was a divine spellcaster of his class level.

Table 2–2: The Scout (Sct)

Class Level	Base Attack Bonus	Fort Save	Ref Save	Will Save	Special
1st	+0	+2	+2	+0	Track, nature sense
2nd	+1	+3	+3	+0	Wild healing
3rd	+2	+3	+3	+1	Woodland stride
4th	+3	+4	+4	+1	Trackless step, uncanny dodge
5th	+3	+4	+4	+1	Trap sense +1
6th	+4	+5	+5	+2	*Locate object* 1/day, wild healing +5
7th	+5	+5	+5	+2	Improved uncanny dodge
8th	+6/+1	+6	+6	+2	Swift tracker, trap sense +2
9th	+6/+1	+6	+6	+3	Venom immunity
10th	+7/+2	+7	+7	+3	Wild healing +10
11th	+8/+3	+7	+7	+3	*Locate creature* 1/day, trap sense +3
12th	+9/+4	+8	+8	+4	Evasion
13th	+9/+4	+8	+8	+4	*Commune with nature* 1/day
14th	+10/+5	+9	+9	+4	Wild healing +15, trap sense +4
15th	+11/+6/+1	+9	+9	+5	—
16th	+12/+7/+2	+10	+10	+5	*Find the path* 1/day
17th	+12/+7/+2	+10	+10	+5	Trap sense +5
18th	+13/+8/+3	+11	+11	+6	Wild healing +20
19th	+14/+9/+4	+11	+11	+6	—
20th	+15/+10/+5	+12	+12	+6	*Wind walk* 1/day, trap sense +6

Tinker

Description: The tinker builds and invents everything from crazy multipurpose knives to siege engines. Dwarves and goblins are the primary members of this class, as they produce rifles, zeppelins, and other technological innovations currently found in Azeroth.

Despite a reputation for being dangerous companions, gained mostly due to reckless goblins, tinkers are not *usually* danger-prone. The real trouble arises when they mess with gunpowder or try to build a better steam engine, and even then mishaps and explosions do not occur as often as many believe.

Races: Primarily goblins and dwarves. Orcs and tauren are the least likely to take this class, due to their disinterest in mechanical things.

Alignment: Any.

Affiliation: Any.

Abilities: A tinker favors Intelligence in order to cultivate his knowledge and craft devices.

Dexterity is always a favorite for that inevitable dive for cover. Wisdom may be a liability, depending on how one views the mind of an inventor.

Hit Die: d6.

Class Skills: The tinker's class skills (and the key ability for each skill) are Appraise (Int), Concentration (Con), Craft (Int), Decipher Script (Int), Disable Device (Int), Forgery (Int), Gather Information (Cha), Knowledge (all but arcana and religion) (Int), Open Lock (Dex), Profession (Wis), Search (Int), Use Magic Device (Cha), and Use Technological Device* (Int). See Chapter 4: Skills in the *PHB* for skill descriptions.

*See "New Skill," below.

Skill Points at 1st Level: (8 + Int modifier) x 4.

Skill Points at Each Additional Level: 8 + Int modifier.

Class Features

Weapon and Armor Proficiency: A tinker is proficient with all simple weapons.

Bonus Feats: A tinker starts play with a bonus technology-oriented feat in addition to the feat that any 1st-level character receives and the bonus feat granted to a human character (if relevant). The tinker gains an additional bonus technology feat at 5th level and every 5 tinker levels thereafter (10th, 15th, and 20th). These bonus feats must be drawn from the feats noted as technology feats (see "Feats," below). A tinker must still meet all prerequisites for a bonus technology feat.

These technology-oriented bonus feats are in addition to the feats that a character of any class receives every 3 levels (see *PHB*, Table 3–2: Experience and Level-Dependent Benefits). A tinker is not limited to the list of technology feats in that circumstance.

Scavenge (Ex): Tinkers can often find whatever they need out of random piles of spare parts and carry an astonishing variety of gadgets and gewgaws wherever they go. If a tinker needs to build something on the fly, he can make a roll to build whatever he needs at +10 DC. The tinker makes a Search check to locate parts and a Craft (technological device) check to build items.

At 4th level, he adds a +2 bonus to his scavenge checks, and then +2 every 4 levels beyond that (+4 at 8th, +6 at 12th, +8 at 16th, and +10 at 20th). A successful check means that the tinker has the items necessary to build the gadget and can jury-rig it in a tenth the normal time. On the other hand, due to the slipshod nature of the components and the need to improvise (wildly), the gadget will last only for a number of uses equal to the tinker's level or for a number of hours of continued use equal to the tinker's level (for instance, a 10th-level tinker could create a cannon that would fire 10 times or a steam-powered, three-wheeled vehicle that runs for 10 hours).

Bomb-Bouncing (Ex): At 2nd level, a tinker perfects an improved technique of bomb throwing. When throwing a grenade-like weapon, he imparts a spin to the throw that doubles the thrown object's range increment.

Evasion (Ex): At 2nd level, a tinker can avoid even magical and unusual attacks with great agility. If he makes a successful Reflex saving throw against an attack that normally deals half damage on a successful save (such as a *fireball* or an exploding siege engine), he instead takes no damage. Evasion can be used only if the tinker is

wearing light armor or no armor. A helpless tinker (such as one who is unconscious or paralyzed) does not gain the benefit of evasion.

Coolness Under Fire (Ex): At 3rd level, the tinker can take 10 on any roll that involves operating or building a mechanical device when circumstances would otherwise prevent it. This ability does not apply to attack rolls, so the tinker cannot take 10 while firing a blunderbuss.

The tinker can use coolness under fire once per day at 3rd level. At 6th level and every 3 levels thereafter, he can use it one additional time per day (to a maximum of 6 times per day at 18th level).

Fire Resistance (Ex): At 4th level, the tinker has become so used to working with intense heat, steam, and explosive forces that he gains fire resistance 5. Each time the tinker is subjected to such damage (whether from a natural or magical source), that damage is reduced by 5 points before being applied to the tinker's hit points. This resistance increases by 5 for every 5 tinker levels thereafter (10 at 9th, 15 at 14th, and 20 at 19th).

Fire resistance absorbs only damage. The tinker could still suffer unfortunate side effects such as suffocating when a fire consumes all the oxygen in the area. Fire resistance is not a supernatural or spell-like ability, so it stacks with *protection from energy* and *resist energy*.

Improved Evasion (Ex): At 11th level, a tinker's evasion ability improves. He still takes no damage on a successful Reflex saving throw against attacks such as a *fireball* or exploding invention, but henceforth he takes only half damage on a failed save. A helpless tinker (such as one who is unconscious or paralyzed) does not gain the benefit of improved evasion.

Table 2–3: The Tinker (Tnk)

Class Level	Base Attack Bonus	Fort Save	Ref Save	Will Save	Special
1st	+0	+0	+2	+2	Bonus technology feat, scavenge
2nd	+1	+0	+3	+3	Bomb-bouncing, evasion
3rd	+2	+1	+3	+3	Coolness under fire 1/day
4th	+3	+1	+4	+4	Fire resistance 5, scavenge +2
5th	+3	+1	+4	+4	Bonus technology feat
6th	+4	+2	+5	+5	Coolness under fire 2/day
7th	+5	+2	+5	+5	—
8th	+6/+1	+2	+6	+6	Scavenge +4
9th	+6/+1	+3	+6	+6	Coolness under fire 3/day, fire resistance 10
10th	+7/+2	+3	+7	+7	Bonus technology feat
11th	+8/+3	+3	+7	+7	Improved evasion
12th	+9/+4	+4	+8	+8	Coolness under fire 4/day, scavenge +6
13th	+9/+4	+4	+8	+8	—
14th	+10/+5	+4	+9	+9	Fire resistance 15
15th	+11/+6/+1	+5	+9	+9	Coolness under fire 5/day, bonus technology feat
16th	+12/+7/+2	+5	+10	+10	Scavenge +8
17th	+12/+7/+2	+5	+10	+10	—
18th	+13/+8/+3	+6	+11	+11	Coolness under fire 6/day
19th	+14/+9/+4	+6	+11	+11	Fire resistance 20
20th	+15/+10/+5	+6	+12	+12	Bonus technology feat, scavenge +10

Prestige Classes

As a general rule, the prestige classes detailed in the *DMG* and other books are uncommon or non-existent in the world of **Warcraft**. You must secure the GM's permission before you can play one of those prestige classes in the **Warcraft RPG**.

There are prestige classes unique to the world of **Warcraft**. Some are found only among certain races, although the GM may allow individual exceptions if a character meets the other class requirements. Some prestige classes are called by

different names depending on whether the hero is affiliated with the Alliance or the Horde. For example, an Alliance character with the mounted warrior prestige class is called a knight, while a Horde character is called a wolf rider. The different affiliation terms are listed within the description, but each prestige class is referred to only by its class name to avoid confusion.

Beastmaster

Description: The beastmaster is a wilderness warrior who has developed an uncanny rapport with animals. Though truly fearsome in battle, the beastmaster can be quite gentle when dealing with creatures of the wild. A beastmaster typically travels with one or more animal companions who show incredible loyalty to their humanoid friend. Though a beastmaster prefers to spend time in the wild with his animal companions, he is not averse to venturing into civilized lands when the need arises. As long as animals may be found where he travels, the beastmaster will feel at home.

Hit Die: d12.

Requirements

Affiliation: Horde or night elf.

Skills: Handle Animal 5 ranks, Survival 8 ranks.

Feats: Animal Affinity, Toughness.

Class Skills

The beastmaster's class skills (and the key ability for each skill) are Climb (Str), Craft (Int), Handle Animal (Cha), Heal (Wis), Intimidate (Cha), Jump (Str), Knowledge (nature) (Int), Spot (Wis), Survival (Wis), and Swim (Str). See Chapter 4: Skills in the *PHB* for skill descriptions.

Skill Points at Each Level: 4 + Int modifier.

Class Features

Weapon and Armor Proficiency: Beastmasters are proficient with simple and martial weapons and with light and medium armor.

Animal Companion (Ex): At 1st level, the beastmaster may attract an animal companion. This class ability functions the same as for a *PHB* druid, except that the character's beastmaster level is used where a druid level is required (*PHB*, Chapter 3: Classes, "Druid").

Wild Empathy (Ex): A beastmaster can use body language, vocalizations, and demeanor to improve the attitude of an animal (such as a bear or a giant lizard). This ability functions just like a Diplomacy check made to improve a person's attitude toward the character (*PHB*, Chapter 4: Skills). The beastmaster rolls 1d20 + beastmaster level + Charisma modifier to determine the wild empathy check result. The typical domestic animal has a starting attitude of indifferent, while wild animals are usually unfriendly.

To use wild empathy, the beastmaster and the animal must be able to study each other, which means that they must be within 30 feet of one another under normal conditions. Generally, influencing an animal in this way takes 1 minute, but as with influencing people, it might take more or less time.

A beastmaster can also use this ability to influence a magical beast with an Intelligence score of 1 or 2, but he suffers a –4 penalty on the check.

Animal Friendship (Sp): At 2nd level, the beastmaster gains the spell-like ability to befriend one or more animals in addition to the animal companion noted above, as long as the additional animals' total Hit Dice do not exceed his beastmaster level. *Animal friendship* is a spell-like ability, and the beastmaster casts as a healer of the same class level. This ability is a mind-affecting effect, and the animal receives a Will save (DC 11 + the beastmaster's Wisdom modifier) to resist the effects if it so desires.

The beastmaster may befriend one animal per day in this manner. As with the animal companion, he may leave current animal friends to find others.

Empathic Link (Su): At 3rd level, the beastmaster forms an empathic link with his animal companion out to a distance of 1 mile. The beastmaster cannot see through the companion's eyes, but the two can communicate empathically. Because of the link's limited nature, only general emotional content (fear, hunger, happiness, curiosity) can be communicated. Note that the low Intelligence of a low-level beastmaster's companion limits what the creature can communicate or understand, and even intelligent animals see the world differently from humans, so misunderstandings are always possible.

Natural Weaponry (Su): At 4th level, the beastmaster can grow claws and fangs or horns (player's choice). Once the player chooses fangs

Table 2–4: The Beastmaster (Bst)

Class Level	Base Attack Bonus	Fort Save	Ref Save	Will Save	Special
1st	+1	+2	+0	+0	Animal companion, wild empathy
2nd	+2	+3	+0	+0	*Animal friendship* 1/day
3rd	+3	+3	+1	+1	Empathic link
4th	+4	+4	+1	+1	Natural weaponry
5th	+5	+4	+1	+1	Speak with animals
6th	+6	+5	+2	+2	*Magic fang* 1/day
7th	+7	+5	+2	+2	Improved natural weaponry
8th	+8	+6	+2	+2	*Magic fang* 2/day
9th	+9	+6	+3	+3	*Scry on companion*
10th	+10	+7	+3	+3	*Greater magic fang* 3/day

or horns, the choice cannot be reversed. A beastmaster is considered proficient with these natural weapons. When making a full attack, a beastmaster uses his full base attack bonus with his 2 claw attacks but takes a –5 penalty on his bite or gore attack. Otherwise, the beastmaster can make only a single claw attack or a bite or a gore attack with a normal attack; if using a weapon, the beastmaster cannot make additional claw, bite, or gore attacks. Damage is listed below:

Size	Claw Damage	Bite/Gore Damage
Small	1d3	1d4
Medium	1d4	1d6
Large	1d6	1d8

The claws do not affect tasks requiring fine manipulation, but the overall appearance gives the beastmaster a +2 circumstance bonus to Intimidation checks. Growing and retracting the claws is considered a move action. Natural weaponry can be used only if the beastmaster is wearing light armor or no armor.

Speak with Animals (Su): At 5th level, the beastmaster may comprehend and communicate with animals and magical beasts. This ability functions as the spell *speak with animals*, although the beastmaster may do so at will.

Magic Fang (Sp): At 6th level, the beastmaster may cast *magic fang* on his animal companion once per day. This rate increases to 2/day starting at 8th level and becomes *greater magic fang* and may be cast 3/day starting at 10th level. The beastmaster casts *magic fang* as a healer equal to his class level.

Improved Natural Weaponry (Su): At 7th level, the beastmaster's claws and fangs or horns grow even longer and more wicked than before. When making a full attack, a beastmaster uses his base attack bonus with his claw attacks but takes a –2 penalty on bite or gore attacks. Damage is listed below:

Size	Claw Damage	Bite/Gore Damage
Small	1d4	1d6
Medium	1d6	1d8
Large	1d8	2d6

Claws of this size apply a –2 circumstance penalty to tasks requiring fine manipulation, and the overall appearance bestows a +4 circumstance bonus to Intimidation checks. Growing and retracting the claws is considered a free action. Improved natural weaponry can be used only if the beastmaster is wearing light armor or no armor.

Scry on Companion (Sp): Starting at 9th level, the beastmaster may scry on his animal companion (as if casting the *scrying* spell) once per day. The beastmaster's effective caster level equals his class level.

Druid of the Wild

Description: Druids of the wild are tied to the living aspects of nature — flora and fauna. They do not dabble in elemental forces; such powers are the purview of shamans. A druid of the wild grows such a strong affinity with nature that she may assume the form of animals and even supernatural beasts.

Traditionally, druids chose the path of a specific animal totem, becoming either druids of the claw or druids of the talon. Indeed, legends suggest that there were even more orders of druid than these two. After the Legion's invasion, the druids began to use the powers of all totems, combining their strengths against their enemies and becoming the druids of the wild.

A druid of the wild who turns away from nature or changes to a prohibited alignment loses all spells and druidic abilities and cannot gain levels in druid of the wild until she atones.

Hit Die: d8.

Requirements

Race: Night elf and tauren only.

Alignment: Any non-evil.

Affiliation: Any.

Skills: Knowledge (nature) 5 ranks, Survival 5 ranks.

Spellcasting: Able to cast 3rd-level divine spells.

Class Skills

The druid of the wild's class skills (and the key ability for each skill) are Concentration (Con), Craft (Int), Handle Animal (Cha), Heal (Wis), Hide (Dex), Knowledge (nature) (Int), Profession (Wis), Survival (Wis), and Swim (Str). See Chapter 4: Skills in the *PHB* for skill descriptions.

Skill Points at Each Level: 4 + Int modifier.

Class Features

Weapon and Armor Proficiency: Druids of the wild are proficient with all simple weapons, small martial melee weapons, shortbow, and longbow. They are also proficient with all natural attacks (unarmed strike, claw, bite, and so forth), regardless of the forms they assume (see wild shape, below). They are proficient with light and medium armors, but are prohibited from wearing metal armor (thus, they may wear

only padded, leather, or hide armor). They are skilled with shields but must use only wooden ones.

A druid of the wild who wears prohibited armor or wields a prohibited weapon is unable to use any of her supernatural or spell-like powers while doing so and for 24 hours thereafter. (**Note:** A druid of the wild can use wooden items that have been altered by the *ironwood* spell so that they function as though they were steel.)

Spells: Druids of the wild continue to advance in spellcasting ability. When a new druid of the wild level is gained, the character gains new spells per day as if she had also gained a level in a divine spellcasting class she belonged to before she added the prestige class. She does not, however, gain any other benefit of a character of that class (improved chance of controlling or rebuking undead, metamagic or item creation feats, and so on). In other words, she adds her druid of the wild level to the level of her original divine spellcasting class purely to determine spells per day and caster level.

Healer is the core divine spellcasting class in the **Warcraft RPG**. If the druid of the wild prestige class is used outside the **Warcraft RPG**, it could apply to clerics, druids, paladins, and rangers.

A druid of the wild casts divine spells and may prepare and cast any spell on the druid of the wild *and* healer spell lists, provided she can cast spells of that level. She prepares and casts spells the way a healer does (see above).

Spontaneous Casting: A druid of the wild can channel stored spell energy into summoning spells that she has not prepared ahead of time. The druid of the wild can "lose" a prepared spell in order to cast any *summon nature's ally* spell of the same level or lower.

A druid of the wild may still use spontaneous casting from her core class, but only for spell levels gained through that class. A 7th-level healer/8th-level druid of the wild can cast 8th level spells, but she may only spontaneously cast *cure* spells of up to 4th level (the highest caster level available to a 7th-level healer).

Green Sleep (Ex): When the night elves were charged with guarding the Well of Eternity in ancient times, part of the price for their access to nature was that druids of the wild would spend much of their time in the Emerald Dream. As a result, all druids of the wild know how to send their souls into this extraplanar realm, thus entering a state of hibernation. See Chapter Five, "The Universe Beyond," for specifics on the Emerald Dream.

A druid of the wild can enter this state of hibernation and send her soul into the Emerald Dream at will. While in hibernation, her body requires no food, water, or air. She cannot, however, emerge from hibernation without someone to awaken her.

Wild Shape (Su): At 1st level, a druid of the wild gains the ability to turn herself into a storm crow and back again once per day. This ability functions like the *polymorph* spell, except as noted here. The effect lasts for 1 hour per class level, or

Wild Shape Benefits

Storm Crow: SZ M animal; Init +3 (Dex); Spd 10 ft., fly 60 ft. (average); AC 15 (+3 Dex, +2 natural); Atk bite melee, claw melee (1d6 bite, 1d4 claw); Face/Reach 5 ft. by 5 ft./5 ft.; Str 10, Dex 17, Con 12.

Stag: SZ L animal; Init +1 (Dex); Spd 50 ft.; AC 14 (−1 size, +1 Dex, +4 natural); Atk 2 hooves melee, gore melee, or bite melee (1d6+6 hoof, 1d8+9 gore, 1d4+3 bite); Face/Reach 5 ft. by 10 ft./5 ft.; Str 22, Dex 13, Con 17.

Nightsaber Panther: SZ L animal; Init +3 (Dex); Spd 40 ft.; AC 15 (−1 size, +3 Dex, +3 natural); Atk 2 claws melee, bite melee (1d4+5 claws, 1d8+2 bite); Face/Reach 5 ft. by 10 ft./5 ft.; Str 21, Dex 17, Con 15.

Dire Bear: SZ H animal; Init +1 (Dex); Spd 40 ft.; AC 16 (−2 size, +1 Dex, +7 natural); Atk 2 claws melee, bite melee (2d4+10 claw, 2d8+5 bite); Face/Reach 10 ft. by 20 ft./10 ft.; Str 31, Dex 13, Con 19.

Treant: SZ H plant; Init −1 (Dex); Spd 30 ft.; AC 20 (−2 size, −1 Dex, +13 natural); Atk Melee 2 slams (2d6+9 slam); Face/Reach 10 ft. by 10 ft./15 ft.; Str 29, Dex 8, Con 21.

Note: The above statistics are tailored for use by a druid of the wild when in wild shape.

until the druid of the wild changes back. Changing form (to animal or back) is a standard action and does not provoke an attack of opportunity.

A druid of the wild loses her ability to speak while in animal form because she is limited to the sounds that a normal, untrained animal can make. She can, however, communicate with other animals of the same general grouping as her new form.

A druid of the wild can use this ability more times per day at 3rd, 5th, 7th, and 9th level, as noted on Table 2–5: The Druid of the Wild (Drw). In addition, the druid of the wild may assume the shape of a stag at 3rd level, a nightsaber panther at 5th level, a dire bear at 7th level, and/or a treant at 9th level.

Woodland Stride (Ex): At 1st level, a druid of the wild may move through any sort of undergrowth (such as natural thorns, briars, overgrown areas, and similar terrain) at her normal speed and without taking damage or suffering any other impairment. Thorns, briars, and overgrown areas enchanted or magically manipulated to impede motion still affect her, however.

Nature Sense (Ex): At 2nd level, a druid of the wild gains a +2 bonus on Knowledge (nature) and Survival checks.

Trackless Step (Ex): At 3rd level, a druid of the wild leaves no trail in natural surroundings and cannot be tracked. She may choose to leave a trail if so desired.

Venom Immunity (Ex): At 5th level, a druid of the wild gains immunity to all organic poisons, including monster poisons but not mineral poisons or poison gas.

Timeless Body (Ex): After attaining 7th level, a druid of the wild no longer takes ability score penalties for aging (*PHB*, Table 6–5: Aging Effects) and cannot be magically aged. Any penalties she may have already incurred remain in place, however. Bonuses still accrue, and the druid of the wild still dies of old age when her time is up. Time spent in green sleep does not count toward aging.

Dreamwalking (Sp): At 10th level, the druid of the wild may enter the Emerald Dream once per day, provided she is in a natural area such as a forest or a desert. This ability does not work in

Table 2–5: The Druid of the Wild (Drw)

Class Level	Base Attack Bonus	Fort Save	Ref Save	Will Save	Special	Spells
1st	+0	+2	+0	+2	Wild shape 1/day, green sleep, woodland stride	+1 level of divine spellcasting class
2nd	+1	+3	+0	+3	Nature sense	+1 level of divine spellcasting class
3rd	+2	+3	+1	+3	Trackless step, wild shape 2/dayc	+1 level of divine spellcasting class
4th	+3	+4	+1	+4	—	+1 level of divine spellcasting class
5th	+3	+4	+1	+4	Venom immunity, wild shape 3/day	+1 level of divine spellcasting class
6th	+4	+5	+2	+5	—	+1 level of divine spellcasting class
7th	+5	+5	+2	+5	Timeless body, wild shape 4/day	+1 level of divine spellcasting class
8th	+6	+6	+2	+6	—	+1 level of divine spellcasting class
9th	+6	+6	+3	+6	Wild shape 5/day	+1 level of divine spellcasting class
10th	+7	+7	+3	+7	Dreamwalking	+1 level of divine spellcasting class

cities or blighted areas. Travel to and from the Emerald Dream functions as per *plane shift*. See Chapter Five, "The Universe Beyond," for specifics on the Emerald Dream.

Druid of the Wild Spell List

Druids of the wild choose their spells from a list geared toward plants and nature. The druid of the wild may also choose spells from the healer spell list (see above).

0 level — *flare, know direction.*

1st level — *calm animals, charm animal, detect animals or plants, detect snares and pits, entangle, faerie fire, goodberry, hide from animals, magic fang, obscuring mist, pass without trace, roar*, shillelagh, speak with animals, summon nature's ally I.*

2nd level — *animal messenger, animal trance, barkskin, delay poison, hold animal, reduce animal, spider climb, summon nature's ally II, summon swarm, tree shape, warp wood, wood shape.*

3rd level — *diminish plants, dominate animal, greater magic fang, neutralize poison, plant growth, poison, remove disease, thorn shield*, snare, speak with plants, spike growth, summon nature's ally III.*

4th level — *antiplant shell, blight, command plants, flame strike, freedom of movement, giant vermin, repel vermin, summon nature's ally IV.*

5th level — *animal growth, awaken, baleful polymorph, commune with nature, insect plague, summon nature's ally V, tree stride, wall of thorns.*

6th level — *antilife shell, find the path, force of nature*, ironwood, liveoak, repel wood, spellstaff, summon nature's ally VI, transport via plants.*

7th level — *animate plants, changestaff, creeping doom, summon nature's ally VII, sunbeam, transmute metal to wood.*

8th level — *animal shapes, greater force of nature*, control plants, summon nature's ally VIII, whirlwind.*

9th level — *shambler, shapechange, summon nature's ally IX.*

Elven Ranger

The elven ranger is an elite wilderness warrior unique to the elves. Elven ranger orders exist amongst both high elves and night elves.

Elven rangers are elite archers and skirmishers, capable of doing tricks with the bow that few others can hope to match. Their ability to fight in the wilderness is equaled only by the Horde's orc hunters.

Alliance Name: Elven ranger (high elf), sentinel (night elf).

Hit Die: d8.

Requirements

Race: Elf (high or night) only.

Alignment: Any.

Affiliation: Alliance only.

Base Attack Bonus: +5.

Skills: Knowledge (nature) 6 ranks, Survival 6 ranks.

Feats: Point Blank Shot, Track.

Class Skills

The elven ranger's class skills (and the key ability for each skill) are Climb (Str), Concentration (Con), Craft (Int), Heal (Wis), Hide (Dex), Jump (Str), Knowledge (military tactics) (Int), Knowledge (nature) (Int), Listen (Wis), Move Silently (Dex), Profession (Wis), Spot (Wis), Survival (Wis), Swim (Str), and Use Rope (Dex). See Chapter 4: Skills in the *PHB* for skill descriptions.

Skill Points at Each Level: 4 + Int modifier.

Class Features

Weapon and Armor Proficiency: Elven rangers are proficient with all simple and martial weapons and with light and medium armor. In addition, elven rangers are proficient in the use of arrows as a melee weapon, meaning they do not suffer the standard −4 penalty for using an arrow in melee.

Spells: Beginning at 1st level, an elven ranger gains the ability to cast a small number of divine spells. She may prepare and cast any spell from the elven ranger spell list, provided that she can cast spells of that level. Her base daily spell allotment is given on Table 2–6: The Elven Ranger (Elr). In addition, she receives bonus spells per day if she has a high Wisdom score (see *PHB*, Table 1–1: Ability Modifiers and Bonus Spells). When the elven ranger gets 0 spells of a given level, she gets only bonus spells.

An elven ranger prepares and casts spells under the same guidelines as a healer (see above).

Extended Range (Ex): Starting at 1st level and for each level thereafter, an elven ranger adds 10 feet to the range increment of bows or crossbows she uses (added after all multipliers). Thus, a 10th-level elven ranger with a composite longbow and the Far Shot feat would have a (110 feet x 1.5) + 100 feet = 265-foot range increment.

Favored Enemy (Ex): At 1st level, an elven ranger may select a type of creature as a favored enemy, chosen from among those given on Table 2–7: Elven Ranger Favored Enemies. Due to her extensive study of her foes and training in the proper techniques for combating them, the

Table 2–7: Elven Ranger Favored Enemies

Type (Subtype)	Examples
Aberration	murloc
Animal	storm crow
Construct	harvest golem
Dragon	red dragon
Elemental	water elemental
Fey	wisp
Giant	sea giant
Humanoid (aquatic)	naga
Humanoid (dwarf)	Ironforge dwarf
Humanoid (elf)	high elf
Humanoid (gnoll)	gnoll
Humanoid (gnome)	gnome
Humanoid (human)	human
Humanoid (orc)	orc
Magical Beast	gryphon
Monstrous Humanoid	harpy
Ooze	mana surge
Outsider (demon)	pit lord
Plant	treant
Undead	ghoul
Vermin	spitting spider

elven ranger gains a +2 bonus to Bluff, Listen, Sense Motive, Spot, and Survival checks when using these skills against this type of creature. Likewise, she gets a +2 bonus to weapon damage rolls against such creatures. This damage bonus with ranged weapons applies only against targets within 30 feet (the elven ranger cannot strike with deadly accuracy beyond that range). The bonus does not apply to damage against creatures that are immune to critical hits.

At 3rd level and every two levels thereafter (at 5th, 7th, and 9th level), the elven ranger may select an additional favored enemy from those given on the table. In addition, at each such interval, the bonus against any one favored enemy (including the one just selected, if so desired) increases by 2. For example, a 3rd-level elven ranger has two favored enemies; against one she gains a +4 bonus to Bluff, Listen, Sense Motive, Spot, and Survival checks and weapon damage rolls, and against the other she gains a +2 bonus. At 5th level, she has three favored enemies, and she gains an additional +2 bonus, which she can allocate to the bonus against any one of her three favored enemies. Thus, her bonuses could be either +4, +4, +2 or +6, +2, +2.

If the elven ranger chooses humanoids or outsiders as a favored enemy, she must also choose an associated subtype, as indicated on the table. If a specific creature falls into more than one category of favored enemy (for instance, murlocs are both aberrations and aquatic humanoids), the elven ranger's bonuses do not stack; she simply uses whichever bonus is higher. See the MM and the **Manual of Monsters** for more information on types of creatures.

Archery Combat Style (Ex): At 1st level, the elven ranger receives the Rapid Shot feat, even if she does not have the normal prerequisites for that feat. The benefits of archery combat style apply only when she wears light or no armor; she loses all benefits of her combat style when wearing medium or heavy armor.

Heightened Perception (Ex): At 2nd level, the elven ranger's senses grow much sharper than those of the average elf. An elven ranger adds a +2 bonus to Listen and Spot checks.

Woodland Stride (Ex): At 2nd level, an elven ranger may move through any sort of undergrowth (such as natural thorns, briars, overgrown areas, and similar terrain) at her normal speed and without taking damage or suffering any other impairment. Thorns, briars, and overgrown areas enchanted or magically manipulated to impede motion still affect her, however.

Keen Arrows (Ex): At 4th level, all arrows or bolts the elven ranger fires are considered *keen* in addition to any other properties they might have. A keen arrow's threat range is doubled, so a normal arrow in an elven ranger's hands would have a threat range of 19–20/x2. If an elven ranger fires an arrow or bolt that already has the *keen* special ability, these effects do not stack.

Swift Tracker (Ex): Beginning 4th level, an elven ranger can move at her normal speed while following tracks without taking the standard –5 penalty. She takes only a –10 penalty (instead of the normal –20) when moving at up to twice her normal speed while tracking.

If a character already has swift tracker from a second class, these modifiers are adjusted to –2 and –5 penalties, respectively.

Bow Strike (Ex): At 6th level, an elven ranger may use her bow in melee combat like a quarterstaff in a manner that does not damage the bow.

Improved Archery Style: At 6th level, the elven ranger receives the Manyshot feat, even if she does not have the normal prerequisites for the feat. As before, the benefits of improved archery style apply only when she wears light or no armor.

Anticipation (Ex): At 8th level, the elven ranger is adept at noticing enemies' tiny movements and other visual and auditory clues. This ability allows her to react more quickly in combat, granting her a +4 bonus to all Initiative checks. In addition, she may select one target to observe each round; for the remainder of that round, this target cannot make attacks of opportunity against the elven ranger when she leaves or enters that opponent's threat area. Finally, this opponent cannot flank the elven ranger, although she may still be flanked by other enemies.

Arrow Cleave (Ex): At 10th level, an elven ranger who deals a creature enough damage with an arrow or bolt to drop it (typically by dropping it to below 0 hit points, killing it, and so forth) receives a second attack with that projectile against another creature directly in the path of the arrow. The creature must be in the same range increment as the original target, and the second attack is at the same bonus as the original attack that dropped the previous creature.

Archery Style Mastery (Ex): At 10th level, the elven ranger's aptitude with archery improves again. She is treated as having the Improved Precise Shot feat, even if she does not have the normal prerequisites for that feat.

As before, the benefits of archery style mastery only apply if the elven ranger is wearing light or no armor.

Table 2–6: The Elven Ranger (Elr)

Class Level	Base Attack Bonus	Fort Save	Ref Save	Will Save	Special
1st	+1	+2	+2	+0	Spells, 1st favored enemy, archery combat style, extended range
2nd	+2	+3	+3	+0	Heightened perception, woodland stride, extended range
3rd	+3	+3	+3	+1	2nd favored enemy, extended range
4th	+4	+4	+4	+1	Keen arrows, swift tracker, extended range
5th	+5	+4	+4	+1	3rd favored enemy, extended range
6th	+6	+5	+5	+2	Bow strike, improved archery style, extended range
7th	+7	+5	+5	+2	4th favored enemy, extended range
8th	+8	+6	+6	+2	Anticipation, extended range
9th	+9	+6	+6	+3	5th favored enemy, extended range
10th	+10	+7	+7	+3	Arrow cleave, master archery style, extended range

Spells per Day:

Class Level	1st	2nd	3rd	4th
1st	0	—	—	—
2nd	1	—	—	—
3rd	1	0	—	—
4th	1	1	—	—
5th	1	1	0	—
6th	1	1	1	—
7th	2	1	1	0
8th	2	1	1	1
9th	2	2	1	1
10th	2	2	2	1

Elven Ranger Spell List

Elven rangers draw their spells from their relationship with nature and the spirits of nature. As such, their spell lists are focused on archery, wilderness, animals, and stealth.

1st level — alarm, delay poison, detect poison, detect snares and pits, detect undead, entangle, faerie fire, hide from animals, jump, longstrider, magic fang, magic weapon, pass without trace, read magic, resist energy, shadow meld*, speak with animals, summon nature's ally I.

2nd level — barkskin, bear's endurance, cat's grace, cure light wounds, detect chaos/evil/good/law, flaming arrows, glitterdust, hold animal, owl's wisdom, produce flame, protection from energy, sleep, snare, speak with plants, spike growth, summon nature's ally II, wood shape.

3rd level — command plants, cure moderate wounds, darkvision, diminish plants, greater magic fang, invisibility, neutralize poison, plant growth, poison, remove disease, remove paralysis, see invisibility, sentinel*, summon nature's ally III, tree shape, water walk, water breathing.

4th level — animal growth, commune with nature, cure serious wounds, freedom of movement, greater magic weapon, invisibility purge, invisibility sphere, nondetection, polymorph self, tree stride.

METZEN · '01

Gladiator

Description: A gladiator has devoted himself to the mastery of close combat. This single-minded devotion to weaponry and fighting styles makes him much feared by his enemies. A gladiator prides himself on having equal proficiency over every weapon imaginable. Most also strive to become peerless experts in a weapon of their choice. This chosen weapon weaves and sings in the gladiator's hand, carving a swath through all foes.

Most gladiators come from the ranks of fighters and barbarians, who find the discipline and rigors of training a welcome challenge to master. Other classes require much more work to become a true gladiator.

Alliance Name: Gladiator.
Horde Name: Blademaster.
Hit Die: d10.

Requirements

Affiliation: Any.
Base Attack Bonus: +5.
Skills: Bluff 2 ranks, Intimidate 5 ranks.
Feats: Cleave, Power Attack.

Class Skills

The gladiator's class skills (and the key ability for each skill) are Bluff (Cha), Climb (Str), Craft (Int), Intimidate (Cha), Jump (Str), Knowledge (military tactics) (Int), Perform (Cha), Sense Motive (Wis), and Swim (Str). See Chapter 4: Skills in the *PHB* for skill descriptions.

Skill Points at Each Level: 2 + Int modifier.

Class Features

Weapon and Armor Proficiency: Gladiators are proficient with all simple and martial weapons and with light and medium armor.

Supreme Cleave (Ex): At 1st level, the gladiator can take a 5-foot step between attacks when using the Cleave or Great Cleave feat, if he has not otherwise moved in that round. This ability can be used once per round and counts as the gladiator's 5-foot step for the round.

Command (Ex): At 2nd level, the gladiator can call upon on his powers of leadership to rally his allies, giving a +1 morale bonus to attack rolls for all allies within 20 feet of the gladiator. This bonus increases to +2 at 4th level, +3 at 6th level, +4 at 8th level, and +5 at 10th level. This ability is usable once per day and lasts a number of rounds equal to 1 + the gladiator's Charisma bonus.

Two-Handed Mastery (Ex): At 3rd level, the gladiator adds double his Strength modifier to damage rolls when wielding a two-handed weapon (instead of 1.5 times his Strength modifier).

Strike Like the Wind (Su): At 4th level, the gladiator becomes one with the flow of battle such that he may turn invisible. This is considered a move action and lasts for a number of rounds per day equal to his gladiator level. Each round, including any on which the strike like the wind ability is activated, counts against this limit. This ability otherwise functions as per the *invisibility* spell.

Critical Strike (Ex): At 5th level, the gladiator's overwhelming strength and power cause greater than normal critical strikes. Once per day, when scoring a critical threat, the gladiator may declare it as a critical strike. If the critical confirms, the gladiator deals 1d4 points of temporary Strength damage to the target in addition to the normal (critical) damage.

The gladiator may attempt a critical strike twice per day at 7th level and three times per day at 9th level. Each critical strike declared counts against the number available for that day regardless of whether the critical confirms.

Maximum Damage (Ex): At 6th level, once per day, the gladiator may declare maximum damage prior to rolling to hit a target. If the attack succeeds, the weapon automatically inflicts its full damage. This amount applies only to the weapon's damage, including damage from a critical hit. Damage from a sneak attack, critical strike Strength, or any other variable damage is determined normally.

The gladiator may apply maximum damage twice per day at 8th level and three times per day at 10th level.

Mirror Image (Sp): At 7th level, the gladiator may activate a mirror image as a move action (this functions per the *mirror image* spell). The images last a total number of rounds per day equal to his gladiator level. Each round, including any on which the *mirror image* ability is activated, counts against this limit.

Improved Strike Like the Wind (Su): At 8th level, the gladiator's strike like the wind ability may be performed as a free action.

Blade Whirlwind (Su): At 10th level, the gladiator becomes a spinning tornado of blades. He is *hasted* per the *haste* spell and gains an additional 5 feet of reach and a +4 enhancement bonus to Strength. Blade whirlwind may be performed once per day and lasts a number of rounds equal to the gladiator's class level. As with *haste*, this ability counters and is countered by *slow*.

Improved Mirror Image (Su): At 10th level, the gladiator's mirror image ability may be performed as a free action.

Table 2–8: The Gladiator (Gla)

Class Level	Base Attack Bonus	Fort Save	Ref Save	Will Save	Special
1st	+1	+2	+0	+0	Supreme Cleave
2nd	+2	+3	+0	+0	Command
3rd	+3	+3	+1	+1	Two-handed mastery
4th	+4	+4	+1	+1	Strike like the wind
5th	+5	+4	+1	+1	Critical strike 1/day
6th	+6	+5	+2	+2	Maximum damage 1/day
7th	+7	+5	+2	+2	Critical strike 2/day, *mirror image*
8th	+8	+6	+2	+2	Improved strike like the wind, maximum damage 2/day
9th	+9	+6	+3	+3	Critical strike 3/day
10th	+10	+7	+3	+3	Blade whirlwind, improved mirror image, maximum damage 3/day

Horde Assassin

Description: These silent, deadly killers first appeared under Gul'dan's demon-backed reign over the Horde. They struck down any who dared oppose the Horde — including anyone within the Horde's ranks who might defy the demonic lords. Horde assassins were renowned for making no sound when administering an execution and leaving no witnesses. Ever.

Though the Horde has cast off the shackles of demon rule, Horde assassins still ply their trade. They still work to keep the Horde strong, though they are no longer the heartless killers from the time of the Burning Legion. Now, they track down and dispatch those who would bring back demonic influence and those who threaten the security of the Horde. These assassins are publicly considered a last resort, to be called only in the direst of circumstances. In practice, Horde chieftains have few reservations about their use.

Requirements

Alignment: Any non-good.
Affiliation: Horde only.
Skills: Hide 8 ranks, Move Silently 8 ranks.

Class Skills

The Horde assassin's class skills (and the key ability for each skill) are Balance (Dex), Bluff (Cha), Climb (Str), Craft (Int), Disable Device (Int), Disguise (Cha), Escape Artist (Dex), Hide (Dex), Intimidate (Cha), Jump (Str), Listen (Wis), Move Silently (Dex), Open Lock (Dex), Profession (Wis), Search (Int), Sense Motive (Wis), Spot (Wis), Swim (Str), Tumble (Dex), and Use Rope (Dex). See Chapter 4: Skills in the *PHB* for skill descriptions.

Skill Points at Each Level: 4 + Int modifier.

Class Features

Aside from the differences noted here, the Horde assassin (Hda) otherwise functions the same as the assassin prestige class (*DMG*, Chapter 6: Characters, "Prestige Classes").

Hunter

Description: Elven rangers are not alone in their mastery of the wilderness. While an elven ranger prefers the bow, the hunter would rather get up close. A hunter is skilled in stealth, slipping through the woods like a ghost. Orcs of the Horde first learned the ways of the hunter from forest trolls on Lordaeron and tauren have been masters of the hunt since the dawn of the world.

Hit Die: d8.

Requirements

Affiliation: Horde only.

Base Attack Bonus: +5.

Skills: Survival 8 ranks.

Feats: Track, Weapon Focus (any melee or thrown).

Class Skills

The hunter's class skills (and the key ability for each skill) are Climb (Str), Concentration (Con), Craft (Int), Handle Animal (Cha), Heal (Wis), Hide (Dex), Jump (Str), Knowledge (military tactics) (Int), Knowledge (nature) (Int), Listen (Wis), Move Silently (Dex), Profession (Wis), Spot (Wis), Survival (Wis), and Swim (Str). See Chapter 4: Skills in the *PHB* for skill descriptions.

Skill Points at Each Level: 4 + Int modifier.

Class Features

Weapon and Armor Proficiency: Hunters are proficient with all simple and martial weapons and with light and medium armor and shields.

Spells: Beginning at 1st level, a hunter gains the ability to cast a small number of divine spells. He may prepare and cast any spell from the hunter spell list, provided that he can cast spells of that level. His base daily spell allotment is given on Table 2–8: The Hunter (Hnt). In addition, he receives bonus spells per day if he has a high Wisdom score (see *PHB*, Table 1–1: Ability Modifiers and Bonus Spells). When the hunter gets 0 spells of a given level, he gets only bonus spells.

A hunter prepares and casts spells under the same guidelines as a healer (see above).

Favored Terrain (Ex): At 1st level, the hunter selects a type of environment — aquatic, desert, forest, hills, marsh, mountains, plains, or underground — as a favored terrain. Due to his extensive study of this type of environment and his training in the proper techniques for surviving in it, the hunter gains a +2 circumstance bonus to Hide, Knowledge (nature), Listen, Move Silently, Spot, and Survival checks relating to this type of environment.

At 3rd, 5th, 7th, and 9th levels, the hunter selects a new favored terrain. In addition, at each such interval, the bonus for any one favored terrain (including the one just selected, if so desired) increases by 2. For example, a 3rd-level hunter has two favored terrains; for one he gains a +4 circumstance bonus to Hide, Knowledge (nature), Listen, Move Silently, Spot, and Survival checks, and for the other he gains a +2 circumstance bonus. At 5th level, he has three favored terrains, and he gains an additional +2 circumstance bonus, which he can allocate to the bonus against any one of his three favored terrains. Thus, his circumstance bonuses could be either +4, +4, +2 or +6, +2, +2.

Weapon Combat Style (Ex): At 1st level, the hunter receives the Weapon Specialization feat for any one weapon that he has Weapon Focus for, even if he does not have the normal prerequisites for that feat.

The benefits of weapon combat style apply only when he wears light or no armor. He loses all benefits of his combat style when wearing medium or heavy armor.

Extended Throwing Range (Ex): Although hunters prefer to get up close to fight, they are quite skilled at using thrown weapons. Starting at 1st level and for each level thereafter, the hunter adds 5 feet to the range increment for a thrown weapon. For example, in the hands of a 6th-level hunter, a throwing axe's range increment becomes 40 feet (10 feet base + [6 x 5 = 30 feet]).

Heightened Stealth (Ex): At 2nd level, the hunter learns secrets of hiding and silent movement. He receives a +2 bonus to Hide and Move Silently checks.

Woodland Stride (Ex): At 2nd level, a hunter may move through any sort of undergrowth (such as natural thorns, briars, overgrown areas, and similar terrain) at his normal speed and without taking damage or suffering any other impairment. Thorns, briars, and overgrown areas enchanted or magically manipulated to impede motion still affect him, however.

Keen Weapon (Ex): At 4th level, the hunter's chosen weapon is considered *keen* in addition to any other properties it may have.

A *keen* weapon's critical threat range is doubled, so a normal battleaxe in a hunter's hands has a threat range of 19–20/x3. If the hunter's weapon already has the *keen* ability, the effects do not stack.

Combat Reflexes (Ex): At 6th level, the hunter gains the Combat Reflexes feat, granting him an additional number of attacks of opportunity each round equal to his Dexterity bonus. If the hunter already has Combat Reflexes, the effects do not stack.

Improved Weapon Style (Ex): At 6th level, the hunter receives the Greater Weapon Focus feat for any one weapon that he has Weapon Focus for, even if he does not have any of the other prerequisites for the feat. The benefits of improved weapon style apply only when he wears light or no armor.

Camouflage (Ex): A hunter of 7th level or higher can use the Hide skill in any sort of natural terrain, even if the terrain does not grant cover or concealment.

Swift Tracker (Ex): Beginning 8th level, a hunter can move at his normal speed while following tracks without taking the standard –5 penalty. He takes only a –10 penalty (instead of the normal –20) when moving at up to twice normal speed while tracking.

If a character already has swift tracker from a second class, these penalties are adjusted to −2 and −5, respectively.

Greater Critical (Ex): At 10th level, the hunter increases the critical damage multiplier by one step when using his chosen weapon. In the aforementioned battleaxe example (see keen weapon, above), critical damage becomes 19–20/x4.

Weapon Combat Mastery (Ex): At 10th level, the hunter receives the Greater Weapon Specialization feat for any one weapon that he has Weapon Focus for, even if he does not have any of the other prerequisites for the feat. The benefits of weapon combat mastery apply only when he wears light or no armor.

Hunter Spell List

Like the shamans of the Horde, hunters call upon the spirits of the land, wind, and fire to aid them in their hunts and tasks. Their spells focus on the elements and the land.

1st level — *alarm, delay poison, detect animals or plants, detect poison, detect snares and pits, endure elements, jump, longstrider, magic stone, obscuring mist, read magic, resist energy, shadow meld*.*

2nd level — *bear's endurance, cat's grace, cure light wounds, fog cloud, owl's wisdom, protection from energy, snare, soften earth and stone, wind wall.*

3rd level — *bloodlust*, cure moderate wounds, darkvision, neutralize poison, remove disease, resist energy, shockwave*, stone shape, water breathing, water walk.*

4th level — *air walk, commune with nature, control water, cure serious wounds, freedom of movement, nondetection.*

Table 2–9: The Hunter (Hnt)

Class Level	Base Attack Bonus	Fort Save	Ref Save	Will Save	Special
1st	+1	+2	+0	+0	Spells, 1st favored terrain, weapon combat style, extended throwing range
2nd	+2	+3	+0	+0	Heightened stealth, woodland stride
3rd	+3	+3	+1	+1	2nd favored terrain
4th	+4	+4	+1	+1	Swift tracker, keen weapon
5th	+5	+4	+1	+1	3rd favored terrain
6th	+6	+5	+2	+2	Combat reflexes, improved combat style
7th	+7	+5	+2	+2	Camouflage, 4th favored terrain
8th	+8	+6	+2	+2	Swift tracker
9th	+9	+6	+3	+3	5th favored terrain
10th	+10	+7	+3	+3	Greater critical, weapon combat mastery

Spells per Day:

Class Level	1st	2nd	3rd	4th
1st	0	—	—	—
2nd	1	—	—	—
3rd	1	0	—	—
4th	1	1	—	—
5th	1	1	0	—
6th	1	1	1	—
7th	2	1	1	0
8th	2	1	1	1

Infiltrator

Description: This select group has proven invaluable to keeping the Alliance from being fatally fragmented by internal rivalries or shattered by the efforts of the Horde. The infiltrator is a manipulator, charmer, and spy who pursues a life of intrigue, politics, and diplomacy throughout Alliance territories and beyond.

Hit Die: d6.

Requirements

Affiliation: Alliance only.

Skills: Bluff 8 ranks, Disguise 8 ranks.

Class Skills

The infiltrator's class skills (and the key ability for each skill) are Appraise (Int), Balance (Dex), Bluff (Cha), Climb (Str), Craft (Int), Decipher Script (Int), Diplomacy (Cha), Disguise (Cha), Escape Artist (Dex), Forgery (Int), Gather Information (Cha), Hide (Dex), Intimidate (Cha), Jump (Str), Listen (Wis), Move Silently (Dex), Open Lock (Dex), Perform (Cha), Profession (Wis), Search (Int), Sense Motive (Wis), Sleight of Hand (Dex), Speak Language, Spot (Wis), Swim (Str), Tumble (Dex), Use Magic Device (Cha), Use Technological Device (Int)*, and Use Rope (Dex). See Chapter 4: Skills in the *PHB* for skill descriptions.

* See "New Skill," below.

Skill Points at Each Level: 6 + Int modifier.

Class Features

Weapon and Armor Proficiency: Infiltrators are proficient with all simple weapons and light armor.

Canny Defense (Ex): An infiltrator's intellect is so honed that she can judge the angle and thrust of a blow sufficiently to deflect or otherwise avoid the attack. When unarmored and wielding a melee weapon, the infiltrator adds 1 point of Intelligence bonus (if any) per infiltrator class level to her AC. For instance, a 2nd-level infiltrator with an Intelligence score of 16 (+3 bonus) adds a +2 to her AC when wielding her sword, while a 3rd-level or higher infiltrator adds +3 to her AC. This bonus to AC applies even against touch attacks, but not if the infiltrator is flat-footed or otherwise denied her Dexterity bonus.

Smooth Talker (Ex): At 1st level, the infiltrator gains a +2 bonus to Bluff and Sense Motive checks.

Connections (Ex): The infiltrator has friends in high and low places. Starting at 1st level, once per day, in any inhabited environment—even one that she has never been to before—the infiltrator can check to see if she has a connection in the area. Roll 1d20 + infiltrator class level + Charisma bonus; the DC depends on the importance of the desired connection:

DC	NPC Importance
10	City guard, fence, shopkeeper
15	Captain of the guard, thieves' guild lieutenant, merchant
20	City ruler, ambassador from the Horde, merchant prince
25	Archmage, Lord Captain of the Knights of the Silver Hand
35	Jaina Proudmoore, Thrall, Tyrande Whisperwind

Having 5 ranks or higher in the appropriate Knowledge skill provides a +2 synergy bonus to this check, as appropriate: i.e., Knowledge (religion) will help if the infiltrator is looking for a priest, but will do no good if she's looking for a guard captain.

Uncanny Dodge (Ex): Starting at 2nd level, an infiltrator retains her Dexterity bonus to AC (if any) even if she is caught flat-footed or struck by an invisible attacker. She still loses her Dexterity bonus to AC if immobilized, however.

If an infiltrator already has uncanny dodge from a different class (an infiltrator with at least 4 levels of scout, for example), she automatically gains improved uncanny dodge instead (see below).

Flawless Disguise (Ex): Starting at 3rd level, the infiltrator adds a +4 bonus to all Disguise checks and can take 10 on Disguise checks no matter the circumstance.

Suggestion **(Sp):** Starting at 4th level, an infiltrator can cast *suggestion* once per day as a sorcerer of her class level. The Will save DC is 13 + the infiltrator's Charisma bonus. At 6th level, she can cast *suggestion* twice per day. At 8th level, she can also cast *mass suggestion* (DC 16 + Charisma bonus) once per day.

Improved Uncanny Dodge (Ex): Starting at 5th level, the infiltrator can no longer be flanked; she can react to opponents on opposite sides of her as easily as she can react to a single attacker.

This defense denies a rogue the ability to sneak attack the infiltrator by flanking her, unless the attacker has at least 4 more rogue levels than the target has infiltrator levels.

If a character already has uncanny dodge (see above) from a second class, the character automatically gains improved uncanny dodge instead, and the levels from the classes that grant uncanny dodge stack to determine the minimum rogue level required to flank the character.

Slippery Mind (Ex): At 7th level, the infiltrator gains the ability to wriggle free from magical effects that would otherwise control or compel her. If an infiltrator with this ability is affected by an enchantment spell or effect and fails her saving throw, she can attempt the saving throw again 1 round later at the same DC. She gets only this one extra chance to succeed on her saving throw.

Hide in Plain Sight (Ex): At 9th level, the infiltrator can use the Hide skill even while being observed. As long as she is within 10 feet of some sort of shadow, an infiltrator can hide herself from view in the open without actually having anything to hide behind. She cannot, however, hide in her own shadow.

Dominate **(Sp):** At 10th level, the infiltrator gains the ability to cast *dominate monster* once per day. This works precisely like the spell, and the Will save DC is 19 + the infiltrator's Charisma bonus (if any).

Table 2–10: The Infiltrator (Inf)

Class Level	Base Attack Bonus	Fort Save	Ref Save	Will Save	Special
1st	+0	+0	+2	+0	Canny defense, smooth talker, connections
2nd	+1	+0	+3	+0	Uncanny dodge
3rd	+2	+1	+3	+1	Flawless disguise
4th	+3	+1	+4	+1	*Suggestion* 1/day
5th	+3	+2	+4	+2	Improved uncanny dodge
6th	+4	+2	+5	+2	*Suggestion* 2/day
7th	+5	+2	+5	+2	Slippery Mind
8th	+6	+3	+6	+3	*Mass suggestion* 1/day
9th	+6	+3	+6	+3	Hide in plain sight
10th	+7	+3	+7	+3	*Dominate* 1/day

WARCRAFT
THE ROLEPLAYING GAME

Mounted Warrior

Description: These fighters are trained to utilize their steeds to utmost tactical advantage in battle. Their skill in both riding and combat makes them devastating foes. While they have little interest in unmounted melee combat, they are not to be taken lightly when faced on foot.

Alliance Name: Knight (human, high elf), Huntress (night elf female).

Horde Name: Raider (orc).

Hit Die: d10.

Requirements

Affiliation: Any.

Base Attack Bonus: +5.

Skills: Ride (warhorse or nightsaber panther) 8 ranks [Alliance]; Ride (dire wolf) 8 ranks [Horde].

Feats: Mounted Combat.

Class Skills

The mounted warrior's class skills (and the key ability for each skill) are Climb (Str), Craft (Int), Diplomacy (Cha), Handle Animal (Cha), Jump (Str), Knowledge (military tactics) (Int), Profession (Wis), Ride (Dex), and Swim (Str). See Chapter 4: Skills in the *PHB* for skill descriptions.

Skill Points at Each Level: 2 + Int modifier.

Class Features

Weapon and Armor Proficiency: Mounted warriors are proficient with all simple and martial weapons, with all types of armor (heavy, medium, and light), and with shields (except tower shields).

Special Mount: Upon reaching 1st level, a mounted warrior can call an unusually intelligent, strong, and loyal mount to serve him. This mount must be a heavy warhorse for a knight, a nightsaber panther for a huntress, or a dire wolf for a raider.

Should the mounted warrior's mount die, he cannot call another until 30 days have passed or until he gains a mounted warrior level, whichever comes first. (This condition applies even if the current mount is somehow returned from the dead.) The mounted warrior suffers a –1 penalty on attack and weapon damage rolls during this 30-day period. The new mount has all the accumulated abilities due a mount of the mounted warrior's level.

The GM will provide information about the mount that the mounted warrior finds.

Mounted Expertise: At 2nd level, the mounted warrior becomes highly skilled at fighting while mounted. He can modify his melee attack rolls and Armor Class, suffering a penalty to one to enhance the other. Before making any rolls when using the attack action or the full attack action while mounted in melee, he may shift points between his attack roll and his Armor Class. A penalty subtracted from an attack roll applies as a dodge bonus to his AC; a penalty subtracted from Armor Class applies as a bonus on all attack rolls for that round. This number may not exceed his base attack bonus. The changes to attack rolls and AC last until his next action.

Bonus Feats: At 3rd, 6th, and 9th level, the mounted warrior receives a bonus feat. These bonus feats may be chosen from the following list: Animal Affinity, Expert Rider*, Mounted Archery, Mounted Sharpshooter*, Ride-By Attack, Spirited Charge, and Trample.

* These new feats are detailed in "Feats," below.

Improved Mounted Combat: At 4th level, the mounted warrior may attempt a Ride check (as a reaction) twice per round to negate a successful hit on his mount. At 8th level, the mounted warrior may attempt a Ride check 3 times per round against successful hits on his mount.

Mounted Command (Ex): Starting at 5th level, the mounted warrior can direct a number of allied mounts equal to his class level. These mounts must be within 100 feet of the mounted warrior and must be of the same type that he rides (warhorse, nightsaber panther, or dire wolf). He makes a Ride check for each of the other mounts instead of the mount's own rider doing so; this check applies even if a mount lacks a rider. If the other mount's rider tries to keep control of his mount, resolve using wrestle for control (see "Skills," *Ride*, below). Otherwise, the mount can be directed to perform the following maneuvers: fight with warhorse, leap, spur mount, and wrestle for control. The mounted warrior may also bring a panicked mount under control, except if the panic is the direct result of a spell (such as *fear* and the like). Using mounted command is a standard action.

The number of mounts that the mounted warrior can command increases with his character level: 6 mounts at 6th level, 7 mounts at 7th level, 8 mounts at 8th level, 9 mounts at 9th level, and 10 mounts at 10th level. This ability may be used a number of times per day equal to 1 + the mounted warrior's Charisma bonus.

Woodland Ride (Ex): At 7th level, a mounted warrior may ride through any sort of undergrowth (such as natural thorns, briars, overgrown areas, and similar terrain) at the mount's normal speed and without taking damage or suffering any other impairment. Thorns, briars, and overgrown areas that are enchanted or magically manipulated to impede motion still affect the mount, however.

Shock Charge (Ex): At 10th level, the mounted warrior can deliver a devastating mounted attack. When mounted and using the charge action, he gains an additional +2 bonus on the attack roll and his threat range is doubled. These bonuses stack with any other modifiers to attack and threat range.

Table 2–11: The Mounted Warrior (Mow)

Class Level	Base Attack Bonus	Fort Save	Ref Save	Will Save	Special
1st	+1	+2	+0	+0	Special mount
2nd	+2	+3	+0	+0	Mounted expertise
3rd	+3	+3	+1	+1	Bonus feat
4th	+4	+4	+1	+1	Improved mounted combat 2/round
5th	+5	+4	+1	+1	Mounted command
6th	+6	+5	+2	+2	Bonus feat
7th	+7	+5	+2	+2	Woodland ride
8th	+8	+6	+2	+2	Improved mounted combat 3/round
9th	+9	+6	+3	+3	Bonus feat
10th	+10	+7	+3	+3	Shock charge

The Mounted Warrior's Mount

The standard mount for a human or high elf knight is a heavy warhorse, the standard mount for a night elf huntress (or hunter, although most are female) is a nightsaber panther, and the standard mount for an orc raider is a dire wolf.

Mow Level	Bonus HD	Natural Armor Adj.	Str Adj.	Int	Special
1–2	+2	4	+1	6	Extra trick
3–4	+4	6	+2	7	Extra trick, improved evasion
5–7	+6	8	+3	8	Extra trick, share saving throws
8–10	+8	10	+4	9	Extra trick, blood bond

Mounted Warrior's Mount Basics: The mounted warrior's mount is different from a standard animal of its type in many ways. Use the base statistics for a creature of the mount's kind as given in **Manual of Monsters**, but make the following changes:

Mow Level: The character's mounted warrior class level. If the mount suffers a level drain, treat it as a mount of a lower-level mounted warrior.

Bonus HD: Extra eight-sided (d8) Hit Dice, each of which gains a Constitution modifier, as normal. Extra Hit Dice improve the mount's base attack and base save bonuses. A special mount's base attack bonus is equal to that of a healer of a level equal to the mount's HD. A mount has good Fortitude and Reflex saves (treat it as a character whose level equals the animal's HD). The mount does not gain extra skill points or feats for bonus HD.

Natural Armor Adj.: The number listed here adds to the mount's existing natural armor bonus. It represents the preternatural toughness of an experienced mounted warrior's mount.

Str Adj.: Add this figure to the mount's Strength score.

Int: The mount's Intelligence score.

Extra Tricks: The mount may learn one trick per mounted warrior level for free, without the need for a Handle Animal skill check (*PHB*, Chapter 4: Skills, "Handle Animal"). All unusual mounts (such as nightsaber panthers) are assumed to already have the "accept a rider" trick.

Improved Evasion (Ex): If the mount is subjected to an attack that normally allows a Reflex saving throw for half damage, it takes no damage on a successful saving throw and only half damage on a failed saving throw. Improved evasion is an extraordinary ability.

Share Saving Throws: For each of its saving throws, the mount uses either its own base save bonus or the mounted warrior's, whichever is higher. The mount applies its own ability modifiers to saves, and it does not share any other bonuses on saves that the mounted warrior might have (such as from magic items or feats).

Blood Bond (Ex): The bond between the mounted warrior and his mount grows strong enough that the mount gains a +2 bonus on all attack rolls, checks, and saves if it witnesses the mounted warrior being threatened or harmed. This bonus lasts as long as the threat is immediate and apparent.

Paladin Warrior

Description: Although this prestige class shares similarities with the paladin core class found in the *PHB*, the paladin warrior is very distinct in the world of **Warcraft**.

The paladin warrior does not battle "evil" in the general sense. This prestige class is for those select holy warriors who defend Azeroth from the advance of undead and demons specifically. While the presence of evil is reprehensible to a paladin warrior, destruction and entropy are his true enemies. Above all else, a paladin warrior vows to uphold his faith in the Holy Light. Empowered by the Light, these mighty warriors brandish weapons and holy fire in battle against all who would trample the meek and innocent.

Paladin warriors universally belong to the Knights of the Silver Hand. See "Faiths" in Chapter Three: Adventuring for more information.

Hit Die: d10.

Requirements

Race: Human and Ironforge dwarf only.

Alignment: Any good.

Affiliation: Alliance only.

Base Attack Bonus: +5.

Skills: Diplomacy 5 ranks, Knowledge (religion) 3 ranks.

Feat: Weapon Focus (warhammer).

Special: An initiate must seek out a paladin warrior for training and initiation. Typically, the paladin warrior assigns the supplicant a quest to accomplish that will certainly be a tremendous challenge to achieve.

Class Skills

The paladin warrior's class skills (and the key ability for each skill) are Climb (Str), Concentration (Con), Craft (Int), Diplomacy (Cha), Handle Animal (Cha), Heal (Wis), Jump (Str), Knowledge (military tactics) (Int), Knowledge (the planes) (Int), Knowledge (religion) (Int), Knowledge (undead) (Int), Profession (Wis), Ride (Dex), and Swim (Str). See Chapter 4: Skills in the *PHB* for skill descriptions.

Skill Points at Each Level: 2 + Int modifier.

Class Features

Weapon and Armor Proficiency: Paladin warriors are proficient with all simple and martial weapons, with all types of armor (heavy, medium, and light), and with shields.

Spells: Beginning at 1st level, a paladin warrior gains the ability to cast divine spells. He may prepare and cast any spell from the paladin warrior spell list, provided that he can cast

spells of that level. A paladin warrior's caster level is equal to his class level. His base daily spell allotment is given on Table 2–11: The Paladin Warrior (Plw). In addition, he receives bonus spells per day if he has a high Wisdom score (see *PHB*, Table 1–1: Ability Modifiers and Bonus Spells). When the paladin warrior gets 0 spells of a given level, she gets only bonus spells.

A paladin warrior prepares and casts spells under the same guidelines as a healer (see above), except that the paladin warrior cannot use spontaneous casting to substitute a *cure* spell in place of a prepared spell.

Lay on Hands (Su): Beginning at 1st level, a paladin warrior with a Charisma score of 12 or higher can heal wounds (his own or those of others) by touch. Each day, he can heal a total number of hit points of damage equal to his total character level (not including any racial level adjustment) x his Charisma bonus. A paladin warrior may choose to divide his healing among multiple recipients, and he does not need to use it all at once. Using *lay on hands* is a standard action.

Alternatively, the paladin warrior can use any or all of this healing power to deal damage to undead or outsiders. Using *lay on hands* in this way requires a successful melee touch attack and does not provoke an attack of opportunity. The paladin warrior decides how many of his daily allotment of points to use as damage after successfully touching the undead or outsider target.

Detect Outsiders (Sp): At will, a paladin warrior can detect demonic creatures exactly as with the spell *detect evil*, except that it focuses upon the presence of demons and other outsiders.

Detect Undead (Sp): At will, a paladin warrior can *detect undead*, as the spell.

Turn Undead and Outsiders (Su): Starting at 1st level, the paladin warrior has the power to turn or destroy undead and outsiders (*PHB*, Chapter 8: Combat, "Turn or Rebuke Undead"). He turns undead as a *PHB* cleric equal to his paladin warrior levels, and may attempt to turn a number of times per day equal to 3 + his Charisma modifier. A paladin warrior with 5 or more ranks in Knowledge (religion) gets a +2 bonus on turning checks against undead or outsiders.

Aura of Courage (Su): Beginning at 2nd level, a paladin warrior is immune to fear (magical or otherwise). Each ally within 10 feet of him gains a +4 morale bonus on saving throws against fear effects. This ability functions while the paladin warrior is conscious, but not if he is unconscious or dead.

Smite Undead and Outsiders (Su): Starting at 3rd level, a paladin warrior may attempt to smite an undead or outsider once per day with one normal melee attack. He adds his Charisma bonus (if any) to his attack roll and deals 1 extra point of damage per paladin warrior level. If the paladin warrior accidentally smites a creature that is not undead or an outsider, the smite has no effect, but the ability is still used up for that day.

At 6th level and again at 9th level, the paladin warrior may smite undead and outsiders one additional time per day, as indicated on Table 2–11: The Paladin Warrior (Plw).

Divine Health (Ex): Upon reaching 4th level, a paladin warrior gains immunity to all diseases, including supernatural and magical diseases (such as mummy rot and lycanthropy).

Remove Disease (Sp): At 4th level, a paladin warrior can produce a *remove disease* effect, as the spell, once per day.

Divine Grace (Su): At 5th level, a paladin warrior gains a bonus equal to his Charisma bonus (if any) on all saving throws.

Greater Turning (Su): Once per day at 6th level, the paladin warrior can perform a greater turning against undead or outsiders in place of a regular turning attempt. The paladin warrior adds his class level to his turning check result, and turning damage is 2d8 + paladin warrior level + Charisma modifier.

Extra Turning (Ex): At 7th level, the paladin warrior gains the Extra Turning feat for free, allowing him to turn undead or outsiders 4 additional times per day. If the paladin warrior already has Extra Turning, the effects stack.

Banishing Strike (Su): Once per day at 8th level, a paladin warrior may declare a banishing strike against an undead or a demon with one normal melee attack. On a successful hit, the target must make a Will save (DC 10 + the paladin warrior's level + Charisma modifier) or be banished instantly from the plane of Azeroth. Spell resistance does not function against a banishing strike. If the attack fails, the ability is still used up for that day.

Power Turning (Su): Once per day at 10th level, the paladin warrior can perform a power turning against undead or outsiders in place of a regular turning attempt. This ability functions as a greater turning, except that the affected undead and/or outsiders are always destroyed, regardless of Hit Dice.

Code of Conduct: A paladin warrior must be of good alignment and loses all class abilities if he ever willingly commits an evil act. Additionally, a paladin warrior's code requires that he respect legitimate authority, act with honor (not lying, not cheating, not using poison, and so forth), help those in need (provided they do not use the help for evil or chaotic ends), and punish those who harm or threaten innocents.

A paladin warrior who violates this code loses all class abilities and may not progress in levels as a paladin warrior until he atones for his violations. This atonement requires undertaking a quest (see *geas/quest*); if successful, the burden of his violation is removed as if the *atonement* spell was cast.

Paladin Warrior Spell List

Paladin warriors have a spell list geared toward fighting demons and the undead, as well as bolstering their allies' strengths and minimizing their weaknesses.

1st level — bane, bless, bless weapon, command, cure light wounds, detect poison, detect undead, divine favor, endure elements, magic weapon, protection from chaos, shield of faith.

2nd level — aid, bull's strength, cure moderate wounds, delay poison, eagle's splendor, endurance, owl's wisdom, remove paralysis, resist energy, shield other, spiritual weapon, undetectable alignment.

3rd level — cure serious wounds, discern lies, dispel magic, greater magic weapon, magic circle against chaos, prayer, remove blindness/deafness, searing light.

4th level — break enchantment, cure critical wounds, death ward, dispel chaos, dispel evil, freedom of movement, holy sword, neutralize poison, restoration.

Table 2–12: The Paladin Warrior (Plw)

Class Level	Base Attack Bonus	Fort Save	Ref Save	Will Save	Special
1st	+1	+2	+0	+0	*Lay on hands, detect outsiders, detect undead,* turn outsiders/undead
2nd	+2	+3	+0	+0	Aura of courage
3rd	+3	+3	+1	+1	Smite undead/outsider
4th	+4	+4	+1	+1	Divine health, *remove disease* 1/day
5th	+5	+4	+1	+1	Divine grace
6th	+6	+5	+2	+2	Greater turning, smite undead/outsider 2/day
7th	+7	+5	+2	+2	Extra Turning
8th	+8	+6	+2	+2	Banishing strike 1/day
9th	+9	+6	+3	+3	Smite undead/outsider 3/day
10th	+10	+7	+3	+3	Power turning

Spells per Day:

Class Level	1st	2nd	3rd	4th
1st	0	—	—	—
2nd	1	—	—	—
3rd	1	0	—	—
4th	1	1	—	—
5th	1	1	0	—
6th	1	1	1	—
7th	2	1	1	0
8th	2	1	1	1
9th	2	2	1	1
10th	2	2	2	1

Priest

Description: While healers are common devotees of the faiths of Azeroth, priests are true adherents of their chosen religion. Whether a worshipper of the Holy Light or a follower of Elune, the priest has delved deep to become a conduit for divine power.

Hit Die: d8.

Requirements

Alignment: Any non-evil.

Affiliation: Alliance only.

Skills: Knowledge (religion) 6 ranks.

Spellcasting: Able to cast 3rd-level divine spells.

Class Skills

The priest's class skills (and the key ability for each skill) are Concentration (Con), Craft (Int), Diplomacy (Cha), Gather Information (Cha), Heal (Wis), Knowledge (arcana) (Int), Knowledge (religion) (Int), Profession (Wis), and Spellcraft (Int). See Chapter 4: Skills in the *PHB* for skill descriptions.

Skill Points at Each Level: 2 + Int modifier.

Class Features

Weapon and Armor Proficiency: Priests are proficient with all simple weapons and light armor.

Aura (Ex): A priest has a particularly powerful aura corresponding to her faith's alignment (see the *detect evil* spell for details).

Spells: A priest's training focuses on divine spells. When a new priest level is gained, the character gains new spells per day as if she had also gained a level in whatever divine spellcasting class she belonged to (typically, the healer class in the **Warcraft RPG**) before she added the prestige class. She does not, however, gain any other benefit a character of that class would have gained (bonus metamagic or item creation feats, paladin warrior abilities, and so on). Put another way, she adds her priest level to the level of whatever other divine spellcasting class she has, then determines spells per day and caster level accordingly.

If a character had more than one divine spellcasting class before she became a priest, she must decide to which class she adds each level of priest for the purpose of determining spells per day.

A priest prepares and casts spells from the priest spell list under the same guidelines as a healer (see above), including being able to use spontaneous casting to "lose" a prepared spell for a *cure* spell.

Domain Spells: Priests gain access to the Healing and Protection domains (*PHB*, Chapter 11: Spells). Each domain gives the priest access to a domain spell at each spell level she can cast, as well as a granted power. The priest gets the granted powers from both domains. With access to two domain spells at a given spell level, a priest prepares one or the other each day in her domain spell slot. If a domain spell is not on the priest spell list, a priest can prepare it only in her domain spell slot.

Divine Defense: Starting at 1st level, a priest's faith grants her a +1 sacred bonus on saving throws against all necromancy spells. This includes any circumstance where a necromancy spell channels another spell, like using *spectral hand* to deliver *shocking grasp*. This bonus increases to +2 at 4th level, +3 at 7th level and +4 at 10th level.

Turn Undead (Su): Starting at 1st level, the priest has the power to turn or destroy undead (*PHB*, Chapter 8: Combat, "Turn or Rebuke Undead"). She turns undead as a *PHB* cleric equal to her divine spellcaster levels + priest levels + paladin warrior levels (if any). She may attempt to turn a number of times per day equal to 3 + her Charisma modifier. A priest with 5 or more ranks in Knowledge (religion) gets a +2 bonus on turning checks against undead.

Divine Urge (Su): At 3rd level, the priest can impose her divine will upon another once per day. This functions exactly as if the priest cast *suggestion* at her full divine spellcaster level. At 6th level, she can use divine urge twice per day.

Mass Divine Urge (Su): At 9th level, the priest can impose her will on a group once per day. This functions exactly as if the priest cast *mass suggestion* at her full divine spellcaster level.

Priest Spell List

Priest spells build upon the healer spell list, adding more offensive and defensive firepower to the mix, as well as protections from undead and demonic powers. These spells listed are in addition to the healer spell list.

1st level — *detect undead, hide from undead, magic weapon, protection from evil.*

2nd level — *align weapon (good), consecrate, lesser restoration, undetectable alignment.*

3rd level — *magic circle against evil, searing light.*

4th level — *dismissal, restoration.*

5th level — *flame strike, mark of justice, plane shift.*

6th level — *forbiddance, undeath to death.*

7th level — *ethereal jaunt, holy word.*

8th level — *dimensional lock, holy aura.*

9th level — *astral projection, etherealness, gate, starfall*.*

Table 2–13: The Priest (Pre)

Class Level	Base Attack Bonus	Fort Save	Ref Save	Will	Special	Spells per Day
1st	+0	+2	+0	+2	divine defense +1	+1 level of divine spellcasting class
2nd	+1	+3	+0	+3	—	+1 level of divine spellcasting class
3rd	+2	+3	+1	+3	divine urge 1/day	+1 level of divine spellcasting class
4th	+3	+4	+1	+4	divine defense +2	+1 level of divine spellcasting class
5th	+3	+4	+1	+4	—	+1 level of divine spellcasting class
6th	+4	+5	+2	+5	divine urge 2/day	+1 level of divine spellcasting class
7th	+5	+5	+2	+5	divine defense +3	+1 level of divine spellcasting class
8th	+6	+6	+2	+6	—	+1 level of divine spellcasting class
9th	+6	+6	+3	+6	mass divine urge 1/day	+1 level of divine spellcasting class
10th	+7	+7	+3	+7	divine defense +4	+1 level of divine spellcasting class

Shaman

Description: In contrast to the priest (who focuses on life energy) and the druid of the wild (who builds a rapport with plants and wildlife), the shaman attunes himself to the forces of nature. He draws his power from the elements and spirits of earth and sky. While a shaman's powers come from his relationship with the spirits of the elements, these spirits should not be confused with actual elementals — although a shaman can gain the power to command such beings through the force of his will alone.

Though divine spellcasters, shamans do not shy from physical conflict.

Hit Die: d8.

Requirements

Affiliation: Any.

Base Attack Bonus: +4.

Spellcasting: Able to cast 1st-level divine spells.

Class Skills

The shaman's class skills (and the key ability for each skill) are Climb (Str), Concentration (Con), Craft (Int), Heal (Heal), Intimidate (Cha), Jump (Str), Knowledge (nature) (Int), Knowledge (religion) (Int), Profession (Wis), Spellcraft (Int), Survival (Wis), and Swim (Str). See Chapter 4: Skills in the *PHB* for skill descriptions.

Skill Points at Each Level: 2 + Int modifier.

Class Features

Weapon and Armor Proficiency: Shamans are proficient with all simple weapons as well as with light and medium armor and shields.

Spells: A shaman's training focuses on divine spells. When a new shaman level is gained, the character gains new spells per day as if he had also gained a level in whatever divine spellcasting class he belonged to (typically, the healer class in **Warcraft**) before he added the prestige class. He does not, however, gain any other benefit a character of that class would have gained (bonus metamagic or item creation feats, paladin warrior abilities, and so on). Put another way, he adds his shaman level to the level of whatever other divine spellcasting class he has, then determines spells per day and caster level accordingly.

If a character had more than one divine spellcasting class before he became a shaman, he must decide to which class he adds each level of shaman for the purpose of determining spells per day.

A shaman prepares and casts spells from the shaman spell list under the same guidelines as a healer (see above), including being able to use spontaneous casting to "lose" a prepared spell for a *cure* spell.

Weather Sense (Su): At 1st level, the shaman gets a +2 circumstance bonus to his DC 15 Survival check to know what the weather will be like for the next 24 hours. This bonus increases by 2 every other shaman level thereafter to a total of +10 at 9th level, as indicated on Table 2–14: The Shaman (Sha).

Elemental Companion (Su): At 3rd level, the shaman may summon a Small elemental companion. Choose from the Small elemental familiars described under "Familiars" in the *DMG*, Chapter 6: Characters (see also the *MM* or **Manual of Monsters** for Small elemental statistics). This summoned Small elemental cannot be turned, rebuked, or commanded by any third party. The elemental serves as a companion to and can communicate intelligibly with the shaman. At every third level the shaman gains, his elemental companion's Hit Dice increase by 2 (also affecting base attack and base save bonuses).

The shaman may have only one elemental companion at a time. If the elemental companion is destroyed or if the shaman dismisses it, the shaman must attempt a DC 15 Fortitude save. If the saving throw fails, the shaman loses 200 XP per HD the elemental had. A successful saving throw reduces the loss by half. A destroyed or dismissed elemental cannot be replaced for a year and a day.

Elemental Mastery (Su): At 10th level, the spirits of the elements are the shaman's to command. He rebukes and controls elementals the same as a *PHB* evil cleric rebukes or commands undead: use the shaman's divine spellcaster levels +

the shaman's class levels to determine the equivalent of a turning check, and apply the relevant elemental Hit Dice to the undead HD chart (*PHB*, Chapter 8: Combat, "Turn or Rebuke Undead").

He may also bolster elementals he controls in the same way that a *PHB* evil cleric bolsters undead. The shaman may attempt to control elementals a number of times per day equal to 3 + his Charisma modifier.

Shaman Spell List

These spells listed are in addition to the healer spell list.

1st level — *burning hands, magic stone, obscuring mist, stasis trap**.

2nd level — *fog cloud, frost armor*, produce flame, soften earth and stone, wind wall.*

3rd level — *bloodlust*, frost nova*, gaseous form, healing ward*, resist energy, serpent ward*, shockwave*, stone shape, water breathing.*

4th level — *air walk, control water, immolation*, spike stones, wall of fire.*

5th level — *control winds, fire shield, ice storm, wall of stone.*

6th level — *chain lightning, cone of cold, fire seeds, stoneskin.*

7th level — *acid fog, control weather, fire storm, earthquake.*

8th level — *horrid wilting, incendiary cloud, iron body, whirlwind.*

9th level — *elemental swarm (air, earth, fire, or water).*

Table 2–14: The Shaman (Sha)

Class Level	Base Attack Bonus	Fort Save	Ref Save	Will Save	Special	Spells per Day
1st	+0	+2	+0	+2	Weather sense +2	+1 level of divine spellcasting class
2nd	+1	+3	+0	+3	—	+1 level of divine spellcasting class
3rd	+2	+3	+1	+3	Elemental companion, weather sense +4	+1 level of divine spellcasting class
4th	+3	+4	+1	+4	—	+1 level of divine spellcasting class
5th	+3	+4	+1	+4	Weather sense +6	+1 level of divine spellcasting class
6th	+4	+5	+2	+5	Elemental companion +2 HD	+1 level of divine spellcasting class
7th	+5	+5	+2	+5	Weather sense +8	+1 level of divine spellcasting class
8th	+6	+6	+2	+6	—	+1 level of divine spellcasting class
9th	+6	+6	+3	+6	Elemental companion +4 HD, weather sense +10	+1 level of divine spellcasting class
10th	+7	+7	+3	+7	Elemental mastery	+1 level of divine spellcasting class

Warlock

Description: Warlocks are arcane spellcasters devoted to trafficking with demons and other dark beings. Warlocks initially appeared on Azeroth some 30 years ago, when the first of their kind, Gul'dan, led the Horde across the dimensional gulf from the world of Draenor while in servitude to the Burning Legion.

Some high elves turned to this path after their glorious home of Quel'Thalas was destroyed in the Third War. This new breed of warlock seeks to control the powers that ravaged their homeland and use them for vengeance. Night elves shun this prestige class, given its roots in the arcane. Any who might take on the mantle of warlock would be forever sundered from their night elf heritage — socially, physically, and spiritually.

Hit Die: d4.

Requirements

Alignment: Any evil.

Affiliation: Any.

Spellcasting: Able to cast 3rd-level arcane spells. Must not have "Conjuration" as a forbidden school.

Class Skills

The warlock's class skills (and the key ability for each skill) are Bluff (Cha), Concentration (Con), Craft (Int), Diplomacy (Cha), Intimidate (Cha), Knowledge (arcana) (Int), Profession (Wis), and Spellcraft (Int). See Chapter 4: Skills in the *PHB* for skill descriptions.

Skill Points at Each Level: 2 + Int modifier.

Class Features

Weapon and Armor Proficiency: Warlocks are proficient with all simple weapons.

Spells: A warlock focuses on summoning demonic proxies (imps, Infernals, and other outsiders). These demonic minions take on the bulk of tasks and combat for him.

A warlock's training focuses on arcane spells. When a new warlock level is gained, the character gains new spells per day as if he had also gained a level in whatever arcane spellcasting class he belonged to before he added the prestige class. He does not, however, gain any other benefit a character of that class would have gained (bonus metamagic or item creation feats, sorcerer or wizard abilities, and so on). Put another way, he adds his warlock level to the level of whatever other arcane spellcasting class he has, then determines spells per day and caster level accordingly.

If a character had more than one arcane spellcasting class before he became a warlock, he must decide to which class he adds each

level of warlock for the purpose of determining spells per day.

Enhanced Conjuring: Upon becoming a warlock, a character increases his devotion to the conjuration school. In exchange, the warlock must sacrifice study in two schools, just as if he were a specialist (*PHB*, Chapter 3: Classes, "School Specialization"). He can never again learn spells from either prohibited school. He can still use any prohibited spells he knew prior to becoming a warlock, including using items that are activated by spell completion or spell trigger.

In return, the warlock can prepare one additional conjuration spell per spell level each day. He also gains a +2 bonus on Spellcraft checks to learn conjuration spells (*PHB*, Chapter 10: Magic, "Arcane Spells," *Adding Spells to a Wizard's Spellbook*).

If the warlock was already a conjurer, he must choose two additional forbidden schools and gains yet another conjuration spell, for a total of two additional conjuration spells per spell level each day. Similarly, his bonus on Spellcraft checks for learning conjuration spells increases to +4. The warlock may end up with two school specializations or with the conjuration specialty twice.

Demonic Companion (Su): At 1st level, the warlock may summon an imp companion. This summoned demon follows the same rules as an improved imp familiar, as detailed under "Familiars" in the *DMG*, Chapter 6: Characters.

If the demonic companion is destroyed or if the warlock dismisses it, the warlock must attempt a DC 15 Fortitude save. If the saving throw fails, the warlock loses 200 XP per warlock level; success reduces the loss to half that amount. In addition, the warlock must make a DC 15 Will save or suffer 1d6 points of temporary Constitution damage as the companion's sudden loss rips away a portion of the warlock's life force. Such is the price for dealing with infernal powers. A destroyed or dismissed demonic companion cannot be replaced for a year and a day.

Each time a warlock loses a demonic companion, he gains a mark of chaos: burning red eyes, strange sigils marked on his skin, and so on. These marks apply a –1 penalty to any Charisma-related checks

when dealing with anyone who can see the deformities and who does not also serve demonkind.

Improved Ally: A warlock is adept at convincing creatures from other planes to do his bidding. When a warlock casts a *planar ally* spell (including the *lesser* and *greater* versions), he makes a Diplomacy check to convince the creature to aid him for a reduced payment. If the warlock's Diplomacy check adjusts the creature's attitude to helpful (see the "Influencing NPC Attitudes" sidebar in Chapter 4: Skills of the *PHB*), the creature will work for 50% of the standard fee, as long as the task is one that does not go against its nature. For example, a 2nd-level warlock that gets a Diplomacy check result of 15 while negotiating with an initially friendly planar ally can convince a 6-HD creature to perform a 7-hour task for only 1,500 gp an hour (normally 3,000 gp an hour).

The warlock's improved ally class feature only works when the planar ally shares at least one aspect of alignment with the warlock. The warlock may only have one such ally at a time, but he may bargain for tasks from other planar allies normally.

Demonic Lore (Ex): At 3rd level, warlocks receive a +4 bonus to all Knowledge checks that relate to demons and the Twisting Nether.

Augment Summoning: At 4th level, a warlock gamins the Augment Summoning feat (see Chapter 5: Feats in the *PHB*).

Extended Summoning: At 6th level and higher, all spells from the summoning subschool that the warlock casts have their durations doubled, as if the Extend Spell feat is applied to them. The levels of the summoning spells do not change, however. This ability stacks with the effect of the Extend Spell feat, which does change the spell's level.

Planar Cohort: An 8th-level warlock can use any of the *planar ally* spells to call a creature to act as his cohort. The called creature serves loyally and well as long as the warlock continues to advance a cause important to the creature. For example, an 8th-level warlock could use a *planar ally* spell to call a nathrezite dreadlord to act as his cohort. As long as the warlock undertakes tasks that would increase the Burning Legion's power and influence on Azeroth, the nathrezite will serve the warlock.

To call the planar cohort, the warlock must cast the relevant spell, paying the XP costs normally. Convincing the creature to serve as a planar cohort requires an offering of 1,000 gp x the creature's HD, and the improved ally class feature cannot be used to reduce or eliminate this cost. The planar cohort cannot have more Hit Dice than the warlock and must have an ECL no higher than the warlock's character level –2. So, a 7th level conjuror/8th level warlock can summon demons of ECL 13 or lower from the Twisting Nether.

A warlock can have only one planar cohort at a time, but he can continue to make agreements with other called creatures normally. A planar cohort replaces a warlock's existing cohort if he has one by virtue of the Leadership feat (see the *PHB* and the *DMG*).

Demon Mastery (Su): At 10th-level, the warlock has gained such power that he may bend demons to his will. He rebukes and controls outsiders the same as a *PHB* evil cleric rebukes or commands undead: use the warlock's arcane spellcaster levels + warlock levels to determine the equivalent of a turning check, and apply the relevant outsider Hit Dice to the undead HD chart (*PHB*, Chapter 8: Combat, "Turn or Rebuke Undead").

The warlock may also bolster outsiders he controls in the same way that a *PHB* evil cleric bolsters undead. The warlock may attempt to control outsiders a number of times per day equal to 3 + his Charisma modifier, which also applies to outsiders that the warlock did not summon himself.

Warlock Spell List

A warlock focuses on conjuring demonic servants to do his bidding. As such, a warlock sacrifices spell variety for increased access to the conjuration school. The spells listed are in addition to any other arcane spells to which the warlock already has access.

1st level — *summon monster I.*
2nd level — *summon monster II.*
3rd level — *summon monster III.*
4th level — *summon monster IV.*
5th level — *contact other plane, flame strike, lesser planar binding, summon monster V.*
6th level — *summon monster VI.*
7th level — *planar binding, summon monster VII.*
8th level — *greater planar binding, summon monster VIII.*
9th level — *summon monster IX.*

Table 2–15: The Warlock (Wrl)

Class Level	Base Attack Bonus	Fort Save	Ref Save	Will Save	Special	Spells per Level
1st	+0	+0	+0	+2	Enhanced conjuring, demonic companion	+1 level of arcane spellcasting class
2nd	+1	+0	+0	+3	Improved ally	+1 level of arcane spellcasting class
3rd	+1	+1	+1	+3	Demonic Lore	+1 level of arcane spellcasting class
4th	+2	+1	+1	+4	Augment summoning	+1 level of arcane spellcasting class
5th	+2	+1	+1	+4	—	+1 level of arcane spellcasting class
6th	+3	+2	+2	+5	Extended summoning	+1 level of arcane spellcasting class
7th	+3	+2	+2	+5	—	+1 level of arcane spellcasting class
8th	+4	+2	+2	+6	Planar cohort	+1 level of arcane spellcasting class
9th	+4	+3	+3	+6	—	+1 level of arcane spellcasting class
10th	+5	+3	+3	+7	Demon mastery	+1 level of arcane spellcasting class

Skills

Thanks to the power of steam and some unusual relationships between the races in the world of **Warcraft**, certain existing skills have some new uses.

Appraise (Int)

Steam technology is new enough that most people are not sure what to make of it yet. The people of Kalimdor still point in surprise at passing flying machines, and a goblin walking through the marketplace on autostilts is sure to turn heads. Unfamiliarity with such technology makes appraising these devices difficult.

Check: Appraising technological devices calls for a base DC 15 Appraise check, but the DC can vary depending on the item's market value. Items with a value between 1,000 and 10,000 gp are DC 20; technological devices with a value over 10,000 gp are DC 25.

Special: An Ironforge dwarf gets a +2 racial bonus on Appraise checks related to stone or metal items, including technological devices. A goblin gets a +2 racial bonus to all Appraise checks. Appraise is a class skill for Ironforge dwarf and goblin characters.

Concentration (Con)

Special: A high elf gets a +2 racial bonus to Concentration checks. Concentration is a class skill for all high elf characters.

Craft (Int)

Gunpowder and Phlogiston: Mechanical devices and steam technology are the latest attraction, leaving alchemy as "the old technology." Alchemists resent the disparaging tone that accompanies "old."

Alchemy remains very useful. Gunpowder is the most powerful explosive in the world of **Warcraft**. Those who know how to make gunpowder guard the secret jealously, ordering false supplies and teaching fake procedures to all but a few promising apprentices. Rumors claim that some powder makers have even purchased the deaths of those who study the process too closely.

Just as mysterious is the gas called phlogiston. This odorless, weightless, almost undetectable gas makes steam technology practical by speeding combustion and increasing the heat produced by steam boilers. Phlogiston allows the creation of small but powerful boilers that can be fitted into guns, backpacks, and other easy-to-carry equipment. In addition to its application in devices, the gas has proven useful in the form of elixirs that can alter an imbiber's abilities for a short time.

Recently, alchemists have worked to combine the two, giving rise to imbued gunpowder. This valuable substance combines the explosive power of gunpowder with a phlogiston accelerant.

Table 2–16: New Items and Craft DCs

Item	Craft Skill	Craft DC
Gunpowder	Alchemy*	15
Imbued Gunpowder	Alchemy*	25
Phlogiston	Alchemy*	20
Phlogiston elixir	Alchemy*	30
Totem, tauren	Carpentry	18
Ammunition, mortar	Technological device*	18
Army knife, goblin	Technological device*	16
Blunderbuss	Technological device*	17
Bomb	Technological device*	17
Bomb, grenade	Technological device*	19
Flintlock pistol	Technological device*	18
Gyroparasol	Technological device*	18
Long rifle	Technological device*	21
Mine shoes, goblin	Technological device*	17
Mortar	Technological device*	16
Pulley gun	Technological device*	20
Steam hammer	Technological device*	20
Ammunition, other types	Weaponsmithing	10
Claws of attack, orcish	Weaponsmithing	18
Halberd, tauren	Weaponsmithing	18
Hammer, dwarven tossing	Weaponsmithing	18
Moonglaive	Weaponsmithing	18
Warblade	Weaponsmithing	18

* You must be a tinker to craft these items.

Creating Technological Devices: Craft (technological device) can be used to build different steam-powered devices. It uses the same rules for item creation and repairs as other Craft skills. To determine the market value and item creation DC of technological devices, see the Creating Technological Devices section below.

Not all the equipment of **Warcraft** requires steamtech prowess, of course. If an item uses gunpowder, steam power, or a complex arrangement of gears and other machinery, it's a mechanical object. Everything else uses traditional Craft specializations such as weaponsmithing, armorsmithing, or calligraphy. Table 2–15: New Items and Craft DCs shows the Craft specializations and item creation DCs for new equipment found in Chapter Three: Adventuring, "Equipment."

Special: A dwarf gets a +2 racial bonus on Craft checks relating to stone, metal, or gunsmithing. A goblin gets a +2 racial bonus on Craft (alchemy) checks and a +4 racial bonus on all Craft (technological device) checks. Craft is a class skill for both races.

Decipher Script (Int; Trained Only)

This skill may be used to read blueprints, design notes, and other technical documents.

Check: Reading a complete technical document with examples and illustrations is a DC 15 Decipher Script check. A document that is at least 50% complete is DC 20, and a fragmentary or badly damaged document is DC 25 or more.

A character who has successfully interpreted a technical document receives a +2 circumstance bonus to Craft (technological device) checks to construct the device that the document describes. This bonus applies only if the document describes the item correctly to begin with and is available for study during the construction process.

Decipher Script can also be used for its traditional purpose of figuring out ancient writing. In Kalimdor, four languages almost always require Decipher Script checks to be interpreted: the demonic language of Eredun, the elemental language of Kalimag, and the ancient Draconic and Titan languages.

Some of these languages are more obscure than others. Eredun seemingly wants to be understood, while linguists tear their hair out trying to parse the inhumanoid grammar and circular references of Titan. The DCs for deciphering various languages are listed below.

Language	Simple Message DC	Standard Text DC	Complex Document DC
Draconic	20	25	30
Eredun	15	20	25
Kalimag	20	25	30
Titan	30	35	40

Diplomacy (Cha)

The wars between the races may be over — for the present, anyway — but the old alliances and enmities still loom in the minds of many. Kalimdor is a land of refugees and survivors; loved ones still grieve over empty places at their tables, and warriors remember friendships forged in the heat of battle. For the majority of people, the war is the most important event that has ever happened, and bringing up memories of it provokes a strong emotional response.

Check: A well-chosen reference to the war can be a powerful negotiating tool. If you show how a person's war experiences support the ideas you are trying to communicate, and can do so without opening up too many old wounds, you can gain a +2 circumstance bonus to a subsequent Diplomacy check. This tactic is not without risks, however. If you trample on or trivialize war memories, the modifier may become a –2 circumstance penalty instead.

Whenever possible, the GM should imagine what war experiences an NPC had and how the memories of the past affect that NPC's attitudes now. Table 2–17: Possible War Experiences offers brief histories for minor characters that the GM may roll or choose from. In addition to giving heroes an angle to winning NPCs over to their side on certain issues, this element can make for entertaining roleplay and turn a brief NPC reference into a useful recurring character.

Still, be careful of going overboard. You don't need to deal with Felos the dwarf's flashbacks of fixing flying machines under fire every time the PCs want to purchase new tools.

Table 2–17: Possible War Experiences

D10 Roll	War Experience
1	The character grieves for the loss of a loved one and blames another race for that person's death
2	The character feels lost in the new land of Kalimdor and looks with nostalgia at the life left behind.
3	The character's mind was damaged by the horrors of war, leading to unc ontrollable urges and fears.
4	The character was wounded and still suffers pain or disability from the injuries.
5	The character feels cheated by the war and its aftermath and wants recom pense for undergoing trials and suffering.
6	Though apparently unharmed, the character wants to leave the war in the past and get on with life.
7	Surviving the war has left the character with an appreciation of life and empathy for others.
8	The character developed an intense camaraderie with others caught in the war, and will do anything for those people.
9	The character looks back on the war as a glorious time and wishes to reclaim the excitement the past.
10	The character owes his life or that of loved ones to the actions of an enemy and feels a sense of debt or friendship because of it.

Special: Goblins and humans get a +2 racial bonus to Diplomacy checks. Diplomacy is a class skill for both races.

Disable Device (Int; Trained Only)

Most technological devices look (or often sound) like they are on the verge of exploding, but they are surprisingly robust.

Check: The difficulty of safely shutting down — or sabotaging — a technological device is

Table 2–18: Malfunction DCs

Device	DC
No Malfunction Rating	30
Malfunction Rating 1	27
Malfunction Rating 2	24
Malfunction Rating 3	21
Malfunction Rating 4	18
Malfunction Rating 5	15

based on its Malfunction Rating, as noted on Table 2–18: Malfunction DCs.

In addition to the DCs listed in the *PHB* (Chapter 4: Skills, "Disable Device"), the DC for trying to disable technological devices may be subject to the modifiers on Table 2–19: Modifiers to Disable Device.

Action: Attempting to disable or sabotage a technological device takes 1d6 minutes. If the character is forced to complete work before the time is up, the job is rushed and subject to the −2 adjustment to the DC listed on Table 2–19.

Table 2–19: Modifiers to Disable Device

Situation	DC Modifier*
Character built the device he is disabling	−2
Device fails when a particular condition is fulfilled, such as exceeding a certain speed	+2
Device uses gunpowder or other explosive materials	−2
Masterwork artisan's tools	−2
No artisan's tools, or improvised tools	+2
Disable attempt is a "rush job"	+2

* All applicable modifiers to the DC are cumulative.

Escape Artist (Dex; Armor Check Penalty)

Escape Artist can be a lifesaver when trying to escape a vehicle that thunders out of control, has crashed, or is doing something other than what you want it to.

This skill is also useful for getting *into* vehicles, especially those built with more attention to engine power than passenger comfort. Many goblin vehicles require the skills of a contortionist to enter, especially if you are bigger than the average goblin.

Check: Escaping from a vehicle calls for a base DC 20 Escape Artist check; the DC increases by 1 for every 10 miles per hour the vehicle is traveling, or was traveling when it crashed. Climbing into a flying machine or a walking buggy calls for a DC 20 Escape Artist check. A creature larger or smaller than Medium takes a size bonus or penalty on Escape Artist checks for getting into or out of vehicles: Fine +16, Diminutive +12, Tiny +8, Small +4, Large –4, Huge –8, Gargantuan –12, Colossal –16.

Forgery (Int)

The technology of **Warcraft** is an art, not an industrial process. Each master crafter has a distinct way of shaping and assembling parts that can be identified in all equipment her studio creates. Top designers earn top coin for their unique creations, which means that a lucrative income can be had making copies of technological devices.

Check: Copying technology requires two types of checks. The forger must build a facsimile of the device to be copied using the technological item creation rules and the usual Craft checks. Most forgers save money by building devices with fewer capabilities and shoddier components. These changes reduce the Technology Score and increase the Malfunction Rating of the item (see Chapter Three: Adventuring), lowering the market value and raw materials cost.

The forger then makes a Forgery check, which opposes the Forgery check of any character who tries to determine the device's authenticity. The success or failure of the check is determined as usual, with the "reader" of the device receiving bonuses or penalties depending on familiarity with the type of "document" (in this case, the device) or the "handwriting" (distinctive style) of its creator.

Note that most devices quickly prove their shoddy workmanship, giving their users ample reason to be suspicious of who really made them. Of course, examining what's left of a gun that has just exploded in your face can be difficult. Authenticating destroyed equipment imposes a –5 penalty on the Forgery check of the character performing the examination.

Gather Information (Cha)

Special: Half-elves and humans receive a +2 racial bonus to Gather Information checks. Gather Information is a class skill for both races.

Handle Animal (Cha; Trained Only)

Special: Orcs receive a +2 racial bonus to Handle Animal checks while working with wolves. Tauren receive a +2 bonus to all Handle Animal checks. Handle Animal is a class skill for both races.

Intimidate (Cha)

Much in the world of **Warcraft** is intimidating, generally for the usual reasons. (Why you should not make a tauren angry is not hard to figure out.) One particular source of fear and respect is common to all, regardless of who you are or where you're from: firearms and explosives. Just brandishing a flintlock pistol gets people's attention, and showing that you are willing and able to use it can make a compelling argument.

Check: You can do a number of things with a firearm or an explosive that give you a +2 circumstance bonus on an Intimidate check. Examples include firing a flintlock pistol into the air, leveling a blunderbuss at a character's midsection, lighting the fuse on a bomb, and cheerfully describing the destructive capabilities of your favorite firearm.

If you want to get creative — say, by firing a ball past a target's ear (or other sensitive body part) — make a ranged touch attack against the target. If you succeed, take the difference between your attack roll result and the target's touch attack AC and add that as a circumstance bonus to your Intimidate check. If you "miss" the ranged touch attack, you may have fired *too* close to the target: make a normal ranged attack roll; if you succeed, then you have actually hit the target for damage.

Special: Although great intimidation tools, firearms are one-shot weapons that take 1 round to reload. When firing a gun to scare someone, having an extra weapon to ensure that you can carry out your threat is wise.

An orc gets a +2 racial bonus to Intimidation checks. Intimidation is a class skill for all orcs.

Knowledge (Int; Trained Only)

Knowledge (military tactics) plays an important role in the world of **Warcraft**. It represents both the formal study of warfare and the practical experience of surviving and winning battles. Some of the tasks Knowledge (military tactics) can accomplish are:

Assess odds: Given accurate information about your forces, an enemy's forces, and the terrain they may do battle in, you can develop a logical conclusion about the relative strengths of the opposing forces and your chances of prevailing against them in battle.

Evaluate forces: You can examine a military force to determine its strengths and weaknesses. This is easier to do for your own forces than for an enemy's, but you may use the "evaluate own force" DC if you can infiltrate the enemy's forces and gain a position of trust within them. To make this skill check, you must study that unit you are evaluating for 1 hour, examining it physically and gathering opinions of it from fellow soldiers. If you succeed at the check, you learn how ready the unit is for battle, what combat tasks it is most suited to perform, what problems it has, and how these problems might be solved or (in the case of enemies) exacerbated.

Evaluate terrain: You can examine a potential battlefield and figure out how to use it to your advantage. To make this skill check, you must study the area for 1 hour, either in person or with the help of detailed and accurate maps. If you succeed at the check, you locate the best positions for your forces to take, anticipate potential ambushes, map out good paths of advance or retreat, and locate safe places for supplies and reserves.

Predict tactics: You may attempt to predict the tactics of a military opponent before a conflict. You must know who leads the enemy forces and what their military experience is. (If you do not know the background of your opponent, a DC 15 Gather Information check can help.) The DC of the Knowledge (military tactics) check is 20 + the enemy leader's character level. If you succeed at the check, you deduce the battle plan that your opponent is most likely to use against your forces.

Train troops: You may construct and lead training regimens to keep troops at the peak of their effectiveness. To benefit from this ability, the troops must undergo regular exercise, combat drills, and testing under your direction. If they have received a training session within 2 days before going into battle, you may make a skill check (DC 20) just before the battle begins. If the skill check succeeds, your troops receive a +1 morale bonus to initiative, attack rolls, Will saves, and AC at the battle's beginning for a number of rounds equal to 1 + your Intelligence bonus.

Task	DC
Assess odds	15
Evaluate enemy force	25
Evaluate own force	15
Evaluate terrain	20
Predict tactics	20 + opposing leader's character level
Train troops	20

Special: High elves receive a +2 racial bonus to Knowledge (arcana) skill checks. Night elves receive a +2 racial bonus to Knowledge (nature) skill checks. Knowledge (arcana) is a class skill for all high elf characters, while Knowledge (nature) is a class skill for all night elf characters.

Listen (Wis)

Special: Goblins receive a +2 racial bonus to Listen checks. Listen is a class skill for all goblins.

Move Silently (Dex; Armor Check Penalty)

Steam technology is noisy. Most technological devices are concertos of hisses, squeaks, and whirring gears.

Special: Any attempt to Move Silently with a technological device active suffers a –4 circumstance penalty.

Open Lock (Dex; Trained Only)

The steam technology revolution has changed the art of lockpicking. Many locks no longer use the traditional hardware of keys, tumblers, and bolts. Instead, they use intricate combinations of levers, dials, gears, and puzzle pieces to draw massive bolts open and closed.

Special: Doors in **Warcraft** resemble bank vaults, and lockpicks provide no bonus to open them.

Perform (Cha)

Life can be hard in a world that knows only war, but music and dance are still important to many. Each race favors its own songs and instruments; the races of **Warcraft** are just beginning to listen to each other's music.

Tauren play strangely delicate bone flutes and dance shuffling steps under the light of the moon. Dwarves and orcs love percussive instruments: Ironforge dwarves play chimes and orcs play drums, and an understanding of each other's music is one of the few things they have in common. Humans play an endless variety of instruments, but favor the lute. The high elves specialize in magical instruments such as the singing crystals of Stranglethorn, and the always experimental goblins create new sounds with massive clockwork organs and steam fiddles. Even the night elves sing haunting melodies as they move between the trees.

Orcish War Drums: These instruments deserve special mention. Each orc tribe has a priceless collection of drums covered with the skins of its mightiest enemies, and young warriors train for years to learn the tribe's traditional war rhythms. The war drums are the heart of a tribe's battle formation; their sound drives the tribe's warriors into a terrifying frenzy. See Drums of Courage in "Feats," below, for the potential effects of orcish war drums in battle.

Ride (Dex)

The races of **Warcraft** ride a variety of beasts. Humans are most comfortable on horses, but other races' mounts include gryphons, hippogryphs, kodo beasts, wolves, wyverns, and the nightsaber and frostsaber cats. Each type of these mounts counts as different for purposes of familiarity. Most mounts perform the same kinds of maneuvers and require the same kinds of equipment as horses. Wyverns and saber cats, however, refuse to accept saddles, bridles, and other tack; any character wishing to ride one of these mounts must master the art of riding bareback (see the Ride Bareback feat in the "Feats" section, below).

Check: Land-based and flying mounts are very different. If you are familiar with a land-based mount but try to ride a flying mount, or vice-versa, you suffer a –5 penalty to your Ride checks. Kalimdor boasts many expert riders capable of spectacular tricks in the saddle. Some of the more typical stunts skilled riders can perform are listed below and are subject to armor check and bareback riding penalties:

Task	Ride DC
Fire from the saddle	20
Jump into the saddle (stationary)	20
Jump into the saddle (moving)	25
Stand in the saddle	20
Swing into the saddle	20
Wrestle for control	15*
*This usage is also an opposed roll.	

Fire from the Saddle: Firearms and mounted warriors do not mix well yet, and anyone who tries to shoot from the saddle is asking for trouble. A firearm attack while mounted applies a –4 penalty to the attack roll. Make your Ride check after making the attack roll. If you fail, your mount panics. You may not do anything else until you make a new Ride check to regain control of your mount. This procedure is identical to the check for controlling a mount in battle (*PHB*, Chapter 4: Skills, "Ride"), but applies to all mounts, including those trained for battle.

Jump into the Saddle: You may leap from a position above or next to your mount and land upon it ready to ride. Make a Ride check. If you fail, you hit the ground and take damage as if you had fallen the distance that you jumped. This Ride check is more difficult if the mount is moving. This usage is a move action.

Stand in the Saddle: You may stand up on your mount's back. Make a Ride check. If you successfully stand in the saddle, you get a +2 circumstance bonus to ranged attack rolls and Jump checks; however, you also get a –2 penalty to Ride checks.

If you fail, you fall off your mount (see the soft fall maneuver in the *PHB*, Chapter 4: Skills, "Ride"). This usage is a move action.

If you fail a Ride check while standing, make another Ride check to stay seated in the saddle. If you fail this subsequent check, you fall off your mount. This usage is a free action.

Swing into the Saddle: When a moving mount passes through your threatened area, you may use an attack of opportunity to swing up into the saddle. If you fail, make a DC 15 Reflex save or fall prone.

Wrestle for Control: You may struggle with another rider to take control of a mount. The rider with the highest Ride skill check has control of the mount. A rider who fails falls off (see the soft fall maneuver in the *PHB*, Chapter 4: Skills, "Ride"). Multiple riders may continue to wrestle for control until any opposition falls off or gives up. This usage is a standard action.

Sense Motive (Wis)

Special: Half-elves receive a +2 racial bonus to Sense Motive checks. Sense Motive is a class skill for all half-elves.

Speak Language (None; Trained Only)

While all heroes can speak Common and can read and write all the languages that they speak (except for barbarians), the languages available in the **Warcraft** universe are seldom the same as those listed in the *PHB*.

Known languages, typical speakers, and alphabets (as relevant) are provided on Table 2–20: Languages of Azeroth. Any languages from the *PHB* that are not listed do not have an equivalent in **Warcraft**.

Restricted Language: A restricted language is almost impossible for a starting hero to know, either because no one remains to speak it or

Table 2–20: Languages of Azeroth

Language	Typical Speakers	Alphabet
Common	Humans, half-elves, half-orcs	Common
Darnassian*	Night elves	Darnassian
Draconic*	Dragons, a few night elves	Runic
Dwarven	Dwarves	Runic
Eredun*	Demons, a few corrupted orcs	Eredic
Gnome	Gnomes	Common
Goblin	Goblins	Common
Kalimag*	Elementals	Runic
Low Common	Ogres, gnolls, furbolgs, kobolds, other humanoids and giants	None
Orc	Orcs, half-orcs	Common
Nazja*	Naga	Darnassian
Taur-ahe	Tauren	Pictoforms
Thalassian	High elves, half-elves	Darnassian
Titan*	None at present	Runic

*This language is restricted.

because that race is so reclusive that the PC has not received the opportunity to learn it. A character may not know a restricted language unless it is listed specifically as an automatic or bonus race or class language. The GM may allow a hero to learn a restricted language if there is a plausible reason for the PC to come across it.

Draconic and Kalimag are obscure tongues spoken only by a few scholars. The native speakers — dragons and elemental beings, respectively — are seldom encountered.

Eredun, the speech of the Burning Legion, is all but eradicated. It lives in the minds of cultists and those few brave enough to study it. Eredun has a life of its own — its words writhe in the minds of those who know it, eating away sanity and morality. Any non-evil character that learns Eredun must make a DC 12 Will save each year. If the save fails, the character suffers 1 point of permanent drain to Wisdom and his alignment shifts one step toward evil. The annual Will save continues even after the character becomes evil.

Gnomes are little known among the residents of Kalimdor, and many assume that they are nothing more than myth. As such, anyone claiming to speak the language of gnomes is dismissed as a drunken lout.

Sailors speak of the mysterious and dangerous naga. Some even claim to know phrases in the aquatic race's language, heard on the wind as their ships sailed the seas. These folks get the same consideration as those who profess to speak Gnome.

Tauren do not have an alphabet as other races do; their written language is made of elaborate pictograms.

Titan is understood only by deduction. Scholars are trying to restore the language based on matching with the modern Dwarven tongue rare evidence found at dwarven excavations of Titan ruins.

Spellcraft (Int; Trained Only)

Special: A high elf gets a +2 racial bonus to Spellcraft checks. Spellcraft is a class skill for all high elves.

Spot (Wis)

Read Lips: This usage functions as described in Chapter 4: Skills of the *PHB*, but it is worth noting that read lips sees a fair amount of use among dwarves and goblins. Deafness is an occupational hazard among seasoned tinkers, after all, and even young tinkers find themselves resorting to lip reading after a particularly "successful" experiment.

Survival (Wis)

Special: Night elves and tauren receive a +2 racial bonus to Survival checks. Survival is a class skill for both races.

New Skill

Use Technological Device (Int)

The technological devices of **Warcraft** all work in much the same way — pull the levers, twist the knobs, and hope the contraption you're using doesn't explode. The goblins call this a "system of operations," which means that you can operate many dubious devices with just one skill.

This flexible skill operates many different technological devices. There are exceptions — most weapons work automatically and are aimed with attack rolls, while a few items require specialized skill or ability checks — but most devices are easy to figure out if you understand the basic technology behind them. Use Technological Device represents that understanding.

Use Technological Device does not measure the ability to build or repair devices — the Craft (technological device) skill fills this role.

Check: Technological devices listed in Chapter Three: Adventuring indicate any relevant DCs required for operation. Other typical DCs are listed on Table 2–21: Use Technological Device DCs.

Some devices are more difficult to operate than others. Vehicles are notoriously complicated and require a special Vehicle Proficiency to operate correctly (see "Feats," below). Any character that does not have the appropriate proficiency suffers a –4 penalty to Use Technological Device checks for that device.

Special: Use Technological Device is a class skill for rogues and tinkers.

Table 2–21: Use Technological Device DCs

DC	Task
5	Extremely simple or self-operating devices — at this difficulty, you're just looking for the "on" switch.
10	Simple devices with one or two controls, such as an alarm system that protects a variable area.
12	Simple devices such as bombs that require some care but little knowledge.
15	Typical devices such as a goblin treecutter that requires some direction but mostly operate themselves.
20	Complex devices such as a pulley gun that require careful operation.
25	Complex and dangerous tools such as power saws, which require constant attention to use properly.
30	Calculating devices and other complex machines that require extensive programming and supervision.

Feats

This section provides several feats for use in a **Warcraft** campaign. As well, it presents two new kinds of feat: Technology feats, which deal with the building of and tinkering around with technological devices; and Tauren feats, available only to tauren and tied to their shamanistic traditions. A tinker can take any Technology feat as a bonus feat.

Bash [General]

One blow from your weapon can leave an opponent stunned and reeling.

Prerequisites: Str 13, Power Attack, base attack bonus +4.

Benefit: You can declare a bash attempt before taking a full attack action with a bludgeoning weapon. For the successful attack of your choice, roll damage normally; the foe struck by your attack must then make a Fortitude save (DC 10 + the damage rolled). The foe suffers no damage from the blow, but on a failed save he is stunned for 1 round. A stunned character can't act, loses any Dexterity bonus to AC, and takes a –2 penalty to AC. You can use Bash only once per round and no more than once per level per day.

When you use Bash, you forfeit any bonus or extra attacks granted by other feats or abilities (such as the Cleave feat or the *haste* spell). Constructs, oozes, plants, undead, incorporeal creatures, and creatures immune to critical hits cannot be stunned.

Special: A fighter may select Bash as one of his fighter bonus feats.

Battle Cry [General]

You can terrify opponents with a fearsome battle cry. Most characters must be berserk with rage to use this ability. (Orcs are so intimidating

that this ability works even when they're in a good mood.)

Prerequisite: Cha 13, ability to rage.

Benefit: As a move action, you can sound a battle cry that strikes fear into the hearts of your opponents. Each foe within 30 feet of you at the time of the battle cry must make a Will save (DC 10 + half your character level + your Charisma bonus); add 2 to the Will save DC if you have at least 5 ranks in Intimidate. A foe who fails this saving throw suffers a –2 morale penalty to attack rolls, Will saves, and AC for 1 round. This penalty does not stack unless a character with Collective Fury is involved in the battle. Battle Cry produces a mind-affecting effect.

Special: Non-orc characters may take this feat, but can only use it while raging. Each use reduces a non-orc character's total rage time by 1 round.

Battle Language [General]

You can use short phrases and gestures to communicate orders and vital information during the chaos of battle.

Prerequisites: Bluff 3 ranks.

Benefit: In combat, you can support a friend who also has this feat to take "aid another" actions. You must be within 100 feet of your friend, and you must be able to see each other. Attempting to help a companion in this manner is a move action. The sender makes a DC 15 Bluff check, and if successful, the recipient gains a +2 circumstance bonus either to his next attack roll or to his AC against an opponent's next attack (your choice). This bonus stacks with other aid another attempts, but not with other Battle Language attempts.

Designed for efficiency and not secrecy, the limited options of Battle Language make it relatively easy to decipher in combat. If you observe two or more opponents using Battle Language, you can make a Sense Motive check opposed by a sender's Bluff check to intercept the message. If successful, you understand the message sufficiently to negate the "aid another" bonus.

Normal: "Aid another" actions can be taken only when in melee combat range to distract or interfere with an opponent.

Special: If you have 5 or more ranks in Knowledge (military tactics), you receive a +2 synergy bonus to send or intercept Battle Language. A fighter may select Battle Language as one of his fighter bonus feats.

Block Spell [Metamagic]

You may channel magic energy to block the effects of a spell.

Prerequisites: Iron Will, Magic Energy Control, caster level 5th.

Benefit: When you are the target of a spell, you may disrupt the casting and counter its effects. Make a Spellcraft check (DC 15 + the spell's level). If you succeed, you identify the spell and may automatically counter it by spending a spell slot that is at least one spell level higher than the spell you are attempting to disrupt. You do not need to have an appropriate counterspell prepared and ready to cast.

Normal: Most spells can only be countered by casting the same spell, a spell with a diametrically opposed effect, or *dispel magic*.

Brilliant Leadership [Metamagic]

You inspire and challenge other spellcasters that follow you, encouraging them to explore their talents to the fullest.

Prerequisites: Leadership, able to cast 3rd-level spells.

Benefit: Each day, any of your followers who are spellcasters may prepare or cast extra spells. Each follower gets one extra spell per day for each spell level, up to two spell levels below the highest spell level you can cast. For example, if you can cast 5th-level spells, your follows can gain 1 extra spell per level up to 3rd-level spells.

Build Firearms [Technology]

You have a talent for building and using firearms.

Benefit: You get a +2 bonus to Craft (technological device) checks when crafting a firearm. Your Technological Limit for building firearms is increased by 2. (On technological limit, see "Creating Technological Devices" in Chapter Three: Adventuring.)

Special: Once per week, instead of making the usual attack roll, you may declare an automatic critical threat using a firearm that you have built. You must still roll to confirm the critical, as normal.

A tinker may select Build Firearms as one of his tinker bonus feats.

Build Siege Weapons [Technology]

You have a talent for building — or sabotaging! — large weapons and engines of destruction.

Benefit: You get a +2 bonus to Craft (technological device) checks when building catapults, cannons, mortars, and other siege weapons. Your technological limit for building these weapons is increased by 2.

Special: You may make a Craft (technological device) check to sabotage any technological device or weapon that is larger than Medium. The DC for the check equals the DC to create the item. If you succeed, the item becomes useless until repaired. If you succeed by 5 or more, you can rig the item to suffer a catastrophic malfunction the next time it is used, destroying the item and (at the GM's discretion) endangering whoever is using it.

A tinker may select Build Siege Weapons as one of his tinker bonus feats.

Build Small Devices [Technology]

You have nimble fingers and a gift for fine workmanship.

Prerequisites: Dex 13.

Benefit: You get a +2 bonus to Craft (technological device) checks when building a device of Tiny, Diminutive, or Fine size. Your technological limit for building such devices is increased by 2.

Special: You can build devices that are easily concealed or disguised as other objects. If you choose to conceal or disguise a device, then any character trying to find it must make a Spot check. Any character trying to discover what the device does must make a Use Technological Device check. The DC of these checks is equal to 10 + your Craft (technological device) skill modifier.

A tinker may select Build Small Devices as one of his tinker bonus feats.

Build Teamwork [Technology]

You work well with others and can use teamwork to speed the construction of technological devices.

Prerequisites: Leadership, at least 2 other technology feats.

Benefit: When you are assisted in a Craft check by at least 3 other people who each have at least 1 rank in a Craft skill, the result of a successful Craft check is doubled. This feat has no effect on an unsuccessful Craft check.

A tinker may select Build Teamwork as one of his tinker bonus feats.

Build Vehicles [Technology]

You have a talent for building and operating vehicles.

Benefit: You get a +2 bonus to Craft (technological device) and Use Technological Device checks when building or using a vehicle. Your technological limit for building vehicles is increased by 2.

Special: Once per day for 1d6 minutes, you may double the speed of a vehicle you are driving. When this period is over, you may extend it for 1 additional minute by making a DC 20 Use Technological Device check. You may continue to extend the period each minute by making another Use Technological Device check; each subsequent check increases the DC by 1. The vehicle's speed returns to normal the first time you miss a check.

A tinker may select Build Vehicles as one of his tinker bonus feats.

Close Shot [General]

You can use a ranged weapon while avoiding opponents in melee combat.

Prerequisites: Dex 13, Dodge, Point Blank Shot, Precise Shot, base attack bonus +4.

Benefit: You may fire a ranged weapon without provoking an attack of opportunity.

Normal: If you fire a ranged weapon, any opponent that threatens you gets an attack of opportunity.

Special: A fighter may select Close Shot as one of his fighter bonus feats.

Collective Fury [General]

The only sight scarier than one angry orc is a gang of angry orcs. That kind of rage can rout armies and level buildings.

Prerequisites: Cha 13, Battle Cry, Leadership.

Benefit: When a character with Collective Fury rages, all other characters within 30 feet who have the ability to rage gain the benefits of the Battle Cry feat. Multiple Battle Cry effects do not stack.

Special: When an orc with Collective Fury rages, all orcs within 30 feet gain a +2 enhancement bonus to Strength as well as the Battle Cry ability.

Defend [General]

You're trained to fight shoulder-to-shoulder and share the benefits of a shield with a nearby ally.

Prerequisites: Shield Proficiency, base attack bonus +2.

Benefit: If you are fighting with a shield, any ally within 5 feet who is not fighting with a shield gains your shield's AC bonus. You do not lose your shield bonus, and this bonus stacks with the ally's armor bonus as per the normal stacking rules.

Any ally within 5 feet who is fighting with a shield gains a +2 circumstance bonus to AC; this bonus does not stack with itself. If multiple characters with Defend stand within 5 feet of each other and fight with shields, each character gains only the highest shield bonus to AC.

Special: A fighter may select Defend as one of his fighter bonus feats.

Deflect Spell [Metamagic]

You may counter a spell and choose a new target for it.

Prerequisites: Block Spell, Iron Will, Magic Energy Control, Mirror Spell, Reflect Spell, caster level 9th.

Benefit: If you successfully counter a spell — using the same spell, a spell with a diametrically opposed effect, *dispel magic*, or the Block Spell feat — you may deflect the spell at any target you choose. The new target is determined as if you had originally cast the spell yourself.

Special: Two or more spellcasters with Deflect Spell may counter and retarget the spell until no spellcaster succeeds at countering it. The spell then has its normal effect on its current target. (Once you have identified the spell you are trying to counter, you do not need to make any further Spellcraft checks to identify it.)

Delay Malfunction [Technology]

You know how to make last-minute repairs to malfunctioning equipment — adjustments that can prevent a disaster or at least stave it off for a few crucial seconds.

Benefit: When a device malfunctions, you may make a DC 15 Craft (technological device) check. If you succeed, the device operates normally for 1d3 rounds, giving you a chance to finish the job you are doing, make an emergency repair, or get clear before it blows up. If you roll a natural 20 on the check, the malfunction is completely averted. You cannot try again for any specific malfunction, even after a successful use of this feat.

Special: Goblin characters can avoid the malfunction entirely by rolling a natural 19 or 20 on the check.

A tinker may select Delay Malfunction as one of his tinker bonus feats.

Devoted Leadership [General]

Your faith in your followers gives them the confidence they need to survive difficult situations.

Prerequisites: Cha 13, Wis 13, Leadership.

Benefit: Your followers receive a +2 morale bonus to AC, as well as a +1 morale bonus to all saves. Followers must be within a distance of 5 feet x your Charisma bonus to benefit from Devoted Leadership. You can use Devoted Leadership for a number of rounds per day equal to your character level (to a maximum of 20), and the rounds need not be consecutive or used all at once.

Drums of Courage [General]

You can drive your tribe's warriors into a terrifying frenzy by playing the sacred war rhythms as they go into battle.

Prerequisites: Perform (percussion instruments) 5 ranks.

Benefit: As your tribe enters battle, you can play your war drums to inspire courage in its warriors. Make a DC 20 Perform (percussion instruments) check. If successful, all warriors of your tribe who can hear your drums receive a +1 morale bonus to attack and damage rolls and to Will saves. This morale bonus lasts for as long as the warriors hear your drums and for 5 rounds

thereafter. Playing the war drums is a standard action and requires concentration, which means you must take a standard action each round to keep playing.

Emergency Repair [Technology]

You are adept at spotting mechanical problems and making quick repairs.

Prerequisite: Wis 13, Delay Malfunction.

Benefit: As a full-round action, you may make a DC 20 Craft (mechanical object) check to repair a malfunctioning or broken technological device. If you succeed at the check, the device does not destroy itself or endanger its user due to the malfunction. Instead, it operates normally for 1 hour and then ceases functioning until it can undergo normal repairs.

If you roll a natural 20 on the check, the item is completely and permanently repaired.

Special: Goblin characters can completely and permanently repair an item by rolling a natural 19 or 20 on the check.

A tinker may select Emergency Repair as one of his tinker bonus feats.

Enduring Leadership [General]

Your tireless efforts are an example to your followers, and you need but a word to push those followers to the peak of their physical abilities.

Prerequisites: Endurance, Leadership.

Benefit: Once per day before an encounter begins, as a free action you may inspire your followers to exceptional efforts. They receive a +4 morale bonus to their Initiative check, and their speed increases by +10 feet for the duration of the combat.

Special: If you or any of your followers enter into a rage during this combat, then the characters who rage are not fatigued when the rage ends.

Exotic Weapon Proficiency: Thorium Weapons [General]

You can use weapons made out of thorium effectively.

Prerequisite: Appropriate proficiency with non-thorium version of a weapon.

Benefit: You are proficient with a particular weapon made out of thorium and may add half your Strength bonus to damage rolls. Thus, for example, an attack with a one-handed thorium weapon would add 1.5x your Strength bonus, while an attack with a two-handed thorium weapon would add double your Strength bonus.

Normal: Characters who are not proficient with thorium weapons suffer a –4 penalty to attack with them, even if they are proficient with a non-thorium version of the weapon they are using. Characters receive their normal Strength bonus to damage rolls.

Expert Rider [General]

You can perform a variety of physical stunts while on horseback.

Prerequisites: Dex 13, Ride skill.

Benefit: The DCs for all Ride tasks are reduced by 2, and you can take 10 on Ride checks for mounted combat maneuvers.

Normal: You cannot take 10 on skill checks when threatened or distracted.

Special: A fighter can select Expert Rider as one of his fighter bonus feats.

Follower of the Totem [General]

You have been trained in the shamanic traditions of the tauren and can tap into the forces of nature.

Prerequisites: Wis 13, orc or tauren.

Benefit: Once per day as a free action, you may gain a +2 sacred bonus to any ability. This bonus lasts for 1d6+1 rounds.

Special: Tauren characters with this feat are considered to have the Exotic Weapon Proficiency (tauren totem) feat.

Lightning Reload [General]

You reload firearms with well-practiced efficiency.

Prerequisites: Dex 13, Exotic Weapon Proficiency (firearms).

Benefit: If your firearm takes a standard action to reload, you may reload it as a move action. If the firearm takes more than 1 round to reload, you may reload it in half the normal time.

Special: A fighter may select Lightning Reload as one of his fighter bonus feats.

Magic Energy Control [Metamagic]

You understand the flow of magic energy and find it easy to tap into and control.

Prerequisites: Iron Will.

Benefit: You may perform your daily preparation of spells in half the normal time.

Special: A high elf character with this feat no longer suffers from the effects of magic addiction. As a result, he prepares his spells in the normal amount of time, rather than half. A high elf is not actually cured of the addiction, however, so night elves, for instance, can still detect the addiction normally.

Mirror Spell [Metamagic]

You may channel additional arcane energy to duplicate the effects of a spell you have just cast.

Prerequisites: Iron Will, Magic Energy Control, caster level 3rd.

Benefit: When you cast an arcane spell, the spell is treated as if you had cast it twice. The two copies of the spell are resolved simultaneously. They may have the same or different targets, and both copies of the spell are resolved separately.

To use this feat, you must spend a spell slot as if you had used it to cast the duplicate spell. This spell slot must be of the same spell level or higher as the spell you cast.

Mounted Sharpshooter [General]

You have learned how to use a firearm while mounted.

Prerequisites: Dex 13, Ride skill, Expert Rider.

Benefit: You do not suffer any penalty while making ranged attacks with a firearm while mounted. You must still make a Ride check to keep your mount under control.

Normal: If you make a ranged attack with a firearm while mounted, you suffer a –4 penalty to your attack roll.

Special: A fighter can select Mounted Sharpshooter as one of his fighter bonus feats.

Pistol Whip [General]

You can use a firearm as an improvised melee weapon without damaging it.

Benefit: You are proficient at using a firearm as a melee weapon and can do so without breaking it. Small firearms are treated as light hammers, Medium firearms are treated as clubs, and Large firearms are treated as warhammers.

Normal: Any character may use a firearm as a melee weapon; however, the character is not necessarily proficient with the weapon (determine proficiency based on the weapon the firearm is treated as, noted above), and the firearm is broken if it hits. It cannot be fired until repaired with a Craft (mechanical object) check.

Special: A fighter may select Pistol Whip as one of his fighter bonus feats.

Precision Leadership [General]

By training your followers to coordinate their fire, you have turned individual soldiers into a single deadly ranged weapon.

Prerequisites: Leadership, Point Blank Shot.

Benefit: When making a ranged attack, each of your followers gains a +1 bonus to the attack roll for every 5 followers attacking at the same time. All followers must be near you, within a radius equal to 10 feet x your Charisma bonus, and must attack with the same kind of weapon. The followers must attack the same target, which must be within 100 feet of you.

Special: You and all the other followers that are attacking fire a ranged attack at the same target, then the damage from all the hits is added together before any damage reduction is applied.

Pulverize [Tauren]

A mighty blow to the ground with your tauren totem frightens the spirits of the earth, causing them to shake the ground in their haste to escape.

Prerequisites: Wis 13, Exotic Weapon Proficiency (tauren totem), Follower of the Totem.

Benefit: You can declare a Pulverize attempt on a full attack action with your tauren totem. Instead of making a normal attack roll, you strike the ground with your tauren totem. Roll damage for the attack, but do not apply the damage to any target. Instead, any creature within 20 feet of you must succeed at a Reflex save (DC 10 + the damage rolled) or fall prone. You can use Pulverize only once per round and no more than a number of times per day equal to 1 + your Wisdom bonus.

A prone creature suffers a –4 penalty to melee attack rolls, cannot use a ranged weapon (except for a crossbow), and receives a –4 penalty to AC against melee attacks and a +4 bonus to AC against ranged attacks.

When you use Pulverize, you forfeit any bonus or extra attacks granted by other feats or abilities (such as the Cleave feat or the *haste* spell). A pulverize attempt draws an attack of opportunity.

Reflect Spell [Metamagic]

Instead of dissipating the energy of a countered spell, you may reflect that spell back upon its caster.

Prerequisites: Block Spell, Iron Will, Magic Energy Control, Mirror Spell, caster level 7th.

Benefit: If you are the target of a spell and successfully counter it — using the same spell, a spell with a diametrically opposed effect, *dispel magic*, or the Block Spell feat — then you may reflect the spell back upon its caster. The spell resolves normally against this new target.

Two spellcasters with Reflect Spell may bounce the spell between them until one spellcaster fails to counter it. The spell then has its normal effect on the character who failed to counter it.

Ride Bareback [General]

You do not need a saddle or bridle to guide a mount.

Prerequisites: Ride skill.

Benefit: You do not suffer any penalty on Ride checks when riding bareback.

Normal: Characters that ride bareback suffer a –5 penalty to Ride checks.

Scavenge Materials [Technology]

You are adept at "making do" with whatever materials come to hand.

Prerequisites: Craft 8 ranks.

Benefit: You may build an item using raw materials equivalent to only 1/10 the item's market value. The Craft check DC needed to build the item increases by 10.

Storm Bolt [General]

You can stun opponents with a well-hurled weapon.

Prerequisites: Str 13, Bash, Power Attack, base attack bonus +4.

Benefit: You can declare use of Storm Bolt before taking a full attack action with a ranged bludgeoning weapon. For the successful attack of your choice, roll damage normally, although the foe applies it as nonlethal damage. Also, the foe struck by your attack must make a Fortitude save (DC 10 + the damage rolled) or be stunned for 1 round. A stunned character can't act, loses any Dexterity bonus to AC, and takes a –2 penalty to AC. You can use Storm Bolt only once per round and no more than once per character level per day.

When you use Storm Bolt, you forfeit any bonus or extra attacks granted by other feats or abilities (such as the Manyshot feat or the *haste* spell). Constructs, oozes, plants, undead, incorporeal creatures, and creatures immune to critical hits cannot be stunned.

Special: A fighter may select Storm Bolt as one of his fighter bonus feats.

Sunder Armor [General]

You can strike blows that damage and destroy armor.

Prerequisites: Str 13, Power Attack.

Benefit: You can use a melee attack with a slashing or bludgeoning weapon to strike a piece of armor that your opponent is wearing. Doing so does not provoke an attack of opportunity from your opponent.

If you score a critical hit against your opponent while targeting his armor, roll damage normally and make a Strength check (DC 15 + the targeted armor's armor bonus). If your damage surpasses the armor's hardness and your Strength check succeeds, the armor you have targeted is reduced by 1 point of armor bonus until repaired. You cannot damage magic armor that has an enhancement bonus unless your own weapon has an enhancement bonus equal to or greater than the armor's.

Normal: Targeting an opponent's armor provokes an attack of opportunity.

Special: A fighter may select Sunder Armor as one of his fighter bonus feats.

Trick Shot [General]

You can bounce a ranged attack off a surface and hit a target from an unexpected angle.

Prerequisites: Dex 13.

Benefit: Trace a path from you to a wall or other convenient surface, then from that point to your target. This is the path your attack takes. Figure your target's cover based on the direction your attack is coming from when it reaches the target. With a good angle, most cover, *shield* spells, and other directional forms of protection can be negated. Concealment is not affected by this feat.

You may only bounce the weapon off one surface, and any range penalty is figured based on the total distance of the path from you to the surface to the target.

Hitting a target you cannot see using this feat is possible, but you suffer from the usual 50% miss chance associated with total concealment.

Special: If you are using a moonglaive and are proficient with that weapon, you may bounce it off two surfaces. A fighter may select Trick Shot as one of his fighter bonus feats.

Vehicle Proficiency [Technology]

You are familiar with and can operate vehicles that move over land, through water, or in the air.

Benefit: Choose a specialty: land vehicles, water vehicles, or air vehicles. You may operate a vehicle of the appropriate type by making a Use Technological Device check.

Normal: Characters who operate a vehicle without the appropriate proficiency suffer a –4 penalty to the Use Technological Device check.

Special: You can gain this feat multiple times. Each time you take this feat, it applies to a different specialty. A tinker may select Vehicle Proficiency as one of his tinker bonus feats.

War Stomp [Tauren]

With an imperious blow of your tauren totem, you command the spirits of air and earth to batter your opponents.

Prerequisites: Cha 13, Wis 13, Exotic Weapon Proficiency (tauren totem), Follower of the Totem, Pulverize, base attack bonus +8.

Benefit: You can declare a war stomp attempt on a full attack action. Instead of making a normal attack roll, you stomp powerfully on the ground with your tauren totem, potentially damaging any opponents within 20 feet of you. Choose a number of targets equal to 1 + your Wisdom bonus. Roll 1d6 + your Strength bonus points of damage. Each target must then succeed at a Fortitude save (DC 10 + the damage rolled) or suffer the damage and be dazed for 1 round. A dazed creature can take no actions, but it suffers no penalty to AC. You can use War Stomp only once per round and no more than a number of times per day equal to 1 + your Charisma bonus.

When you use War Stomp, you forfeit any bonus or extra attacks granted by other feats or abilities (such as the Cleave feat or the *haste* spell). Creatures who save successfully are immune to the effects of your War Stomp for 24 hours. A war stomp attempt draws an attack of opportunity.

Hellak Darkhorn, tauren warrior in the service of the Alliance, moved among the ruins, alert for any potential threat that would harm the humans who followed him. He found murloc footprints earlier in the day, but they were small ones, not the strange mutant versions that had become increasingly common. Murlocs were nothing that humans could not handle on their own.

They remained uneasy around him, the humans did. Part of it was that he was so much larger and stronger than they were. Of greater influence, though, was that most of his brethren had thrown their lot in with the orc Horde. Humans saw his bestial features and assumed he was just a mindless follower of the greenskins.

Yet Hellak had learned to mistrust orcs. They seemed too quick to fight — and too willing to fight dirty — to be considered honorable. Then he learned that they came from another world entirely and were led for many years by demon-worshipping warlocks. That was enough for Hellak. His fellow tauren might welcome the orcs as spirit brothers, but he could not abide it.

Though humans were far from lacking in faults, Hellak felt they possessed a core of honor. He had come to them cautiously, serving as a scout for the armored knights and their powerful paladin warriors. The order and organization of their peoples impressed him. Yes, they were distrustful of him, but then one is always distrustful of the new. All the more reason to serve well and speak quietly, reassuring them that not all tauren were to be lumped with orcs.

The hackles rose on the back of his mane when he heard the shift of stones around a corner: he was not alone in the ruins. Hellak froze, his massive chest barely rising as he waited. Another shifting of stones, then footsteps on loose gravel. Not the heavy tread of tauren or trolls, nor as light as the various elven breeds. Human or dwarf, likely, and therefore Alliance.

Hellak moved slowly around the corner, letting his thundering hooves warn of his approach. A female human crouched behind a tree, watching his advance carefully. She was dressed in common adventuring leathers, without insignia or badge. Her eyes were wide, but he saw no fear in them.

Probably a scout like me, Hellak thought, sent ahead to see that the Horde had set no ambushes. Still, though he sensed no fear in her, she was clearly tense. Hellak shook his massive head. When would they learn not to judge based on surface appearances?

Hellak slung his axe into the sheath on his back and approached slowly, his hands out and palms up to show he meant no harm. Hellak knew that he was an imposing figure even unarmed. "Do not fear," he said. "I am a scout working for the Alliance."

The woman moved upon hearing these words, though not as Hellak had anticipated. She stepped from the tree with a spear in hand, driving the tip deep into his chest before he could react. Hellak snarled and swung at her, but she let go of the spear and danced backward, drawing a serrated blade as she did so.

"Fool!" Hellak thundered. "I am on your side!"

He felt a cold chill spread through his veins from the wound, and his legs were quickly growing numb. The weapon is envenomed, Hellak realized, coated with a thick paste that deadens the flesh and stops the heart.

Humans did not use such things. This was a weapon of the Horde.

Hellak raised his head with effort to confront his assailant. The human stood with weapon ready, a snarl on her lips. The tauren staggered forward a step, then collapsed at her feet, the ground rumbling with the force of his fall. He struggled to rise, but the poison worked too swiftly. As the poison stilled his heart, Hellak saw the human smile.

H'jalla Danfour, human warrior in the service of the Horde, knelt before the fallen tauren. The smile lingered on her face as she began sawing off the creature's horns. Her orc masters would pay a hefty bounty for the death of a traitor.

CHAPTER THREE:
ADVENTURING

A hero is made up of more than race and class. This chapter discusses three other key aspects of characters in the **Warcraft RPG**: affiliation, faiths, and equipment.

Affiliation

The choice of affiliation is central in a **Warcraft RPG** campaign. The decision affects not only each individual hero, but also the adventuring party as a whole, since it defines the party's origins and some of the heroes' goals. Deciding the affiliation to which your character belongs determines his homeland and allegiance, his allies and his enemies.

All heroes in an adventuring group must be of the same affiliation, so consulting with the other players and the GM before making your decision is important.

The two affiliations available are the Alliance and the Horde. Some races are listed as "independent" (goblins in the **Warcraft RPG**, for instance, but others will appear in upcoming supplements). They can belong to either affiliation.

The Alliance and the Horde are not actually currently at war with one another, but neither are they on good terms. The coalition the groups formed during the darkest hour of the Third War was transitory at best. Though the leaders hold each other in great respect, the common citizens do not share this feeling. Many human soldiers remember the terrible destruction wrought by orcs in the First and Second Wars. In turn, orcs recall their capture and enslavement by humans. Decades of racial enmity do not evaporate easily, leaving relations between the two factions strained at best. An uneasy truce prevents total war from breaking out, but brief, savage border skirmishes are common. Political platitudes do little to stop individuals on both sides from finding excuses to unleash their vengeance and ancestral hatred upon one another.

Determining Affiliation

The Alliance includes humans, dwarves, high elves, night elves, and the few half-elves that exist. The Horde consists primarily of orcs and tauren. Half-orcs typically belong to whichever

Affiliation and Common Conflicts

Certain realities in the grim world of **Warcraft** are a part of the characters' lives, regardless of affiliation. Heroes on both sides will face danger, adventure, and excitement. They will cross swords with members of the opposing faction — and even with members of their own affiliation. After all, just because two people have a common allegiance does not mean they share the same goals and beliefs.

The lands of Kalimdor are primitive and largely unknown. Discovery and exploration are more important for the Alliance than for the Horde. Native creatures of the land, including centaur, harpies, gnolls, trolls, and so on, are hostile and seldom care about their foes' affiliation. Though the Burning Legion and the forces of the dread Scourge were shattered in the Third War, the pieces remain. Undead creatures, necromancers, and fearsome demons stalk the land. Orcs and night elves suffered corruption at the hands of the Burning Legion, leaving depraved satyrs and corrupted Ancients of Ashenvale to threaten all within their reach. Moreover, the threat of a new enemy — the mysterious naga — looms forbiddingly over the world.

faction they were born into, but have difficulty gaining acceptance regardless of the society they're in. Goblins are seldom drawn into siding with either affiliation.

Affiliation is largely determined by this racial distinction, but it is not absolute. Just because a hero is a night elf does not mean she must belong to the Alliance; similarly, not every tauren is a member of the Horde. Both affiliations are willing to accept members of other races among their ranks. These individuals are exceptions, to be sure, but heroes are exceptions by default. In fact, playing a nonstandard race in the "wrong" affili-

Table 3–1: Affiliation Rating

Affiliation	Alliance	Horde	Burning Legion	Scourge	Independent
Alliance	—	3	—	—	1
Horde	3	—	—	—	1
Burning Legion	6	6	—	2	5
Scourge	6	6	2	—	5
Independent	1	1	—	—	—

Example: A follower of the Burning Legion who encounters a member of the Alliance or Horde suffers a −6 penalty to Bluff, Diplomacy, Gather Information, and Perform checks but enjoys a +6 bonus to Intimidate checks; however, his modifiers are −2/+2 when dealing with a minion of the Scourge.

ation can offer a dynamic history for a character. After all, you must decide why she belongs to the affiliation she's chosen. Still, while "stranger in a strange land" concepts can be fun, be careful that the sum total of the character's concept does not derive from being an exception.

Affiliation Rating

The affiliations to which most races belong have generations of conflict and sometimes vastly different lifestyle philosophies between them. Combine this situation with a world where violence and strife are the norm and you get xenophobia. This reaction is expressed as an Affiliation Rating (AR), which may modify the DCs of social skill checks when members of conflicting groups interact.

Table 3–1: Affiliation Rating lists each affiliation and the AR modifier applied when dealing with other groups. The listed modifier applies as a circumstance penalty to Bluff, Diplomacy, Gather Information, and Perform checks, but it applies as a bonus to Intimidate checks.

Affiliation Rating reflects only first reactions; improving one's standing is possible. For each good deed a character performs (stopping a crime, defeating a monster preying on the community, helping a farmer harvest crops, and so on), that individual dispels some of the stigma relating to his affiliation. His AR with that group or community drops by 1, to a minimum of 0. Such efforts are not uncommon among members of the Alliance or Horde (or independent heroes), but a demon worshipper or undead lackey would likely not bother.

Affiliation Ratings apply only if the person involved clearly belongs to a different affiliation. An Alliance infiltrator working undercover in Durotar or a citizen of Theramore who is secretly a follower of the Burning Legion are treated like typical members of the Horde and the Alliance, respectively. AR modifiers do apply if their true affiliation is discovered… though they probably have larger concerns at that point.

AR modifiers never apply when dealing with friends or allies, such as other PCs or fellow members of an affiliation.

The distinctions between the existing affiliations are described below. See also "Affiliation" in Chapter Six: Campaigning for more information on this subject.

The Alliance

If you are a member of the Alliance, your allies are plentiful and varied. You can count associates among the ranks of the humans, dwarves, night elves, high elves, and half-elves. Your leadership is strong but divided. Jaina Proudmoore, Tyrande Whisperwind, and Malfurion Stormrage are able leaders and command respect, but tension among the Alliance factions remains. The Alliance is based on the storm-swept island of Theramore, off the coast of Kalimdor.

With so many races lumped together, the Alliance is unsurprisingly rife with internal friction. High elves are often aloof and become alienated from others—most notably from the night elves, who see them as corrupt victims of their thirst for arcane magic. Half-elves struggle for acceptance, dwarves are obsessed with their recently discov-

ered heritage, and humans must cope with the decimation of their most powerful empires.

These relationships suffer further strain since few in the Alliance have a land to call their own. The continent of Kalimdor offers a new beginning, but the past lies in ruins. Lordaeron and Quel'Thalas are ravaged graveyards, haunted by ghosts both real and imagined, and ruled over by Arthas the death knight. Aside from the night elves, who still reside on the great Mount Hyjal, and the dwarves, who have claimed Bael Modan, the Alliance peoples mix together in Theramore. This mixing makes for a lively center of commerce and a strong power base, but Theramore has also become cramped and volatile as the races struggle to pursue their various agendas.

The Alliance is the best affiliation because it allows characters to become embroiled in political and social espionage, and focuses on the exploration of unknown lands and the discovery of ancient and powerful secrets.

The Horde

If you are a member of the Horde, your allies are orcs and tauren. You have strong leadership in the living legends Thrall son of Durotan and his tauren friend Cairne Bloodhoof. If you are an orc, you claim the new country of Durotar as your home, with the city of Orgrimmar as the seat of its power. If you are a tauren, you call the plains and mesas of Mulgore your homeland, with the city upon Thunder Bluff as its capitol. The two regions have regular trade, so you may well be from either Durotar or Mulgore as you see fit.

The orcs are in the process of a great reawakening — a grand racial enlightenment. For years, they suffered under the fist of the Burning Legion, carrying out demonic plans and fighting wars that were not their own. They have finally become free of that dominance and now work to reclaim their shamanistic heritage.

Unlike the Alliance, the Horde has claimed a sizeable portion of Kalimdor as a new homeland. Before affiliating with the orcs, the tauren were a nomadic people and easy prey for savage centaur warbands. Tauren have since settled the realm of Mulgore and revel in permanent settlements such as Thunder Bluff, but they are still subject to centaur attacks.

The homeland of Durotar holds particular significance to the orcs since their home world Draenor was ripped apart during the Second War. Still, Durotar is not yet the country that Thrall and the other members of the Horde wish it to be. Much must be done to establish it as a country in its own right and as a true homeland for the orcs.

The Horde is the best affiliation because it combines a noble spiritual heritage, strong leadership, internal unity, and the desire and ability to crush enemies with sword and axe.

Independent

Allegiance to either the Alliance or the Horde is by far the norm, but some races remain steadfastly independent— most notably the goblins of Ratchet. Independent characters have no land to call their own and answer to no one. They may find welcome in the teeming city of Ratchet, but they are met with suspicion by members of both Alliance and Horde.

Yet independence has its advantages. No one will attack you because of your allegiance (though they may attack you because of your *lack* of allegiance…). Independent heroes often work as mercenaries or free agents and may become embroiled in any of the same machinations that drive other affiliations.

Independent is the best affiliation because it allows the greatest flexibility of where a hero can go and what he can do. Still, an independent character should join up with an Alliance or a Horde party. A group of entirely independent heroes is not as likely to enter easily into stories that form the majority of **Warcraft** campaigns. The GM has final say on whether a party of independent heroes will work in the campaign.

Changing Sides

In the course of a campaign, an opportunity may arise wherein your character faces a personal crisis that could result in a change of affiliation. Perhaps your character can no longer ignore the unease he feels when dealing with the secretive high elves. Perhaps he tires of the anger and resentment his orc brethren show toward the Alliance races. Perhaps he made too many enemies in his current affiliation and would prefer to be where they are not. Perhaps he spent many months as a captive of the other side and to his surprise learned to appreciate the new culture in a way he never felt for his own.

Though uncommon, switching affiliations is possible. In fact, leaving the current faction is easy. Joining the other side is the difficult part.

When your character changes sides, his previous allies will abandon him. This choice is a significant life change, one that his shocked friends may even equate with treason. He is turning his back on all that he knows, after all, and is effectively spurning his friends' beliefs. No one likes a turncoat.

This choice is also difficult in game terms. Remember that all heroes in an adventuring party must belong to the same affiliation, so unless all the heroes switch sides at the same time, things will become difficult. If the entire party defects, members of the new affiliation will view it with distrust, if not open derision. Your characters must work very hard to prove themselves. If your character keeps the shift secret from the other heroes, it is possible to create a double agent within a network of "friends" — though this is a difficult and highly dangerous endeavor.

Before getting to the aforementioned complications, remember that the GM must approve any change of affiliation. Think carefully before you request something like this for your character. Changing affiliation can shift the course of the entire campaign, and there may well be no going back once it's done.

Faiths

Five popular approaches to faith are active in the world of **Warcraft**. Humans take a philosophical approach that stresses ethics and spiritual living over cosmology. Night elves, orcs, and tauren seek to understand and sometimes communicate with the spirits of the world that surround them. Dwarves approach the mysteries of their lives with more curiosity than faith. Worshippers of the Burning Legion remain, their spiritual fulfillment derived from power and madness. Finally, the members of Ner'zhul's death-worshipping cult seek fulfillment in the trappings of mortality and undeath.

The Holy Light

The Holy Light is not a religion. It is a philosophy, a way of living that provides spiritual strength and guidance to those who follow it. For those who understand the Holy Light, faith is a matter of practice rather than worship.

The fundamental concept of the Holy Light is that feeling — in both the emotional and physical senses — is evidence of the connection between the self and the universe. If you feel emotion, you know that you exist, that there is some force within you from which those emotions spring. At the same time, you know that the world around you exists. It acts upon you and changes the way that you feel. By acting on your feelings, you can, in turn, change the world. To deny the importance of either the self or the world cuts you off from half of existence.

The Holy Light teaches that once you acknowledge the connection between yourself and the rest of the world, you must acknowledge that your health and happiness are also connected to that of the world. If you wish to be happy, you must try to make the rest of the world happy; if you open yourself up to the beauties of the world, you can unlock your own inner beauty. Yet if you give yourself over to despair, then you diminish the rest of existence. The Holy Light is the energy of the soul lighting up the world around it.

Humans are the primary followers of the Light. High elves and dwarves once followed the Light.

Most Quel'dorei have fallen from its teachings as they succumb to the grip of their magic addiction, while Ironforge dwarves have embraced the pursuit of new truths that lie in their titan origins. A night elf, orc, or tauren even considering the values of the Holy Light is almost unheard of.

The Three Virtues

Those who practice the Light focus their efforts on developing three virtues: respect, tenacity, and compassion. Each virtue is further divided into a principle and a lesson (see the "Principles and Lessons of the Three Virtues" sidebar).

Every creature that has feelings shares the same kind of connection between self and world that you do. If you destroy another being's happiness, you diminish the happiness of the world — and, ultimately, your own as well. The practitioners of the Holy Light understand that conflict and suffering are inevitable, but they seek to minimize the unhappiness of others.

While the self and the world are of equal importance to any self that considers them, the philosophy of Holy Light also acknowledges that the world is much bigger than the self. The events of the world can sweep up a self and change it in a day, but years are needed for one self to change the world through its actions.

Even if years are needed, however, that one self inevitably changes the world. The connection between self and world means that you cannot help but have an effect upon the world, even if that effect is small. You can also inspire the efforts of other selves, each with their own small effect that adds together with others until significant changes happen. Because the world connects to the self and because the self changes, that the world will change to fit the self is inevitable.

The first two concepts lead to the third: compassion. You have only one connection to the world, which limits the effect your happiness can have upon it. By helping another, you make both yourself and that person happy. The effect upon the world is doubled. At the same time, you become stronger, more able to help others. Your ability to affect the world grows.

Compassion must be practiced carefully. Over-eager helpers give aid where it is not needed, preventing the recipients from persevering and developing their own strength. Clumsy helpers provide the wrong help, doing harm instead of good and increasing the suffering of the world. Wise and compassionate characters identify the true needs of others, then supply the support those creatures need to overcome their problems themselves.

Principles and Lessons of the Three Virtues

The principle of respect:
Each thing has its own connection to the world.

The lesson of respect:
Do not harm what you would value if it were yours.

The principle of tenacity:
The world is too large to be remade in a day.

The lesson of tenacity:
Perseverance creates strength.

The principle of compassion:
You accomplish more brightening the lives of others than your own.

The lesson of compassion:
Give aid freely, but do not diminish the one who receives it.

Worship of the Light

The Church of the Light was a tremendous influence in Lordaeron and Quel'Thalas, and the Knights of the Silver Hand its mightiest agents. Then those lands — and the Church — fell before the unstoppable power of the Scourge. The Church of the Light remains strong in the land of Stormwind, but that means little on the continent of Kalimdor. Those who survive in the new world must hold to their faith without the support of an organized church. Some — including the stalwart paladins of the Silver Hand — work to establish a new church on Kalimdor.

Followers of the Light encourage a great deal of debate, and the libraries of Lordaeron were once filled with densely written texts exploring the fine points of ethics and interactions of the three principles. Sadly, most of these texts were destroyed in the war. Scholars are left with those few books they could save and carry to Kalimdor. The commentaries on the Holy Light are being rewritten, and the process is reinvigorating the tradition of philosophical thought. Rather than exploring obscure corners of long-established treatises in search of a crumb of originality, fresh minds are taking ethical thought in new directions.

A few angry thinkers have condemned the reconstruction of the texts, calling the entire philosophy outdated and simplistic. Many have presented new systems of thought, most of which depend on complex systems of divination and ethical resolution. They make a great deal of noise in scholarly circles but have little impact upon the secular folk of Kalimdor. Most prefer to follow the same Holy Light practices that they've enjoyed for years.

Knights of the Silver Hand

Scholars are not the only group with a special interest in the Holy Light. The Knights of the Silver Hand is an organization of paladin warriors who have devoted their lives to the three principles. By placing themselves under the authority of a holy order, paladin warriors seek to multiply their efforts and strengthen each other with their dedication.

The Knights are quick to point out that their way of life is not for everyone. They give up a great deal for their calling, starting with their own independence.

Uther Lightbringer founded the order just before the onset of the Second War. In the past few years, the holy order suffered a tremendous blow to its stability when one of their number, Prince Arthas, was consumed by the forces of evil and became a death knight in service to the undead. Once a great champion of the Alliance, Arthas turned into one of its most dreaded enemies. Though Light triumphed over darkness in the Third War, the paladin warriors cannot forget Arthas's betrayal and just how close their order — and all of Azeroth — came to destruction. They hunt down the remnants of the undead and the Burning Legion that scattered to the dark places of Kalimdor, ensuring with grim determination that such a tragedy will never happen again.

Shamanism and Nature Worship

To orcs, tauren, and night elves, the world is alive with spirits dancing on the edge of perception. Everything that has ever lived owns a unique and enduring spirit, an essential spark that calls out to all the other lives in the world. The shamanistic and druidic races do not dismiss the Holy Light that the humans prize, but they understand that the light comes from countless myriads of brightly shining points. In a rush to embrace the all, the shamans agree, humans quite literally miss the point.

Shamans are puzzled by the goblins, who profess many of the same ideals but do so in a "thank the spirits while you get on to important stuff with gears" fashion. The goblins' casual attitude toward spirits can be very frustrating to the spiritual mind.

Night elves take a personal approach to their spirit relationships. They recognize each spirit that they encounter as an individual life and

persuade or honor them as the occasion demands. They interact mostly with the spirits of nature and do so primarily concerning matters in the immediate vicinity of the spirit with whom they are dealing. When greater matters are at stake, night elves entreat nature deities, a pantheon of greater spirits that represent especially important parts of the night elves' world. Elune the moon goddess is an example of one of these greater spirits.

Orcs and tauren take a more symbolic approach. The spirits they encounter on the wild plains of Kalimdor are less specific, cover a wider range, and are more likely to be spirits of earth and fire than the essences of trees or animals.

Instead of negotiating with individual spirits, tauren carve representative imagery on their totems and draw power from acting in a particular spirit's name. This relationship provides tauren with great strength but little spiritual comfort. For such comfort, they look to the spirits of their ancestors. Each tauren learns at an early age to recite his lineage — an impressive feat, given that most tauren family trees go back at least ten generations. Tauren tell many tales of their ancestors, and most tauren establish a strong bond with one or two of their forebears. A tauren lives his life in honor of these favored ancestors, doing great deeds in their name and meditating on their adventures for guidance in the choices of life.

Orcs do not share the steady faith of tauren and night elves. They are only now learning to accept their old traditions again. The Burning Legion's corrupting influence drew them away from their ancestral traditions, and most of their spirit knowledge was lost. Having thrown off the Burning Legion's dominance, they must learn again how to communicate with the spirits.

Luckily, orcs find this process relatively easy. Some of their lore is preserved in epic tales and children's stories; an orc that remembers his granddame's fables may draw on that insight when dealing with the spirit world. Orc shamans are back on good terms with many ancestral and nature spirits, and they are reintroducing their people to the natural world with prayer, lodge sweats, and vision quests.

The Mystery of the Makers

For humans, the present has always mattered more than the past. They spend little time exploring their origins. As far as they are concerned, they have always been here. (Older races raise an eyebrow at this assertion, but even the elves must admit that human tribes were well established when the elves discovered them.)

In contrast, dwarves have always been curious about their origins. Their oldest dwellings and relics contained hints at an origin myth, but only after their recent arrival upon Kalimdor did the dwarves see the larger truth behind their fragmented legends. Based on scattered ruins they discovered in the wilds of Kalimdor, the dwarves were apparently created by a now-vanished race that ruled the world in ancient days.

Incredible as this possibility is, it barely answers one mystery while giving rise to a host of questions. Who was this ancient race? Why were the dwarves created? What did these titans intend for them to do and should they be doing it? What were their creators like, and what happened to them? When they disappeared, why were the dwarves left behind?

Still, the dwarves' practical nature does not lend itself to blind worship of a progenitor race, regardless of how compelling the evidence may be. They rely upon measurements, mathematics, and the work of their hands. Rather than taking the measure of their creators on faith, the dwarves have embarked on a mammoth investigation of their past.

This evidence of titan progenitors has awakened a powerful excitement within the dwarves of Kalimdor. They rush out to explore the world around them, searching for clues as their time and resources allow. Any possible piece of evidence is studied, tested, and passed on to another dwarf for examination. The information piles up, the theories are tested and shared, and the base of knowledge grows.

The other races look upon the dwarves' efforts with everything from bemusement to treasure-seeking avarice to concern. Some are as curious as the dwarves themselves, while others worry that seeking hidden mysteries may awaken something primordial and dangerous.

Burning Legion

They're still out there. The followers of the Burning Legion are scattered and leaderless, but the survivors still lust for infernal power. They know that new opportunities are never far away, that achieving the power they crave is far from impossible.

What drives these fanatics? Why have they pledged themselves to beings who are dedicated to pillaging and destroying the life on every world they visit? What do they have to gain?

In the past, the Legion's pawns were lured by promises of power, the leveling of social orders and hierarchies, and the chance for eternal life. A rational (if amoral) individual could serve the demons, believing that the world would be a better place under their rule.

No more. The destruction of Lordaeron tore away the last of the veils that obscured the demons' agenda. Any sane follower of the Legion now understands precisely what the demons are looking for: destruction, not domination. Many of those followers quietly buried their unholy symbols and Eredun tomes, changed their names, settled down in the new villages of Kalimdor, and prayed that no one would ever discover their dark past.

Most of the demon cultists who remain faithful are insane. Some began that way, while others lost their minds in the cataclysms of the war. They cling to fragmented memories of their service, performing odd tasks or the same missions over and over again. Sometimes, they do not remember who they are or who they serve, only that they are supposed to kill a small child every 21 days at midnight. These mad servants can be cunning; they can even pass for normal people going about their daily lives. Yet a blankness is in their eyes, and a point in almost every conversation is reached where they stray past the tattered remnants of their self. The uninflected truths they speak then can give even stalwart heroes nightmares.

METZEN

Dangerous as the mad servants can be, they are at least easier to spot than the depraved ones. The mind of this cunning ilk is more bent than shattered. The depraved ones have discovered that they enjoy inflicting pain and that the suffering of others gives them a purpose unlike anything they ever knew before. They know that the Legion intended for them to be destroyed with the rest of the world, but they do not care. They enjoyed the freedom to explore countless depravities that serving the Legion offered. The depraved ones

maintain service to the Burning Legion with death cults and acts of violence. Even if the demons are gone forever, these disciples take pleasure in the deeds that they do in the Legion's name.

The fewest and most dangerous of the Legion's followers are the true disciples. Most notable among them are those who form the Shadow Council (see below). Like the depraved ones, they understand the Legion's true purpose. They believe, however, that they can turn this purpose to their advantage — and, given the power at their command, this arrogance is not without validity. Some are convinced that the Legion will come again and that they can survive and prosper in whatever rubble the demons leave behind. Others are certain that the demons' day is over, but they can build a new power base of their own using the knowledge and gullible followers that remain. They give lip service to serving the Burning Legion while aggrandizing themselves.

True disciples of the Legion pursue many routes to power. Some explore ruins for ancient knowledge and magical artifacts. Sometimes they find what they seek, but more often they awaken horrors that have been sleeping for hundreds or thousands of years. Such horrors may be recruited or simply turned loose to rampage through Kalimdor.

Others recruit followers and build new organizations. They do not speak of the Burning Legion — that would be suicide — but they offer the same enticements the Legion offered to them: power, the reversal of the social order, even eternal life. Some take advantage of the greatest weakness of the Holy Light and "discover" one or more "gods" in which the foolish may place their personal faith. Some start secret schools of magic, offering the power of arcane magic to anyone who does not ask too many questions about its origins.

As their power grows, the Legion's mortal servants may take control of villages and small towns, ruling the population with honeyed promises or threats. Some warlocks turn the towns into abattoirs dedicated to their lords' name.

Others prefer to rule behind the scenes, quietly directing mayors and town councils as they stockpile wealth and magic. This technique works best among the scattered tribes of orcs that used to worship the Burning Legion. Most of these tribes have publicly disavowed their allegiance, but a few influential members remain who have chosen to keep using the magic and secrets they learned from the demons.

The servants of the Legion represent a minor threat… at least for now. Not only are they few and far between, but the leaders of Kalimdor keep a sharp eye out for Legion activity. Any cultist who comes to their attention is dealt with immediately, so the smart servants keep a low profile.

Currently, no evidence suggests that any servant of the Legion has slipped into a position of trust among the leaders of Kalimdor, but that does not mean this development has not occurred. If this hypothetical sleeper agent were to exist, then she would need to be very careful. Any plans the agent has would take years to hatch, but they could shake Kalimdor's growing societies to their foundations.

The Shadow Council

This group was established on the world of Draenor under the leadership of the orc Gul'Dan. Comprised of warlocks in league with the Burning Legion, the Shadow Council was directly responsible for the creation of the Horde. The altruistic Warchief Ogrim Doomhammer disbanded the Council in the course of the Second

War. This eventually led to the orcs discarding their demonic influence and returning to their shamanistic ways under the leadership of Warchief Thrall.

In recent times, a few orc warlocks revived the old tenets of the Shadow Council… and recruited other races into their dark cabal. This new Shadow Council has a secret headquarters in Felwood, a corrupted pocket of Ashenvale Forest on Mount Hyjal. Here, they maintain the land's corruption and work to subvert control of the region from the night elves and druids of the wild.

The Scourge

The Lich King was once an unwilling tool of the Burning Legion. He and his undead forces gained their freedom from the demons after the Battle of Mount Hyjal. Now the Scourge answers to none but the Lich King, and he has a vile agenda for his followers.

Like the Burning Legion, the Scourge has but minor influence upon Kalimdor at present. The Lich King's forces seek to change that, and not just through force at the hands of the undead. They also seek to corrupt the living via the Cult of the Damned, a group of fanatical mortal acolytes. The same issues of madness and lust for power described above for those who still follow the Burning Legion may be applied to these depraved men and women. They know of no deed too dark in their efforts to make the Lich King the supreme power over all of Azeroth. Their work is subtle for the most part, however, for they do not yet have the power to strike openly against the enemy. Instead, the Cult of the Damned lures the weak-willed into their fold through promises of wealth, power and wish fulfillment. They slowly corrupt those with influence through mysterious favors and gifts. And, whenever possible, they turn the attention of Alliance and Horde alike away from the lurking menace of the Scourge to a far more convenient target: one another.

After all, increased strife, bloodshed and death amongst the living races can only benefit the Lich King….

Equipment

This section features details on new materials, weapons, firearms, and steam technology available in the **Warcraft** universe.

Malfunction Ratings

Each mechanical object has a Malfunction Rating between 0 and 5. This number represents the chance that the item will suffer a catastrophic failure when used. If you roll a number *equal to or below* the Malfunction Rating (MR) when making a skill check or attack roll while using the device, the object fails to operate correctly.

Any device with MR 1 or higher requires a skill check or attack roll to use. The skill is usually Use Technological Device, with a DC depending on the task (12 + Technology Score is a good default if no DC is listed; for Technology Score, see "Creating Technological Devices," below). The GM may apply other skills for a simple device that does not require the user to understand the details of its operation. A motorized plow might be best used with a Profession (farmer) check, while most weapons use ranged or melee attack rolls as appropriate.

All devices list any special circumstances if a malfunction occurs. Most items simply stop working until repaired with a Craft (technological device) check (DC as determined by the GM). Dangerous items such as gunpowder weapons often destroy themselves in ways that threaten the users and those near the item — not to mention making repairs more than a little challenging.

A device with MR 0 may have a skill check or attack roll assigned to it, but it is not in danger of malfunction. If a mechanical object has no listed Malfunction Rating, assume it has MR 0.

Materials and Techniques

Every race is familiar with the techniques involved in crafting masterwork equipment (see the *PHB*, Chapter 7: Equipment). Some races, though, have developed expertise in crafting weapons and armor from special materials. Each race receives a +1 bonus to appropriate Craft checks with the respective material or materials listed below in Table 3–2: Favored Materials:

Table 3–2: Favored Materials

Race	Material
Dwarf, Ironforge	Gunpowder
Elf, high	Dragonhide
Elf, night	Darkwood
Goblin	Adamantine
Human	Mithril
Orc	Thorium and arcanite
Tauren	None

Masterwork items, adamantine, darkwood, and mithral (spelled "mithril" in the world of **Warcraft**) follow the same rules as described in the core rulebooks. **Warcraft** also includes several new materials, described below.

Arcanite: This grayish metal looks dull even when tempered, but it holds a keener edge than any other metal on Azeroth. An arcanite weapon gains a +1 enhancement bonus to attack and damage rolls, and its critical threat range is increased by 1.

Arcanite is also extremely flexible and can be worked into a springy armor that turns aside the mightiest blows. Armor that uses arcanite has a percentage chance to reduce critical hits from any weapon, starting at 10% and costing 100 gp per percentage point (thus, 1,000 gp for a 10% reduction), to a maximum of 50%. If a critical hit is confirmed, the wearer of the arcanite-enhanced armor must make a miss chance percentile roll to avoid the critical hit (though the attacker still hits and deals damage normally). This rule applies after doubling the threat range for the Improved Critical feat.

Example: A normal longsword has a 19–20 critical threat range, an arcanite longsword has an 18–20 critical threat range, and a *keen* arcanite longsword has a 17–20 critical threat range.

This useful metal does not come cheaply. For arcanite weapons, add 9,000 gp to the base cost. (This adjusted price is added to the cost of enchanting an arcanite weapon.) All weapons

and armor made with arcanite are considered masterwork.

Arcanite has hardness 15 and hp 30 per inch of thickness.

Dragonhide: Inherently magical, dragonhide counts as a masterwork item for purposes of enchanting armor. It can be used to make hide, leather, and studded leather armors. Armor made from dragonhide has a 0% chance of arcane spell failure. Dragonhide is rare, and any armor that uses it costs 20 times its normal price.

Dragonhide has hardness 10 and hp 30 per inch of thickness.

Thorium: This rare metal combines the weight of lead with the strength of steel. Orcs prize it for weapons because the extra weight allows a skilled user to strike with more force.

Using a thorium weapon properly requires the Exotic Weapon Proficiency (thorium weapons) feat. A character with this feat deals extra damage with a thorium weapon equal to half his Strength bonus. So, a hero with a +3 Strength modifier gets a +4 bonus to damage when using a one-handed thorium weapon, or 1.5x his Strength bonus, and a +6 bonus when using a two-handed thorium weapon (assuming it is not a light weapon), or 2x his Strength bonus.

Thorium armor offers damage reduction 5/+1, but leaves its wearer virtually immobile. It is considered one category heavier, to a maximum of "heavy." Thorium reduces the maximum Dexterity bonus for a piece of armor by 2 (to a minimum of +0); furthermore, both the armor check penalty and the chance of arcane spell failure is doubled.

Weapons made from thorium add 20,000 gp to their normal price and weigh twice as much. Thorium armor also adds 20,000 gp to its normal price. (The adjusted price does not affect the cost of creating a masterwork item or enchanting it.)

Thorium has hardness 15 and hp 30 per inch of thickness.

Firearms

Firearms are a relatively new dwarven invention. Despite the dangers of dealing with volatile explosives, dwarves are fascinated by the possibilities. Dwarven gunmakers constantly tinker with the guns they craft, trying out new designs and upgrades, naming and decorating their weapons.

Firearms and gunpowder obey the rules under Renaissance firearms in the revised *DMG*, Chapter 5: Running a Campaign, "Building a Different World," *Advancing the Technology Level*.

Firearms are treated like other ranged projectile weapons, although they cannot be constructed to benefit from a user's exceptional Strength bonus. Exotic Weapon Proficiency (firearms) grants the character proficiency with all firearms; otherwise, a –4 penalty applies to all attack rolls. (Ironforge dwarves treat firearms as martial weapons.)

The attack bonus from a masterwork firearm stacks with the attack bonus from refined gunpowder (there is no such thing as masterwork firearm ammunition), but does not stack with enhancement bonuses.

The attack and damage enhancement bonuses from a magical firearm stack with the attack and damage bonuses from imbued gunpowder and magical ammunition. These bonuses do not stack for purposes of damage reduction, and the attack bonus of magical ammunition does not stack with the attack bonus of imbued gunpowder.

The MR for firearms and explosives varies depending on the specific weapon. Firearms usually jam or misfire, while explosives go off prematurely or prove to be duds. See "Gunpowder," below, for additional details.

Gunpowder

Firearms use 1 ounce of gunpowder per shot. Gunpowder is sold in small kegs (15-pound capacity, 20 pounds total weight, 250 gp each) and in water-resistant powder horns (2-pound capacity and total weight, 35 gp for a full powder horn); there are 16 ounces per pound. If gunpowder gets wet, it is ruined and does not burn.

Dwarven experimentation has uncovered several improvements on common gunpowder. "Refined" gunpowder is a masterwork mixture that propels ammunition with greater velocity. It provides a +1 bonus to damage rolls. Refined gunpowder costs 50 gp per pound.

"Imbued" gunpowder is an alchemical mixture that protects the gunpowder and enhances its explosive properties. Imbued gunpowder is not ruined by water. Any projectile or bomb that uses imbued gunpowder is treated as a +1 magical weapon. Imbued gunpowder costs 650 gp per pound.

Gunpowder has MR 1. On a malfunction — due to a skill check, attack roll, or saving throw — the gunpowder goes off in an uncontrolled fashion. Anyone within 5 feet must make a Reflex save (DC 18) to avoid the resulting explosion. (Ironforge dwarves receive a +4 racial bonus to this Reflex save; they cause gunpowder accidents just as often as anybody else does, but have more practice at avoiding the effects.) Gunpowder itself inflicts 2d6 points of fire damage. If part of a bomb, cannon, or firearm, the explosion

damage is equivalent to the weapon's normal damage.

See Table 3–3: New Weapons and Table 3–4: Explosive Weapons for available firearms and explosives.

Weapons

Ammunition, Ball: A flintlock pistol uses soft lead balls slightly smaller than a human fist. The balls are sold in sturdy leather sacks of 10.

Ammunition, Bullets: A long rifle uses carefully shaped lead bullets about half an inch in diameter. They are sold in pouches of 10 bullets each.

Ammunition, Mortar Shell: A mortar shell is a metal case filled with a small gunpowder charge that explodes on impact. A shell casing has hardness 0 and hp 2.

Ammunition, Shot: A blunderbuss fires a quarter-pound of tiny lead pellets with each shot. Blunderbuss loads are sold 12 at a time, with each load individually wrapped in a muslin bag.

Blunderbuss: This basic firearm deals 2d6 points of damage to a target in the first range increment and 1d6 points of damage to anyone in a 5-foot wide path beyond that distance, out to maximum range. It holds a single shot and requires a standard action to reload.

If the damage of a blunderbuss is upgraded (see Creating Technological Devices, below), then the weapon inflicts maximum damage to any target in the first range increment. (Note that the range increment can be increased as per the upgrade rules.) After that, the damage is reduced one die for each range increment. Once the damage is reduced to 1d6, the blunderbuss does

1d6 points of damage to anyone in a 5-foot-wide path to the maximum range of the gun.

Ironforge dwarves and goblins treat blunderbusses as martial weapons.

Bomb: Bombs are simple weapons made out of little more than gunpowder and bits of metal poured into a steel ball. They are devastating against people and monsters, less so against buildings. About half the weight of a bomb is gunpowder, while the rest is casing, scrap metal, and a fuse.

All bombs must be primed to explode with a DC 12 Use Technological Device check before being tossed, emplaced, or launched. If the check is successful, the bomb explodes at the end of the round. Failure can lead to a gunpowder explosion (see "Gunpowder," above).

A bomb can be set to explode after a delay of 1 or more rounds. Each round of delay adds 1 to the DC of the Use Technological Device check to prime the bomb. Setting a delay requires attaching a fuse or laying a trail of gunpowder, so it is only effective with bombs that are not thrown or moved.

Bombs can be scaled up. On doing so, see "Upgrades and Adding Functions" in Creating Technological Devices, below.

Bomb, Grenade: This small bomb can be thrown by hand. A character hit by a grenade bomb may make a Reflex save (DC 20) to catch or deflect it. A deflected bomb scatters (see *PHB*, Chapter 8: Combat, "Special Attacks," *Throw Splash Weapon*). A character who catches a grenade bomb and has an action available can throw the bomb as a normal attack action. Keep in mind that after the fuse has been lit, Mr. Grenade is no longer your friend.

Grenade bombs can be scaled up. On doing so, see "Upgrades and Adding Functions" in Creating Technological Devices, below.

Claws of Attack, Orcish: This traditional orc weapon consists of blades that emulate the 12-inch claws of a dire wolf.

Orcs treat orcish claws of attack as martial weapons.

Flintlock Pistol: A flintlock pistol is powerful but inaccurate, not so much a small version of the long rifle as it is like firing a bomb through a short tube. It holds a single shot and requires a standard action to reload.

Ironforge dwarves and goblins treat flintlock pistols as martial weapons.

Halberd, Tauren: Tauren use the axe head and spear-like spike of this traditional weapon to devastating effect. Wise opponents keep their distance from anybody strong enough and furious enough to carry this gigantic halberd.

If you use a ready action to set the tauren halberd against a charge, you deal double damage if you score a hit against a charging character.

You can use the hook on the back of the halberd to make trip attacks. If you are tripped during your trip attempt, you can drop the tauren halberd to avoid being tripped (see *PHB*, Chapter 8: Combat, "Special Attacks," *Trip*).

Tauren treat tauren halberds as martial weapons.

Hammer, Dwarven Tossing: This ancient dwarven melee weapon is lighter than a warhammer and is perfectly balanced as a throwing weapon.

Ironforge dwarves treat dwarven tossing hammers as martial weapons.

Long Rifle: The king of small arms, a long rifle is nearly as long as a dwarf is tall. Thanks to the innovative barrel design, a skilled sharpshooter can use the long rifle to knock an apple off an orc's head from nearly half a mile away — assuming the rifleman can resist the urge to shoot the orc instead. The long rifle holds a single shot and requires a standard action to reload.

Ironforge dwarves and goblins treat long rifles as martial weapons.

Moonglaive: Night elf sentinels favor this three-bladed weapon, which can be used either in melee or as a thrown weapon. The Exotic Weapon Proficiency (moonglaive) feat confers proficiency with both fighting styles. A skilled user can gain feats to ricochet the weapon off opponents and back into her own hands.

Night elves treat moonglaives as martial weapons.

Mortar: Mortars launch grenadelike weapons such as explosive shells in a high arc to land near or on a target. Mortars are treated like firearms in most respects, except that they require their own Exotic Weapon Proficiency feat and use 4 ounces of gunpowder with each shot. The mortar can fire once per round as a standard action and must be reloaded after every shot as a full-round action.

Mortar attacks ignore any cover that is not total cover or that does not protect the target from above; however, a mortar cannot fire at targets within one range increment.

Totem, Tauren: If this massive weapon looks like it's an intricately carved tree trunk, that's because it is. The tauren prefer to spend their time decorating and meditating on their totems, but they are also perfectly willing to hit foes over the head with them. Said foes quickly learn the error of disturbing a meditating tauren.

Tauren treat tauren totems as martial weapons.

Warblade: A warblade is a finely balanced longsword with a vicious curved edge. It counts as a light weapon for Medium creatures.

Table 3–3: New Weapons

Martial Weapon	Cost	MR	Dmg (S)	Dmg (M)	Critical	Range Increment	Weight*	Type**
One-Handed Melee Weapon								
Warblade	20 gp	—	1d6	1d8	x2	—	3 lb.	Slashing
Exotic Weapons	**Cost**	**MR**	**Dmg (S)**	**Dmg (M)**	**Critical**	**Range Increment**	**Weight***	**Type****
Light Melee Weapons								
Claws of attack, orcish	25 gp	—	1d4	1d6	19–20/x2	—	2 lb.	Slashing
Moonglaive	20 gp	—	1d4	1d6	x3	10 ft.	1 lb.	Slashing
One-Handed Melee Weapon								
Hammer, dwarven tossing	15 gp	—	1d4	1d6	x3	10 ft.	7 lb.	Bludgeoning
Two-Handed Melee Weapons								
Halberd, tauren†	50 gp	—	1d8	2d6	x3	—	25 lb.	Piercing and slashing
Totem, tauren	20 gp	—	1d10	2d8	x2	—	50 lb.	Bludgeoning
One-Handed Ranged Weapon								
Flintlock pistol	400 gp	1	2d6	3d6	x3	5 ft.	5 lb.	Piercing
Ammunition, ball (10)	5 gp	—	—	—	—	—	3 lb.	—
Two-Handed Ranged Weapons								
Blunderbuss	250 gp	1	Special	Special	x3	10 ft.	10 lb.	Piercing
Ammunition, bullets (10)	10 gp	—	—	—	—	—	3 lb.	—
Long rifle	800 gp	1	2d6	3d6	x3	300 ft.	20 lb.	Piercing
Ammunition, shot (12 bags)	6 gp	—	—	—	—	—	3 lb.	—
Mortar	75 gp	1	‡	‡	x2	40 ft.	20 lb.	Piercing

*Weight figures are for Medium weapons. A Small weapon weighs half as much, and a Large weapon weighs twice as much.

** When two types are given, the weapon inflicts both types if the entry specifies "and" or either type (player's choice at the time of attack) if the entry specifies "or."

† Reach weapon.

‡ The mortar fires mortar shells; see Table 3–3: Explosive Weapons for specifics.

Table 3–4: Explosive Weapons

Weapon	Cost	MR	Damage	Blast Radius	Range Increment	Weight	Type
Ammunition, mortar shell	25 gp	1	3d6	5 ft.	—	1 lb.	Fire
Bomb, catapult†	150 gp	1	8d6	20 ft.	—	20 lb.	Fire
Bomb, emplaced†	80 gp	1	4d6	10 ft.	—	10 lb.	Fire
Bomb, grenade†	40 gp	1	2d6	5 ft.	10 ft.	1 lb.	Fire

† These explosives require no proficiency to use (although a skill check may be required).

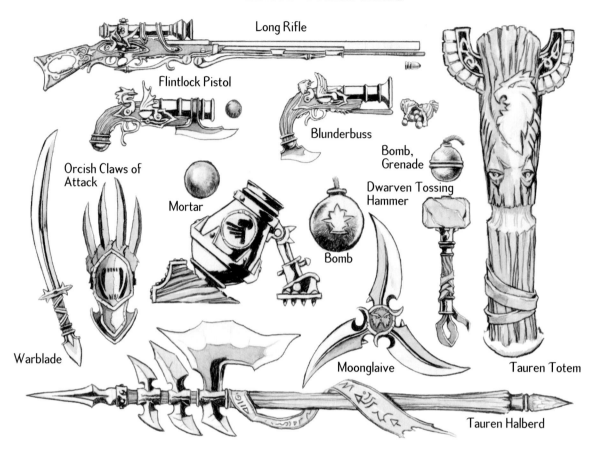

Long Rifle

Flintlock Pistol

Blunderbuss

Bomb, Grenade

Orcish Claws of Attack

Dwarven Tossing Hammer

Mortar

Bomb

Warblade

Moonglaive

Tauren Totem

Tauren Halberd

Technology

Mechanical devices and steam technology are not just about blowing things up. These items can multiply strength, speed up travel, and make tasks easier. The items in this section are examples of the kinds of devices available in the **Warcraft** universe, and rules follow to show how you can turn almost any idea into a functioning device.

Of course, just because a device functions now does not mean it won't *malfunction* later. Yet, then, that's part of the fun of technology, isn't it?

Adventuring Gear

Army Knife, Goblin: It's not stylish and it's useless as a weapon, but no sensible goblin warrior marches without this tool-of-all-trades. The goblin army knife digs trenches, saws wood, hammers nails, lights fires, sounds three different kinds of duck calls, polishes and oils armor, sews clothing, stores 25 feet of spidersilk rope with a test weight of 100 pounds, extends into a fishing rod, and unreels into a 1-person canvas tent. All this utility in just 4 pounds, and it even cuts things!

Operating the intricate system of levers to access each function of the knife takes 3 rounds, but no skill check is required. The knife has hardness 1 and hp 5.

Gyroparasol: This sporty umbrella can protect up to 3 Medium characters from rain and harsh

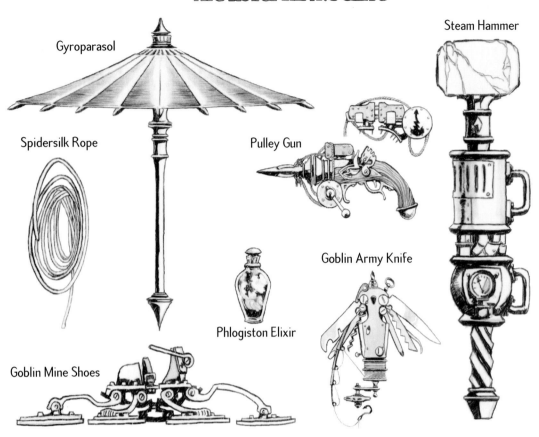

Gyroparasol

Spidersilk Rope

Pulley Gun

Steam Hammer

Goblin Army Knife

Phlogiston Elixir

Goblin Mine Shoes

sunlight. Its cunningly shaped panels also spin when a strong wind rushes through them, while a gyroscopic stabilizer keeps the umbrella steady in its user's hand. This improvement over ordinary umbrellas was designed to keep the gyroparasol from blowing away in storms, but it has proven remarkably useful for slowing down falling heroes.

Opening a gyroparasol is a move action. The device can slow the fall of up to 600 pounds of weight, preventing the first 3d6 points of damage suffered from falling. Holding it properly requires a DC 10 Use Technological Device check. On a malfunction, the gyroparasol's support ribs collapse upward and the device prevents no falling damage. The gyroparasol has hardness 3 and hp 15.

Mine Shoes, Goblin: Once essential for negotiating minefields, goblin mine shoes have been made obsolete by the goblin land mine. They remain exceptionally useful, however, for avoid-

ing pressure plates, pit traps, and other hazards common to old ruins and abandoned fortresses.

Goblin mine shoes are 2-foot wide metal plates that can be strapped onto any normal shoe. A system of gears and hinged plates prevents the shoes from interfering with normal walking and spreads the hero's weight over a much wider area.

Table 3–5: Technology

Adventuring Gear

Item	MR	Cost	Weight
Army knife, goblin	0	50 gp	4 lb.
Gyroparasol	1	150 gp	2 lb.
Mine shoes, goblin	1	400 gp	10 lb.
Pulley gun	1	225 gp	8 lb.
Upgrade	—	175 gp	5 lb.
Rope, spidersilk (50 ft.)	0	25 gp	3 lb.
Steam hammer	0	500 gp	35 lb.

Special Substances and Items

Item	MR	Cost	Weight
Phlogiston elixir	2	25 gp	—

This effect gives the character a chance to avoid any trap that is triggered by being stepped on.

To avoid such a trap, make a Use Technological Device check (DC = the trap's Disable Device DC). If successful, the trap is not triggered, though it is also not disabled.

Running while wearing goblin mine shoes is impossible. Any character with 5 or more ranks of Perform (dance), however, can master some amazing tap dance routines.

On a malfunction, the goblin mine shoes lock in one position when the trap is triggered, preventing the character from making a Reflex save. Goblin mine shoes have hardness 2 and hp 10.

Pulley Gun: Grappling hooks are fine for simple climbing, but sometimes you need to move heavy loads over walls or across chasms. The pulley gun makes this job a breeze. A blast of steam propels a thick metal spike up to 50 feet through the air and deep into any surface up to hardness 8. (The spike penetrates stone but not iron.) The force of impact compresses the spike, causing four tines to dig into the surface and secure it.

An instant after the spike fires, a second blast of steam shoots a pulley-and-rope attachment from a second barrel. This barrel is sighted so that the pulley hits and locks onto the spike. Once the pulley is secure, the 100 feet of attached spidersilk rope can be used to move up to 800 pounds. Resetting the pulley gun after it has been fired takes 4 minutes.

You can get an upgrade of additional ropes and slings that can carry up to 1,600 pounds (enough to move all but the largest of horses). Attaching the upgrade takes 10 minutes. (See "Upgrades and Adding Functions" in Creating Technological Devices, below.)

The pulley gun is a complicated piece of machinery, requiring a DC 20 Use Technological Device check to fire, hit the intended location with the spike shot, and hold the gun steady for the pulley shot. (No attack roll is required.)

If used as a weapon, the pulley gun requires a ranged attack roll. It is considered an exotic weapon with a range increment of 50 feet and inflicts 3d6 points of piercing damage.

On a malfunction, the pulley gun suffers a burst steam line. The user must make a Reflex save (DC 15) or take 2d6 points of heat damage from the steam. The pulley gun has hardness 5 and hp 15.

Rope, Spidersilk: This rope is even sturdier and more lightweight than silk rope. It has 5 hit points and can be burst with a DC 25 Strength check. Most significantly, it has a slightly tacky yet supple texture that aids greatly in climbing, providing a +4 circumstance bonus on Use Rope checks.

Steam Hammer: This portable battering ram knocks down doors, breaks large objects, and pries gates open with its optional crowbar attachment. It is reliable but not useful on stealth missions, given the staggeringly loud sound it makes.

The steam hammer has a +15 Strength bonus and substitutes for your Strength when making checks to break down doors, break objects, and other actions that require heavy smashing.

Using the steam hammer is a full-round action, and rebuilding a head of steam after each use takes 1 minute. The user and anyone within 100 feet is deafened for 1d10 rounds afterward. A deafened character takes a –4 penalty on initiative checks, automatically fails Listen checks, and has a 20% chance of spell failure when casting spells with verbal components.

Any creature within half a mile of the device may make a DC 5 Listen check to hear it being used.

If used as a weapon, the steam hammer requires a melee attack roll. It is considered an exotic weapon and inflicts 5d6 points of bludgeoning damage. The steam hammer has hardness 5 and hp 25.

Special Substances and Items

Phlogiston Elixir: This draught is composed of phlogiston gas mixed with rare herbs and minerals. When you consume the elixir, choose 1 ability to increase and 1 ability to decrease, then roll 1d4+1. Adjust the chosen abilities by the result of the roll; this is an enhancement bonus and penalty. The elixir's effects last for 1 day.

A phlogiston elixir is almost as unstable as the pure substance. Mixing a dose of phlogiston elixir requires a DC 12 Craft (alchemy) check, takes 1 hour to complete, and requires 300 gp for the gas and rare herbs and minerals. The dose remains stable for a number of days equal to the amount by which the Craft (alchemy) check exceeded the DC. After that, the admixture breaks down as if the elixir malfunctioned (see below). A DC 20 Craft (alchemy) check — or ingesting the draught — confirms if the mixture was successful.

On a malfunction, the admixture was off, turning the elixir into an ingested poison (Fort DC 13, initial damage 1 Con, secondary damage 1d4 Con).

Creating Technological Devices

There are many weapons and technological devices in the world of **Warcraft** — from bomb launchers, dragon guns, and gryphonclaw pistols to autostilts, clockwork oxen, goblin zeppelins, flying machines, night scopes, portable field kitchens, rocket submarines, siege engines, and many kinds of walking armor. This amazing technology will be detailed in **Alliance & Horde Compendium**, but that doesn't mean you can't make devices of your own!

Kalimdor is a crucible of developing technology. Dwarven and goblin workshops are springing up across the land, and a host of devices and constructs are taking shape. With all this activity going on, it would be a shame if you got left out

of the fun. The item creation rules below will assist you in developing your own steamtech gadgets.

Step One: Set the Technology Score

Imagination and hard work only go so far. The power of the items you can create is limited by your experience. This factor is handled as a "technological limit," figured as follows:

Technological Limit = 1 + tinker class level + feat modifiers

Any device you build must have a Technology Score (TS) less than or equal to your technological limit. If more than one character works on an item, the device's TS may be less than or equal to the highest technological limit. Items with lower Technology Scores are cheaper and quicker to make than those with higher Technology Scores.

The TS determines the device's maximum capabilities. Not all categories apply to all objects — a gun does not carry cargo, for instance — and an object can be designed to use less than its maximum capabilities. Thus, the object's overall TS is determined by the capability that requires the highest Technology Score. A TS can be increased by later upgrades; see "Upgrades and Adding Functions," below, for more information.

The DC of the Craft (technological device) check needed to build the device is determined as 15 + TS.

Step Two: Define the Task

The first step to designing any item is figuring out what you want it to do. Got a forest you need to chop down? Maybe some goblin treecutters

Table 3–6: Technological Device Limits

Capability	Limit
Maximum AC bonus	Technology Score
Maximum ability modifier	+ (Technology Score x 3)
Maximum cargo	Technology Score x 200 lb.
Maximum damage inflicted/ prevented	(Technology Score)d6 points of damage per round
Maximum hardness	Technology Score
Maximum hit points	Technology Score x 5
Maximum movement speed	Technology Score x 20 miles per hour
Maximum range increment	Technology Score x 50 feet

can help. How about drilling through a castle wall or sailing the seas in a rocket submarine? If you can imagine and describe a task, then a technological device can perform it. Some possibilities include:

• Magnify small or far-away objects.
• Bore through a lock on a door — or the stone wall next to it.
• Fly people and cargo across the continent.
• Test the floors of a ruined temple for traps.
• Entertain a crowd with automated puppetry.
• Assemble a brick wall.
• Forge a hundred swords.
• Communicate with a distant city by using giant semaphore signals.
• Hang glide into a mountain fortress.
• Change the course of a river by digging out its bank.
• Add up large numbers very quickly.

Once you have described the task to be performed, the GM assigns it a DC to represent how difficult it is for the proposed mechanical device to perform the task described.

Task DCs are never used in skill checks. They exist only as a way of evaluating how difficult an item is to construct.

The GM should take into account the scale of the task, how long the task is likely to take, how complicated the actions required to perform the task are, and how the item is expected to operate. These factors make for a wide range of possible DCs — a device that produces a small fire without flint or tinder may be DC 5, for instance,

while "kill every orc on Kalimdor" may be DC 500. The GM may even rule that a task is impossible to perform with the technology available to **Warcraft** characters.

One way you can persuade the GM to set a low DC is to provide a detailed description of how the item is expected to accomplish its task. If you can show that the task is easy, the GM has a good reason to assign a low DC. A Rube Goldberg-style drawing is a wonderful way to prove that a task is not as difficult as it might seem.

Step Three: Decide How Quickly the Item Operates

A task takes time to perform. For most items, this time is the interval between beginning the task and finishing it. For vehicles, this time measures how quickly the vehicle begins operating. For weapons, this is the time required to reload or ready the weapon.

The GM decides the basic time unit for the task — combat rounds, minutes, hours, days, weeks, or months. Use whichever time unit seems most appropriate given the scale of the task and the design of the item.

The person designing the item then chooses a number between 1 and 10. This is the Time Factor, or how many time units are needed for the item to perform its task. The Time Factor is important because slower items are less expensive and can be built more quickly than faster

Table 3–7: Typical DCs for Tasks

DC	Task Description	Examples
10	Simple repetitive chore	Mortar shells; devices that chop down individual trees, wash dishes, or irrigate plants.
15	Complex repetitive chore	Bombs; devices that feed and water livestock, chop down dozens of trees, or add a particular sequence of numbers.
20	Simple responsive systems	Firearms and cannons; alarms and traps; devices that deliver messages; slow ground vehicles.
30	Complex responsive systems	Mechanical guardians with programmed tactics; devices that record and analyze information; air and water vehicles.
50	Simple creative systems	Devices that forge simple weapons, make tools, build walls, or copy books.
75	Complex creative systems	Devices that forge gunpowder weapons, build siege engines, brew alchemical concoctions, erect buildings, or make predictions based on a set of data.
100	Amazing feat of technology	Self-replication; artificial intelligence; devices that hunt down and destroy a particular individual.
200+	World-changing development	Devices that move mountains, destroy species, control weather, or even blow up the world.

items. The faster an item is, the more you pay for it.

Some items work just once and then destroy themselves. These items are considered to have a Time Factor of 10.

Example: Zim the Mad is building a boning machine to prepare his favorite dish: gefilte human. His player presents a charming sketch of a conveyer belt system with 36 strategically placed blades. The GM decides that this is a complex repetitive chore, but the blades are positioned efficiently and will do the job quickly. The GM decides that "minutes" are an appropriate time unit for the job. The player chooses 2 minutes for each use, making this item's Time Factor 2.

Step Four: Determine the Malfunction Rating

You can make something reliable and expensive or save some gold and put up with the occasional life-threatening explosion. Most tinkers prefer thriftiness to personal safety, which means there is a significant chance that their devices will malfunction during normal use.

During the design process, you assign the task a Malfunction Rating from 0 to 5. This number represents the chance that the item will suffer a catastrophic failure when this task is performed. See "Malfunction Rating," above, for specifics on applying an MR to completed items.

Step Five: Figure the Market Value

Once the Technology Score (TS), Task DC, Time Factor, and Malfunction Rating (MR) are determined, the item's market value (in gold pieces) is figured. The Task DC is the most important factor when deciding worth.

Task DC	Multiply by
10	10
15	20
20–30	25
35–50	50
75–100	100
200+	250

The list above shows the number by which you multiply the Task DC to get the Task DC value, which is then applied with the other elements to determine market value, as indicated here:

Market Value $=$ TS x (Task DC value) / (Time Factor + MR)

So, a device with TS 4, Task DC value 500, Time Factor 3, and MR 1 has a market value of 500 gp.

Market value is not set in stone. The GM should round the value to the nearest 25 gp and may adjust it further to reflect special circumstances.

Hardness, Hit Points, and Size

You determine the hardness and hit points. In most cases, these figures represent the maximum that the item's TS allows. (Steam technology may be oversized, but it is generally sturdy.) Building a fragile device that is easy to destroy if it falls into the wrong hands is convenient sometimes, however.

The GM then sets the size and weight of the device based on what functions it performs and the materials from which it is constructed. In most cases, the size of an object is obvious — small hand tools are Tiny and weigh a few pounds at most, steam-powered tree saws are Small and can be held and operated in two hands, while self-propelled mechanical lumberjacks may be Huge and weigh hundreds of pounds. Keep in mind that steam technology tends to involve large pistons, boilers, and other oversized equipment. Most devices are much bigger and bulkier than they would be on 21st-century Earth.

Finally, the GM determines any other information necessary to use the item. Most steam-powered air vehicles have average maneuverability, for instance, though the GM may decide that a particular vehicle is more or less maneuverable. (A flying machine would have "good" maneuverability, for instance.) **Alliance & Horde Compendium** will provide more detailed guidelines.

Building the Item

Once the item creation DC and the market value are set, the item may be built using the standard Craft rules (*PHB*, Chapter 4: Skills, "Craft"). You pay one-third of the item's price in raw materials to get started. Actual construction requires a weekly Craft (technological device) check. Multiply a successful check result by the check's DC and record the total. When the accumulated progress is greater than the device's market value x 10, the item is finally completed!

Technological devices are considered complex items. They require a Craft (technological device) check if created by spells such as *minor creation* or *fabricate*.

Upgrades and Adding Functions

Once you have described how an item operates and what its market value is, you can design new tasks for the item to perform. Adding new tasks is less expensive than creating a new item from scratch. It can be done as part of the item's initial construction or as an improvement to a finished item.

The first task defined for the item is known as the *primary function*. New tasks added during a device's construction are known as *secondary functions*, while new tasks added after the device is complete are known as *upgrades*. Secondary functions and upgrades are designed using the five steps described above, but they are subject to special limitations and conditions.

The Task DC of a secondary function cannot exceed that of the primary function. The effects of a secondary function also cannot exceed the limits of the item's Technology Score. Once you have calculated a secondary function's market value, divide that value by 3 and add it to the current market value of the item. The result is the item's new market value. No matter how many secondary functions a device has, you only make one series of Craft (technological device) checks to build it.

An upgrade may have any Task DC and can increase the item's TS by up to 3. (Increasing the TS also increases the item creation DC.) Once you have calculated the upgrade's market value, divide that value by 2. This is the upgrade's market value, which is then built using a series of Craft (technological device) checks as if it were a new item. When the accumulated progress equals the price of the upgrade x 10, the upgrade is completed and is now a functioning part of the device.

An upgrade can replace an item's primary function — useful if you, say, want to make the barrel of your flintlock pistol bigger so it can fire a projectile the size of your head. The GM must also decide if installing the upgrade alters the device's hardness, hit points, weight, or size.

Example: Building a Flying Machine

Jode is a brilliant Ironforge dwarf tinker with big plans for the future. He wants to explore the mountains looking for arcanite deposits, and he needs a flying machine to leapfrog ahead of his claim-jumping competition.

Jode is a 5th-level tinker with a +10 Craft (technological device) skill modifier and the Build Vehicles feat. His technological limit to build vehicles is 7 (his level gives him 5, and the Build Vehicles feat adds 2). Build Vehicles also gives him a +2 bonus to his Craft (technological device) checks to construct the vehicle, which will speed up construction.

The young dwarf wants to head for the mountains in a few weeks. Not feeling the need to rush things, Jode decides that he doesn't need the fastest flying machine possible. (He can always upgrade the copter later.) He figures 60 miles an hour is fast enough, which is Technology Level 3.

Jode comes up with the following design for the GM's approval: the flying machine has the primary task "fly around in comfort and style." It can travel up to 60 miles an hour, has AC 13, and can carry up to 600 pounds including its pilot. Jode also wants a mounted cannon that inflicts 3d6 points of damage, but the GM rules that this is a secondary task ("shoot vicious predators and claim-jumpers").

The GM gives the primary task a Task DC of 30 (the flying machine is an air vehicle), and the secondary task a Task DC of 20 (the gun is a firearm).

After considering the time involved in turning on magnetos and spinning up the rotor, the GM decides that starting the flying machine requires the "minutes" time increment. Jode doesn't want his poor henchman Chava to be waiting too long, so he decides that 1 minute is quite long enough. The flying machine's primary task is thus Time Factor 1. As for the cannon, the player and GM agree that it should operate every other round, for a Time Factor of 2.

Wanting the flying machine to be absolutely reliable, Jode gives it MR 0. The GM notes that the cannon will fall under the exploding gunpowder rule (see above), but Jode figures that there is no reason not to give the cannon a Malfunction Rating as well. He even decides to push his luck a little, reducing the cost of the cannon by giving it MR 2.

The GM also determines that piloting the flying machine requires a DC 15 Use Technological Device check and is subject to the Vehicle Proficiency (air vehicles) feat. The cannon uses a standard ranged attack roll and is subject to the Exotic Weapon Proficiency (firearms) feat.

The GM now has everything she needs to determine the flying machine's market value. She multiplies the Technology Score (3) by the Task DC value (30 x 25 = 750), then divides the total of 2,250 by the Time Factor (1) plus the Malfunction Rating (0). This gives the flying machine a hefty 2,250 gp price tag.

Assuming construction requires a DC 20 Craft (technical device) check each week and Jode gets exactly 20 each time (20 x 20 = 400), he will need 56 weeks to finish construction! Plus, it's a lot of math to deal with, when all he wants is to get in the air.

Jode decides he can live with a 'copter that's slower (40 miles per hour) and takes longer to start (5 minutes). These changes drop the Technology Score by 1 (and also lower related variables such as AC, hardness, and hit points) and raise the Time Factor by 4, resulting in a 600 gp market value.

Also, the cannon drops to 2d6 points of damage since a secondary task cannot exceed the primary task's Technology Score. Its cost is figured with the same formula as the primary task (2 x 500 / 4 = 250), then divided by 3 since it is a secondary task. This calculation adds 83 to the market value, which the GM rounds down to 80 gp.

These alterations give the flying machine plus mounted cannon a total 680 gp market value. Jode should need between 15 and 20 weeks to reach the 6,800 total (680 gp x 10) he needs from his weekly Craft (technological device) checks.

The final game statistics for Jode's flying machine are listed on Table 3–8: Example Flying Machine. It's a fragile vehicle that requires plenty of coaxing to start, but it's just what Jode needs to zip himself, his henchman Chava, and his equipment around the mountains.

Table 3–8: Example Flying Machine

Top Speed:	40 miles per hour
Maneuverability:	Good
Cargo Capacity:	400 lb.
Operation:	DC 14 Use Technological Device, Vehicle Proficiency (air vehicles)
MR:	0
Startup Time:	5 minutes
AC:	12
Hardness:	2
Hit Points:	10
Size:	Huge (15 ft. long x 8 ft. wide)
Weight:	500 lb.
Weapon:	Cannon
Fires:	Every other round
Operation:	Ranged attack roll, Exotic Weapon Proficiency (firearms)
MR:	2
Damage:	2d6 bludgeoning
Range Increment:	100 feet
Market Value:	680 gp
Item Creation DC:	17

Magic Items

Technology may be powerful, but magic still does things that technology cannot. Technology enhances, multiplies, and destroys, but magic changes. The magic of **Warcraft** alters those who use it, permitting them to draw upon the arcane and natural forces around them. You get many of the same results from using either technology or magic, but magic affects the self in a way that technology cannot.

Most creatures feel the mystical connection that a magic item creates between them and the forces of the universe, but high elves are particularly sensitive to it. A high elf must make a Will save (DC 15) to part voluntarily with a magic item. If the save is failed, the high elf may not give up possession of the item that day. The save DC increases by 1 for every 5,000 gp the item is worth, up to DC 30. Priceless items such as minor artifacts and artifacts are DC 35.

Many of the magic items found in **Warcraft** — *crystal ball*, *belt of giant strength*, *boots of speed*, *potion of invisibility*, *ring of protection*, *ring of regeneration*, and so on — are identical to those listed in Chapter 7: Magic Items of the *DMG*. In addition, some items are unique to the world of **Warcraft**. A few are profiled below, and many others will appear in upcoming books.

Weapons

Goblin Land Mine

Description: The *goblin land mine* combines a gunpowder bomb with the fiendish surprise of invisibility. Once placed and activated, the *mine* sits quietly until an enemy approaches and triggers a ward placed upon the bomb. The ward ignites the gunpowder, producing a devastating explosion.

Powers: The *mine* is a bomb scaled up to 30 pounds with a *glyph of warding* cast upon it. Once activated, it is invisible until triggered. Detonation occurs when the *glyph of warding* is triggered; the *glyph* then ignites the gunpowder, triggering a secondary explosion. The two explosions together deal a total of 8d6 points of fire damage to all targets in a 15-foot radius; a successful Reflex save (DC 15) halves the damage.

Invisibility and *glyph of warding* are incorporated when crafting of the item, with a single command word activating both when the *mine* is placed. The user can set the *glyph* according to creature type, creature subtype, species, physical characteristics, alignment, and faith.

Because the *goblin land mine* also functions as a mechanical, trap-like device, it can be found on a DC 20 Search check, defused on a DC 20 Disable Device check, and is considered a CR 5 encounter.

Faint abjuration; CL 5th; Craft Wondrous Item, *glyph of warding*, *invisibility*, Craft (technological device); Price: 850 gp; Weight 2 lb.

Storm Hammer

Description: The signature weapon of elite gryphon teams, *storm hammers* must be rededicated to their owners each year. The ceremony is held every solstice in the great halls of the gryphon aviaries. The details of the ceremony are secret, but they are said to involve chanting, solemn oaths, and terrible hangovers the next day.

Powers: On a successful hit, this *+1 shock warhammer* deals an additional 1d6 points of electricity damage. The electricity does not harm the *hammer*'s owner, but it does inflict a nasty shock on any other person who attempts to wield it, dealing 1d6 points of electricity damage each round. The subject can avoid this damage by making a DC 20 Reflex save and dropping the *hammer*.

Moderate evocation; CL 8th; Craft Magic Arms and Armor, *lightning bolt*, *shocking grasp*; Price: 8,500 gp; Weight 8 lb.

Vampiric Runeblade

Description: Death knights are few and far between now, but their legacy lives on. The *runeblade* is one example of their terrible power. It channels life force, which bestows a kind of life upon the blade itself. Though not very intelligent, the *runeblade* has a strong survival instinct.

When a death knight who owns a *runeblade* is destroyed, the sword dampens its powers, taking on the appearance of a nondescript magical weapon. It uses its empathic powers to manipulate its next owner — encouraging feelings of possession and anger, discouraging kindness and altruism. Once it gains enough control over its owner, it encourages him to seek out the secret places where death knights still dwell. Only then can the *runeblade* accomplish its goal of gaining a new master.

Powers: A *vampiric runeblade* is a *+1 longsword* that deals an additional 2d6 points of negative energy damage when it hits a living target. The blade's wielder gains temporary hit points equal to the bonus damage inflicted. These extra hit points cannot exceed the wielder's current hit points + 10. The temporary hit points disappear 1 hour later.

The *runeblade* is empathic with Int 10, Wis 12, and Cha 16. It has Ego 9 and is chaotic evil. It can cast *charm person* once per day on a person holding it; the target may resist by making a DC 16 Will save.

Moderate necromancy; CL 7th; Craft Magic Arms and Armor, *charm person*, *vampiric touch*; Price: 200,000 gp; Weight 4 lb.

Potions

Potion of Invulnerability

Description: Strong drink may make warriors feel invulnerable, but this hero's mead makes the feeling real. The potion draws from the life force of the character drinking it, using that energy to strengthen and harden the body.

Powers: The character gains damage reduction 20/adamantine, but suffers 1d4 points of damage per round (this damage cannot be prevented or reduced). The potion's effects last for 10 rounds.

Faint abjuration; CL 5th; Brew Potion, *stoneskin*, creator must be at least a 10th level spellcaster; Price: 2,000 gp.

Potion of Mana

Description: Some spells are too useful to cast just once. This potion helps a spellcaster hold on to the fading memory of a spell, reclaiming it so that it may be cast again.

Powers: A spellcaster who drinks this potion recovers the last spell that she cast. The spell must be between 1st and 3rd level, and the potion must be consumed within 2 rounds after the spell is cast.

Faint transmutation; CL 4th; Brew Potion, *Rarey's mnemonic enhancer*, creator must be at least an 8th level spellcaster; Price: 900 gp.

Potion of Greater Mana

Description: The greater potency of this brew enables the hero who drinks it to recover more powerful spells, but it delivers an equally powerful migraine.

Powers: As *potion of mana*, except that the potion can help the hero who drinks it recover a spell of any level; however, he also suffers damage equal to the spell's level.

Moderate transmutation; CL 7th; Brew Potion, *Morden's lucubration*, creator must be at least an 11th level spellcaster; Price: 9,000 gp.

Wondrous Items

Cloak of Flames

Description: Known in some circles as a holocaust cloak, this heavy garment ignites the rage of its wearer into punishing flames.

Powers: When activated, the *cloak of flames* deals 2d6 points of fire damage per round to any creature within 5 feet of the wearer. On a successful DC 20 Will save, the wearer may also extend the radius of the flames to a maximum of 10 feet. The flames do not harm the wearer or any allies. Opponents, however, can make a DC 17 Reflex save for half damage.

The item activates and deactivates as a free action at the wearer's command, and may be used up to a total of 10 rounds per day.

Faint evocation; CL 5th; Craft Wondrous Item, *fireshield*; Price: 90,000 gp; Weight 4 lb.

Gloves of Celerity

Description: These fingerless gloves draw out the natural quickness of the hero who wears them.

Powers: *Gloves of celerity* provide a +2 luck bonus to initiative and Reflex saves.

Faint transmutation; CL 5th; Craft Wondrous Item, *cat's grace*; Price: 2,000 gp.

The far seer's body was still cooling on the spirit lodge's lower platform when Alayin Glitterhelm managed to break into the inner sanctum. The warding seal was tough, but no match for the combination of arcane knowledge and brute force that the high elf could bring to bear against any problem.

Those same abilities had brought him this far: into the spirit lodge itself. A glib tongue and a passing knowledge of mystic theory had gained him access to the orc far seer in the first place; brute force came into play when it became clear that the orc was unwilling to share his knowledge. A heavy candlestick expertly and forcefully applied to the back of the head left the far seer facedown in a pool of dark blood and Alayin with full run of the place.

Still, speed was of the essence — surely some acolyte, shaman, or penitent would find the body in due time, and the hue and cry would be raised. Until that time, Alayin could ransack the sanctum and steal away those bits that could be utilized by or traded with his magical brethren. Moreover, if the stories Alayin had heard were true, the sanctum contained something else of greater value.

Most of the items, of course, were junk to the high elf's eyes: dolls made of twisted cords, pinned with bits of cloth; carvings of ancient spirits and revered ancestors; shards of mithril, chunks of arcanite, and pieces of thorium left from shattered weapons and broken dreams; pelts, hides, scales, and teeth of a mismatched menagerie of slain beasts, used for purposes that Alayin could only dream of.

In the back, however, among the litter and debris, was the prize that Alayin sought, a great book bound in the hide of a demon and secured with iron clasps: The Book of Khadgar.

Long ago and far away there was more magic in the world, Alayin thought as he pulled the heavy volume from its hiding place. No, that's wrong. There is as much magic as there ever was.

Yet there was once more magical knowledge than in current times, Alayin realized — knowledge held by such powerful magi as Medivh, and within the great arcane halls of the Violet Citadel of the Kirin Tor at Dalaran. The wizard Khadgar grew up within the walls of the latter and served as the assistant (and some say, executioner) of the former. Khadgar vanished utterly in a quest beyond the walls of the Twisting Nether, leaving behind only legends, lies, and a few precious artifacts, such as this tome.

Alayin ran his hands over the tooled leather cover and allowed himself a satisfied grin. A goblin merchant who had stayed with the far seer had learned of the book and its provenance and sold the information (dearly) to a comrade of Alayin's, who in turn proposed that the two of them break in and make it their own. Alayin figured that one could succeed as easily as two, and when his ally met an unfortunate fate, Alayin sought out the orc

spellcaster. The orc was friendly enough, but would not budge on giving up his possessions. So Alayin had no choice but to budge the orc, for the good of all.

So much was lost when Dalaran fell, Alayin mourned. So much knowledge was burned by the undead and trampled beneath their bony feet. The common spells, those known to the warrior-priests, sorceresses, and paladin warriors still saw use, but so much else was lost. Even if this book contained not a single description of a spell, the very theory discussed in its pages would make Alayin the most powerful mage — nay, say it! Archmage — in all of Kalimdor.

Alayin's lust so consumed him that he did not notice the dimming of the lights outside the sanctum, in the spirit lodge itself. The torches flickered and guttered out, and from their sconces arose thick, inky shadows. The shadows snaked around each other and formed into great, solid clouds of blackness.

In the heart of that darkness gleamed feral eyes, and wolf claws made of shadow tapped softly on the spirit lodge's wooden floors. Alayin did not hear them until too late, and then he received only the chance to turn and let out the first words of a curse… or a spell… or a prayer.

Whatever the words Alayin might have uttered, the fragment of the phrase was left unfinished as the feral spirits fed on his flesh. Too late did Alayin Glitterhelm remember that not all of the guardians of magic were made of flesh and blood.

CHAPTER FOUR: MAGIC

Fiery arcane energies tear across the battle-field. Storms of bladelike ice rip through troops and blast apart siege engines. Such magic is an important power in the world of **Warcraft**, and many have come to use it without full knowledge of its dark origins.

In many ways, a counterpoint to the flashy violence of arcane magic, divine magic pervades Azeroth as well. It does not have arcane magic's incredible destructive power, but it is better for subtle uses. Although the magic of health and rejuvenation, it is not without its combat applications. Divine spellcasters can protect the innocent and smite foes with righteous fury. Certain races such as orcs, tauren, and night elves have turned almost exclusively to divine magic as a safer substitute for the arcane.

Each type of magic is explained in detail here, followed by a listing of spells specific to the **Warcraft** universe.

Arcane Magic

The first Well of Eternity existed ten millennia ago, shrouded in the mists of legend and ages past. This large pool was resplendent with liquid magic, and this energy's influence transformed a group of the primitive, primal denizens of the world into the Kaldorei — the beings who would later be known as night elves. The Well intrigued the nascent night elves, and they eventually learned to harness its power. They used their newfound magic to forge a great civilization on the primeval world.

Yet arcane magic has a dark genesis. It was born of demonic power, of terrible creatures that stalk through living nightmares, and it has always borne their accursed taint. The forces of the Burning Legion, led by the fallen titan Sargeras, discovered of the Well of Eternity and the strength it promised. They decided to make it theirs and destroy Azeroth in the process.

They were aided by Queen Azshara of the Kaldorei and her Highborne servitors. She became tainted through her reckless use of arcane magic and summoned the Burning Legion to Azeroth. The demons smashed cities and torched the land, but the great druid Malfurion Stormrage

led a few Kaldorei heroes to victory against the demons. This band of warriors destroyed the Well of Eternity, a feat that sundered the world, and the Kaldorei believed that the taint and danger of the arcane had been banished from Azeroth.

Such was not the case. The renegade night elf Illidan Stormrage, Malfurion's brother, had succumbed to magical addiction. He created a new Well of Eternity at the great Mount Hyjal. Although imprisoned for his crimes, Illidan's act ensured that arcane magic would remain on Azeroth.

Centuries passed and the night elf civilization again grew mighty. Once more, the surviving Highborne obsessed with the use of arcane magic and decried their brothers who would see it forever dormant. These elves, calling themselves the Quel'dorei, or high elves, sought to convince the other night elves of the potency of arcane power and ended up unleashing a savage magical storm that ravaged the land. The Kaldorei banished their cousins from Kalimdor for their recklessness, and the Quel'dorei eventually settled on the continent of Lordaeron. Here they created the mystic kingdom of Quel'Thalas. At its heart was the Sunwell, a new magical wellspring created with waters they took from the Well of Eternity. The Sunwell empowered the high elves and served as the source of their arcane power.

In time, the Quel'dorei discovered that their arcane practices eliminated the deific qualities they bore as night elves. They were no longer immortal; their arcane use divorced them from their night elf heritage. This legacy lasts to current times, for a night elf who practices arcane magic loses his mystical traits and suffers the same racial modifiers as a high elf. (The night elf does not undergo a physical transformation, however.) The Quel'dorei did not regret this change; they gladly traded their Kaldorei lineage for arcane power. Such was their pride that the high elves even contacted the primitive humans of Lordaeron and taught them arcane secrets.

The Burning Legion eventually sensed the arcane energies and was again drawn to Azeroth. Lured by the promise of revenge and the power brimming within the new Well of Eternity, the demonic lord Archimonde led the Legion in a terrible invasion. This was the Third War, a titanic struggle that ended but one year past, in which undead and demons smashed entire kingdoms and courageous men and women became great heroes. The Legion was finally defeated at the Battle of Mount Hyjal, but the battle left a world of ash and cinders in its wake — a reminder of arcane magic's true nature.

The Nature of the Arcane

Arcane magic is a drug. Its use is intoxicating and sends power throbbing through the veins, but it is also addictive, subtly corrupting and even maddening. The high elves' addiction to arcane magic is partly representative of this feature. An even more chilling example is the rise of warlocks among the orcs — their dark manipulations of the Twisting Nether eventually destroyed their entire world of Draenor. Furthermore, when the warlocks were slain after the Horde was defeated upon Azeroth, the orc race suffered a kind of withdrawal from the warlock magics. These grim events serve as reminders that magic has the power to affect an entire race. All practitioners must be wary, for the arcane can turn one away from the light and into the gloom, to become a puppet of dark powers. If one is reckless and uses magic foolishly or excessively, the demonic energies change him. This is a slow, insidious process, as shadow gradually clouds the mind and stifles rational thought. This demonic legacy is one of destruction and manifests itself in a corrupt arcane spellcaster by driving him to violent insanity.

Night elves have known of this danger since the Legion's first invasion over 10,000 years ago. High elves knew of the dangers also and shared this knowledge with the fledgling human nations. Yet the power of the arcane is such that humans and high elves cannot resist its allure. Instead, they have attempted to discover ways to make it safer. Magic wielders have tried to be discreet and select in their use, and a powerful organization, the Guardians of Tirisfal, came into being in order to combat the Burning Legion's sinister forces. Even these precautions ultimately failed, however, as shown when demons came

once more to the world. As long as arcane magic remains in the world, the Burning Legion will return again and again until Azeroth is nothing but a smoking ruin.

The Rules of Corruption

Unlike in other fantasy milieus, arcane magic in **Warcraft** is a dark and dangerous force. Yet no explicit rules govern arcane magic's corrupting effects on characters. We don't want to force your PCs into evil and madness; such decisions should be left up to you.

Arcane magic's sinister nature is left as a theme for you and the GM to explore in your campaign, not as a liability to cripple wizards and sorcerers.

Wielders of the Arcane

Many races wield arcane magic in these grim days, dark and tantalizing as it is. High elves make great use of it — indeed, their civilization and culture were forged in the arcane. Though reunited with their lost brethren, night elves are extremely suspicious of their kin: the stink of the arcane hangs heavy about the Quel'dorei. The high elves distrust their cousins in turn, remembering how their ancestors were persecuted at Kaldorei hands.

Humans also use arcane magic. High elves taught arcane secrets to the burgeoning human kingdoms centuries ago, in return for help battling the savage forest trolls. Humanity took to arcane magic quickly and even constructed the famous magical city of Dalaran, a great center for arcane study. Out of the academies of Dalaran came the human archmagi, wielding fearsome battle magic and possessing incredible knowledge. Dalaran was destroyed during the Third War, but some of the wizards remain on Kalimdor. Some night elves are suspicious of the human factions because of human reliance on magic.

Arcane magic is in the hands of darker forces as well. The undead Scourge wielded terrible powers in the Third War, and those undead still extant possess arcane skills that make the mind reel. The undead are the Legion's creation, but they have thrown off the demons' shackles. Now, the Scourge draws its necromantic powers directly from the Twisting Nether. Necromancers animate fallen corpses into a horrible semblance of life and empower these grotesque creatures with unnatural power and ferocity. The undead have even discovered how to manipulate arcane energies to bring their own necromancers back from the dead in full control of their faculties and sentience, and with chilling new powers — liches, devious undead spellcasters who have traded life for dark power.

Some orcs have control over arcane power, but they are not members of the Horde. These outcasts are warlocks, demon-worshippers who have either been reacquainted with or have never thrown off the taint of the previous generation. Warlocks serve their demonic masters with gleeful violence and fling fire and rage at those they once called kin.

The most terrible of the arcane spellcasters are demons. These creatures hail from the Twisting Nether, the source of the arcane. Dark energies drip from their bodies. They can sense the use of arcane magic's, and they offer it as a lure to those who would do their bidding. The eredar are a race of demonic warlocks, and their might is unquestionable. One has only to look at the charred ruins of Lordaeron and Quel'Thalas to know the Burning Legion's power.

"Distrust" Does Not Mean "Kill on Sight"

Though many night elves distrust both high elves and other arcane spellcasters, combining a night elf and a high elf — or other race who happens to be an arcane spellcaster — in the same party is *not* a recipe for disaster. The night elf character may be suspicious of her companions, or she may not. Some night elves are of a more forgiving nature, and in any case both night elves and high elves (and other arcane spellcasters) are still part of the Alliance. More importantly, the PCs are part of the same adventuring group. Heroic characters can put aside petty differences and develop lasting friendships.

Use of the Arcane

Arcane magic has many uses; the most famous is for battle. Rains of fire and jagged ice, hurtling balls of smoking cinder, and magically created beasts of destruction scar the battlefield. Magic is also used for subtler means of conducting war, from hiding an ally from sight to slowing enemy movement. Arcane magic is also serves for defense and to counter the opposition's spells. Before the ruin wrought by the Burning Legion, new uses for magic were being researched; the most eminent of these discoveries is teleportation. A teleporting wizard can circumvent an enemy's defenses entirely.

Individuals who use arcane magic have little to fear from it, so long as they are careful in its use. Night elves distrust all arcane spellcasters, since the use of the arcane first summoned the demons to this peaceful world and caused the division between the night elves and the high elves. An arcane spellcaster will quickly become aware of the night elves' dislike for him — and he should be wary of those extremists among them who may try to do him harm.

The most dangerous arcane practitioners are demons. They have been defeated and scattered (on Azeroth) but not obliterated, and many demons see the arcane and those who wield it as their path back to dominance. A source of magic must be exceptionally vast or powerful to summon demons from far away, but nearby — where none want a demon to be in any case — demonic forces take note of a magical item or spellcaster.

Some regard the possibility of demonic intervention as beneficial. These arcane spellcasters see the Legion as a tool they can use to further their own ends — a powerful, dangerous and unpredictable tool, but a tool nonetheless. Such individuals — usually warlocks — purposefully attract demonic attention and pretend to serve the Legion, all the while trying to manipulate the demons into serving the spellcaster's purposes. This strategy is extremely dangerous and a course of action usually undertaken only by those already on a magic-induced decline into oblivion. Young wizards and sorcerers are always warned: never believe that you are smarter than the

demons, for along that path lies damnation. Not even the last Guardian of Tirisfal, Medivh, was immune to such temptation.

In ages past, such reckless use of arcane magic brought about its wielder's undoing. As long as one is careful and discreet, arcane magic is a powerful tool and a devastating weapon — but the lure always beckons on the edges of perception to dive into arcane magic's burning depths and give one's self up to the madness.

Divine Magic

The origins of divine magic are varied. Some practitioners draw divine energy from the strength of their own faith, some call to the spirits of their ancestors, some turn to the forces of the earth for divine inspiration, and some claim a divine legacy that runs within their blood. Whatever the source, all divine spellcasters share much in common. They have the ability to ease their allies' wounds and crush their enemies, all while remaining hidden from the shadowy eye of the Burning Legion.

Although gods exist in the world, they do not take the same roles as the gods of other fantasy settings. **Warcraft**'s gods are far more theoretical in nature. They do not manifest themselves upon the world, they do not show divine proof of their existence, and they do not reward their followers with special powers or spells. Indeed, some wonder if these gods even exist at all — and whether the gods might just in fact be a comforting, fictional creation. Even if this is the case, the believers' absolute faith in the gods is enough to tap into a divine spark within themselves, and they draw spells and powers from their own devotion.

The Gods of the Night Elves

Night elves venerate gods where other races do not. They revere Elune, the Moon Goddess; Cenarius, Lord of the Groves; and Malorne the Waywatcher. They also venerate the twin bear gods Ursol and Ursin, and Aviana, the Lady Raven. The mighty bears fought at the night elves' side against the Burning Legion in the War of the Ancients, and the raven goddess was a messenger and patron of the secrets and mysteries of the wild earth.

Respect for these gods is a central aspect of night elf life and influences the culture in profound ways. Many other races have only a passing knowledge of these gods, and some wonder if they truly exist. The gods do not grant spells to their devotees, but they and their mythos provide the faith that allows one to draw divine power from within.

Night elves revere their gods as teachers instead of worshipping them. To outsiders, this reverence is often mistaken for worship, but it is not the same. For example, Cenarius taught his arts to the night elf druids, granting them the power to call upon nature. The druids also draw their totemic powers from the blessings of Ursol, Ursin, and Aviana.

Elune

Over 10,000 years ago, the feral Kaldorei, who would become the night elves, worshipped Elune, the Moon Goddess. They believed she slept within the iridescent waters of the Well of Eternity during the day, and when night fell she rose into the sky in all her pale splendor. The night elves believe that she watches over and protects her children and grants them the ability to meld into the velvet darkness of the night. Priestesses of Elune, such as the famed and ancient Tyrande Whisperwind, represent the grace and might of Elune in the mortal world. They use the power of their faith to fight her enemies and cloak themselves in silvery mail. The fearsome night elf huntresses also draw their strength from Elune, though they do not wield divine spells.

The night elves revere Elune and draw much of their martial strength and divine energy from this devotion. How the belief in Elune began is uncertain, as passing millennia have obscured her origins. Perhaps she does truly grant the night elves their unique ability to shadowmeld; perhaps they draw this power from an association with the Well of Eternity or some other force. In any case, though the actual existence of Elune may be unsure, one thing is certain — she lives in the hearts and minds of her people, and this is all they need to call down her wrath.

Cenarius

Cenarius is the druidic demigod of the Groves. He, unique among deities, is known to have existed in the physical realm. The mighty Cenarius has the torso and head of a night elf and the body of a great gray stag. He is master of the druidic energies that course through the earth and is the father of both the fey dryads and the wise Keepers of the Grove.

It is also widely rumored that he sired the cursed, barbaric centaur that ravage the dusty plains of the Barrens — though this claim has never been substantiated.

The night elves first encountered Cenarius in an age of mists, when they were the Kaldorei and the world was unsullied by the taint of the Legion. The primitive night elves befriended the demigod, and he taught them to venerate the forces of nature and all things living. He has ever been suspicious of the arcane, and he lent his strength to combat the first demonic invasion during the War of the Ancients. After the demons were driven away and the land was sundered beyond recognition, Cenarius took steps to prevent a similar catastrophe from ever again befalling the world. He and the hero Malfurion Stormrage together sealed Malfurion's treacherous brother Illidan in an eternal crypt beneath the earth, and the demigod instructed the night elves in the druidic arts. This magic allows one to summon the primordial energies of the earth and of living things.

Like Horde shamans (see below), night elf druids draw upon the forces of earth and nature to empower their spells. The druids bypass the spirits, however, and tap directly into the primordial energy that flows through the ground and through every living thing. Druids share an intimate bond with nature. Those who wield the druidic magics have the ability to transform themselves into fearsome beasts and to call upon the trees to combat their enemies.

Millennia passed in which Cenarius watched over the night elves from the Moonglades and the Sentinels kept their long vigil. Eventually, as all remember, the demons again invaded the land, and men and orcs came to the continent of Kalimdor. Grom Hellscream drank the tainted blood of Mannoroth, and his corrupted fel orcs clashed with the Cenarius' forces. The powerful demigod, wizened with years and wise beyond all telling, was slain in the forests of his home. His spirit lingers, but his physical self has been forever destroyed.

The Dwarves

The dwarves recently discovered evidence that they are in fact sons and daughters of the titans — great, metallic-skinned, godlike beings who set order to the cosmos and long ago cleansed Azeroth of its vile elemental rulers. According to ancient sources, the titans created dwarves from living stone. The first dwarves assisted the titans with the ordering of the world by dredging out vast caverns beneath the earth. Since this discovery, the dwarves have become obsessed with investigating the mystery of their true genesis and have reawakened powers locked deep inside them for untold ages. The dwarves have learned to change their skin to stone for brief periods of time, and they believe that this is only the first of such powers, the likes of which have not been seen since the titans left the world.

The Horde

Tauren and orcs practice a shamanistic religion that hinges on spirit-worship; often, these spirits are orc and tauren ancestor-spirits. Horde shamans bear great respect and reverence for those who came before them and call upon the spirits for guidance and strength. Many orcs and tauren claim that they can hear or sense the spirits, and they use this awareness to their advantage. Few can argue that the spirits answer when their descendants call, for shamans wield fearsome, primal energies that speak of the anger of the dead. Most believe that the spirits provide direct divine energy to those who call upon them, and their spellcasting ability is not rooted solely in the spellcasters' devotion (as it is with those who revere gods and philosophies).

Shamans also believe that everything — from sentient beings to animals to trees to rocks to the world — has a spirit and that one can speak to these spirits and draw power from them if one knows the way. This is the ancestral shamanism that Thrall rediscovered. Like the ancestor spirits, the earth and elemental spirits desire to aid and protect those who speak to them. Orc shamans have the power of nature in their fists, and earth, wind, and fire come to their call.

Other Races

Humans and high elves follow no gods as such, but most adhere to the philosophy of the Holy Light. Human paladins use their faith in the Light to protect and heal their allies and incinerate their enemies. Like the night elves, the paladins' steadfast devotion grants them divine power — the Holy Light itself is simply a philosophy, a set of ideas created by mortals, but it gives the devoted something to believe in. From this faith comes divine justice. See the "Faiths" section in Chapter 3: Adventuring for more information on the philosophies of the Holy Light.

None question the power of divine magic. Though not as flashy as arcane magic, its applications are myriad. Divine spells are used for everything from attack to defense, from healing to divination. Those who wield divine magic need not fear the suspicions of night elves or the Legion's attentions. It is a safe and powerful energy. While calling upon its essence, one feels both the strength of her own character and a connection with something truly vast. This feeling grants a sense of peace and fulfillment to divine spellcasters — qualities not often seen in

Other Gods

Certain godlike entities exist other than those the night elves revere. In the same way that the night elves draw divine magic from their devotion to Cenarius and Elune, other individuals may bear a faith in their "god" that allows them to tap into a divine source.

Dragons

Before the titans left Azeroth, they imparted some of their power to five great dragons who were to guard the world. These five were Alextrasza the Life-Binder, Malygos the Spell-Weaver, Ysera the Dreamer, Nozdormu the Timeless, and Neltharion the Earth-Warder. These dragons command great power, and Ysera in particular may have followers among the night elves, for she maintains the surreal realm of the Emerald Dream.

The Legion

The Burning Legion is undoubtedly potent, and some of its leaders possess demigod-like power. Those who worship demons draw terrible divine magic from their dark faith.

The Old Gods

Very few mortals know of the Old Gods, and fewer still consider them anything more than a legend. Before the titans came to Azeroth, the malign Old Gods — colossal beings of elemental fury — ruled the world and the savage elementals that dwelt upon it. The titans defeated the Old Gods and chained the raging beings deep beneath the earth where, supposedly, they remain to this day.

Titans

The titans set order to the universe and created the first living creatures on Azeroth. The titans' exact nature remains a mystery to mortals, but some dwarves may revere these beings.

those who tinker with the tainted energies of the arcane.

Spells

Much of the magic of **Warcraft** is necessarily violent and geared toward the battlefield and ancillary tactical uses (espionage, transportation, and so on). Other magics include those for summoning and binding demons, animating corpses as various sorts of undead, and calling upon the powers of the spirits of the elements and nature.

Many *PHB* spells work a bit differently in a **Warcraft RPG** campaign; relevant adjustments are listed below. Following this section are new spells specific to **Warcraft**.

Some spells in this section are now on the necromancer's spell list. The necromancer (Ncr) is a prestige class that will be detailed fully in the forthcoming supplement **Alliance & Horde Compendium**. For the sake of completeness here, however, any spells from the *PHB* now part of the necromancer's spell list are indicated in this section.

Animate Dead
Level: Ncr 4

This spell is no longer on the sorcerer/wizard spell list; it is now on the necromancer spell list. It can be used to animate skeletons or zombies as normal. Refer to the skeleton and zombie templates in **Manual of Monsters**.

Astral Projection

The Astral Plane does not exist in the **Warcraft RPG** setting. Instead, *astral projection* sends the caster's astral form into the Twisting Nether (see "The Universe Beyond" in Chapter Six: Campaigning). *Astral projection* is in all other ways the same as presented in the *PHB*.

Chill Touch
Level: Ncr 1

Chill touch is no longer on the sorcerer/wizard spell list; it is now on the necromancer spell list.

Circle of Death
Level: Ncr 6

Circle of death is no longer on the sorcerer/wizard spell list; it is now on the necromancer spell list.

Contact Other Plane
Level: Wrl 5

This spell is no longer on the sorcerer/wizard spell list; it is now on the warlock spell list. A warlock sends his mind to the Twisting Nether, where he contacts a member of the Burning Legion for answers. All such castings are treated as if the caster were contacting the Astral Plane.

Control Undead
Level: Ncr 7

This spell is no longer on the sorcerer/wizard spell list; it is now on the necromancer spell list.

Create Greater Undead
Level: Ncr 8

This spell is no longer on the sorcerer/wizard spell list; it is now on the necromancer spell list. It adjusts the table included in Chapter 11: Spells of the *PHB* as follows:

Caster Level	Undead Created
15 or lower	Crypt fiend
16-17	Abomination, banshee
18-19	Withered
20	Ghost*

* Ghosts created by this spell have three ghostly powers in addition to their manifestation: malevolence, horrific appearance, and corrupting gaze. See the *MM* entry for more information on all types of undead.

The new undead referenced in this spell will appear in **Manual of Monsters**.

Create Undead
Level: Ncr 6

This spell is no longer on the sorcerer/wizard spell list; it is now on the necromancer spell list. It adds the following table in addition to the one included in Chapter 11: Spells of the *PHB*:

Caster Level	Undead Created
11 or lower	Ghoul (as in **Manual of Monsters**)
12-13	Revenant
14-15	Shade

Death Knell
Level: Ncr 1

This spell is no longer on the sorcerer/wizard spell list; it is now on the necromancer spell list.

Deathwatch
Level: Ncr 2

This spell is no longer on the sorcerer/wizard spell list; it is now on the necromancer spell list.

Enervation
Level: Ncr 4

This spell is no longer on the sorcerer/wizard spell list; it is now on the necromancer spell list.

Ethereal Jaunt

There is no Ethereal Plane in **Warcraft**. That said, this spell otherwise functions the same as described in the *PHB*. The only difference is that the caster never actually leaves the Material Plane, she simply becomes invisible, intangible, and capable of moving in any direction. Other *ethereal* creatures are visible and tangible to the caster and vice versa.

Etherealness

As *ethereal jaunt*, above.

Gate

Gate opens a connection between two planes — so, in **Warcraft**, it opens a connection to the Twisting Nether, to the Elemental Plane (if the caster is aware of it), to other worlds (like Draenor), or to the Emerald Dream (and similar planes attached to other worlds).

Flame Strike
Level: Drw 4, Hlr 5, Wrl 5

When cast as a warlock (arcane) spell, half of *flame strike*'s damage is considered to be fel damage and is therefore not subject to reduction due to *protection from energy (fire)*, *fire shield (chill shield)*, and similar magic. *Resist energy (fire)* also does not provide protection.

Ghoul Touch
Level: Ncr 2

This spell is no longer on the sorcerer/wizard spell list; it is now on the necromancer spell list.

Greater Planar Ally
Level: Hlr 9, Sor/Wiz 8

This spell only summons elementals.

Greater Planar Binding
Level: Wrl 8

This spell is no longer on the sorcerer/wizard spell list; it is now on the warlock spell list.

Lesser Planar Ally
Level: Hlr 5, Sor/Wiz 4

This spell only summons elementals.

Lesser Planar Binding
Level: Wrl 5

This spell is no longer on the sorcerer/wizard spell list; it is now on the warlock spell list.

Planar Ally
Level: Hlr 7, Sor/Wiz 6

This spell only summons elementals.

Planar Binding
Level: Wrl 6

This spell is no longer on the sorcerer/wizard spell list; it is now on the warlock spell list.

Plane Shift

This spell can shift characters to the Twisting Nether, the Emerald Dream, or other material worlds (such as Draenor used to be). If the caster knows of it, he can also shift to the Elemental Plane, although this is not advisable.

Soul Bind
Level: Ncr 9

This spell is no longer on the sorcerer/wizard spell list; it is now on the necromancer spell list.

Summon Monster I–IX
Level: Wrl 1–9

These spells are no longer on the sorcerer/wizard spell list; they are now on the warlock spell list. Additionally, these spells can only be used to summon fiends (demons, natives of the Twisting Nether).

General Note on Positive, Negative, and Shadow Planes

Spells that interact with these planes still interact with these energies in **Warcraft**. These

energies flow throughout Azeroth and the Twisting Nether, however, and are not specific to any particular plane. As such, positive and negative energy work as described in the *PHB*, *DMG*, and *MM*, as do shadow creations.

New Spells

Banish

Target becomes ethereal.

Transmutation
Level: Sor/Wiz 8
Components: V, S
Casting Time: 1 standard action
Range: Close (25 ft. + 5 ft./2 levels)
Target: One creature
Duration: 1 round/level
Saving Throw: Will negates
Spell Resistance: Yes

Description

This spell causes the target to become ethereal, unable to interact with the material world in any way until the duration ends.

Spell Effect

The target becomes invisible and intangible for the spell's duration. The caster can still see her, although he cannot affect her with further spells unless he also shifts into the ethereal. The effects of being ethereal are identical to those described under *ethereal jaunt*, with the additional changes for **Warcraft** as described in "Spells," above.

Bladestorm

The caster creates two magical longswords.

Transmutation
Level: Sor/Wiz 3
Components: V, S, M

Casting Time: 1 standard action
Range: Personal
Duration: 1 round/level (D)
Saving Throw: None
Spell Resistance: None

Description

The caster magically creates a pair of sharp swords, and he becomes a whirling dervish of bladed carnage.

Spell Effect

The caster creates two longswords. The longswords are treated as having an enhancement bonus to attack and damage of +1 per 3 caster levels (maximum +5). Starting on the following round, for 1 round per level, the caster may perform a full attack action, giving up all regular attacks to make one melee attack at the caster's full base attack bonus against each opponent within 5 feet. If the caster does not make a full attack each round, the effect ends.

If the caster is disarmed of one or both of these blades, they reappear in his hands at the start of his next action as long as the spell remains active. The caster is considered proficient with the longsword for the duration of the spell.

Material Components: Two knives, one for each hand. They meld with the caster's arms and are lost when the spell ends.

Blizzard

Sleet, snow, and hail batter the caster's foes.
Evocation [Cold]
Level: Sor/Wiz 3
Components: V, S, M
Casting Time: 1 standard action
Range: Long (400 ft. + 40 ft./level)
Area: Cylinder (20-ft. radius, 40 ft. high)
Duration: Concentration, up to 1 round/2 levels
Saving Throw: None
Spell Resistance: Yes

Description

This spell calls hailstones and cutting ice shards down upon the caster's enemies.

Spell Effect

Freezing sleet, snow, and hail pound down, dealing 1d6 points of impact and 1d6 points of cold damage per round to creatures in the area of effect. The caster may maintain concentration on the spell for up to 5 rounds.

Material Component: A pinch of dust and a few drops of water.

Bloodlust

Spirits give target extra attacks and +4 Strength.
Transmutation
Level: Sha 3, Sor/Wiz 4
Components: V, S, M
Casting Time: 1 standard action
Range: Close (25 ft. + 5 ft./2 levels)
Target: One creature
Duration: 1 round/level
Saving Throw: Fortitude negates (harmless)
Spell Resistance: Yes (harmless)

Description

The caster summons enraged spirits into the target, heightening the target's strength and reflexes for a brief period of time.

Spell Effect

The transmuted creature moves and acts more quickly than normal. This extra speed allows 1 extra attack per round. On his turn, the subject may make this extra attack either before or after his regular action.

The transmuted creature is also imbued with extra strength. The spell grants a +4 enhancement bonus to Strength, adding the usual benefits to melee attack rolls, melee damage rolls, and other uses of the Strength modifier.

Bloodlust is dispelled and countered by *slow*.
Material Component: A drop of blood mingled with earth.

Cannibalize

Caster regains hit points by consuming corpses.
Necromancy [Evil]
Level: Ncr 2
Components: V, S
Casting Time: Concentration, up to 4 rounds
Range: Personal
Target: One corpse
Duration: Instantaneous
Saving Throw: None
Spell Resistance: No

Description

The caster gains some of the traits of a ghoul, especially the creature's bone-cracking jaw and extended tongue. The caster may consume flesh from a corpse to regain health.

Spell Effect

There is no saving throw because this spell works only on dead creatures and heals only the caster. The corpse must be mostly intact and must have a true anatomy (so gelatinous cubes are not allowed).

By consuming the corpse's flesh, the caster regains 1d8 hit points per round of concentration, up to his maximum number of hit points. Once a corpse has been consumed, very little flesh remains and the corpse is no longer considered intact. A corpse can thus be the target of this spell only once.

Carrion Swarm

A swarm of vermin attacks creatures.

Conjuration (Summoning)
Level: Sor/Wiz 5
Components: V, S, M
Casting Time: 1 standard action
Range: Close (25 ft. + 5 ft./2 levels)
Area: Cone
Duration: Instantaneous
Saving Throw: Reflex half
Spell Resistance: Yes

Description

A swarm of bats, poisonous spiders, flying beetles, and other such vermin extend out from the caster's hand to create a cone-shaped area of effect.

Spell Effect

This swarm of vermin causes 1d6 points of damage per caster level (maximum 15d6). The swarm's attacks are non-magical. Creatures that are immune to poison take half damage (one quarter with a successful saving throw). Damage reduction or being incorporeal makes a creature immune to damage from *carrion swarm*.

Material Component: A dead beetle, spider, or other vermin.

Cripple

The target suffers penalties to attacks, damage, Reflex saves, jumping, and Strength.

Transmutation
Level: Sor/Wiz 2
Components: V, S
Casting Time: 1 standard action
Range: Close (25 ft. + 5 ft./2 levels)
Target: One living creature
Duration: 1 round/level
Saving Throw: Will negates
Spell Resistance: Yes

Description

The affected creature moves and attacks at a drastically slowed rate as its limbs wither for the spell's duration.

Spell Effect

The creature can take only a partial action each turn. Additionally, it suffers a –2 penalty to AC, melee attack rolls, melee damage rolls, and Reflex saves. The affected creature jumps half as far as normal.

Additionally, the affected creature suffers a –1d6 penalty to Strength, with an additional –1 per 2 caster levels (maximum additional penalty of –5). The subject's Strength score cannot drop below 1.

Cripple is countered and dispelled by *haste*.

Death Coil

Deals negative energy damage to living targets and heals undead.

Necromancy
Level: Hlr 3, Ncr 3
Components: V, S
Casting Time: 1 standard action
Range: Close (25 ft. + 5 ft./2 levels)
Target: One creature
Duration: Instantaneous
Saving Throw: Will half (see text)
Spell Resistance: Yes

Description

A coil of negative energy projects out from the caster's extended palm and unerringly strikes its target.

Spell Effect

The coil deals 2d8 points of negative energy damage +1 point per caster level (up to +10) to living creatures; a successful Will save halves the damage.

Since undead are powered by negative energy, this spell cures them of a like amount of damage, rather than harms them.

Death Coil, Greater

Level: Hlr 4, Ncr 4

As *death coil*, except that it deals 3d8 points of negative energy damage +1 point per caster level (up to +15).

Death Coil, Lesser

Level: Hlr 2, Ncr 2

As *death coil*, except that it deals 1d8 points of negative energy damage +1 point per caster level (up to +5).

Death Pact

Destruction of an undead creature gives hit points to caster.

Necromancy [Evil]
Level: Ncr 5
Components: V, S
Casting Time: 1 standard action
Range: Touch
Target: One undead creature
Duration: Instantaneous
Saving Throw: Will negates
Spell Resistance: Yes

Description

An undead creature under your control, perhaps from a previously cast *animate dead* spell, is destroyed and crumbles to dust.

Spell Effect

The caster is healed 1 point for each hit point the undead creature had remaining, up to his normal hit point maximum. You lose control of the undead target if its Will save is successful.

Entangling Roots

Grass and weeds entangle and constrict the target.

Transmutation
Level: Hlr 3
Components: V, S
Casting Time: 1 standard action
Range: Medium (100 ft. + 10 ft./level)
Target: One creature
Duration: 1 round/level (D)
Saving Throw: Reflex negates
Spell Resistance: No (see text)

Description

Grass and weeds entwine about the target's legs, holding it fast. If there are no plants under the target, the spell automatically creates some.

Spell Effect

The entangled creature suffers a –2 penalty to attack rolls and a –4 penalty to effective Dexterity. The entangled character cannot move. An entangled character who attempts to cast a spell must make a DC 15 Concentration check or lose the spell. An entangled creature can break free, ending the spell, by using a full-round action to make a DC 25 Strength check or a DC 22 Escape Artist check. The roots have an AC of 10 and hp 22.

While entangled, the victim takes 1d4 points of constriction damage per round.

Force of Nature

A tree changes into a treant that fights for the caster.

Transmutation
Level: Drw 6
Components: V, S
Casting Time: 1 round
Range: Touch
Target: Tree touched
Duration: 1 round/level (D)
Saving Throw: None
Spell Resistance: No

Description

This spell turns the tree touched into a treant that will fight on the caster's behalf for a brief period of time.

Spell Effect

Force of nature must be cast on a living, healthy tree. Statistics for a treant can be found in the MM. If *force of nature* is dispelled, the tree takes root immediately, wherever it happens to be. If released by the spellcaster, the tree tries to return to its original location before taking root.

Force of Nature, Greater

Level: Drw 8

As *force of nature*, but this spell can create 1d4+1 individual treants.

Frost Armor

Grants +4 armor bonus to AC and chills attackers.

Conjuration (Creation) [Force]
Level: Sha 2, Sor/Wiz 2
Components: V, S, F/DF
Casting Time: 1 standard action
Range: Touch
Target: Creature touched
Duration: 1 hour/level (D)

Saving Throw: Will negates (harmless)
Spell Resistance: Yes (see text)

Description

A nearly invisible field of force surrounds the subject of *frost armor*. The temperature is noticeably chillier around the subject.

Spell Effect

Frost armor provides a +4 armor bonus to AC. Unlike mundane armor, *frost armor* entails no armor check penalty, arcane spell failure chance, or speed reduction. Since *frost armor* is made of force, incorporeal creatures can't bypass it the way they do normal armor.

Any creature striking the character with its body or with handheld weapons deals normal damage, but at the same time the attacker becomes chilled. If a creature has spell resistance, it applies to the chilling effect. Note that weapons

with exceptional reach, such as two-handed spears, do not endanger their users in this way.

A chilled creature moves and attacks at a drastically slowed rate for 1 round. Chilled creatures can take only a move action or standard action on their next turn, but not both (nor may they take full-round actions). Additionally, they suffer a –2 penalty to AC, melee attack rolls, melee damage rolls, and Reflex saves. Chilled creatures jump half as far as normal.

Focus: Arcane — a small piece of forged steel; divine — the shaman's totem.

Frost Nova

Explosion of cold damages and chills creatures.
Evocation [Cold]
Level: Sha 3, Sor/Wiz 3
Components: V, S, M
Casting Time: 1 standard action
Range: Close (25 ft. + 5 ft./2 levels)
Area: 10-ft. radius spread
Duration: Instantaneous
Saving Throw: See text
Spell Resistance: Yes

Description

A *frost nova* spell is a burst of ice and cold that detonates with a high-pitched shriek.

Spell Effect

Frost nova deals 1d6 points of cold damage per caster level (maximum 10d6) to all creatures within the area of effect; a successful Reflex save halves the damage. Unattended objects also take this damage. The explosion creates almost no pressure.

The caster points a finger and determines the range (distance and height) at which the *frost nova* is to burst. A frozen, pea-sized bead streaks from the caster's finger and, unless it hit a material body or solid barrier prior to attaining the prescribed range, shatters into the *frost nova* at that point (an early impact results in an early detonation). If the caster attempts to send the bead through a narrow passage such as an arrow slit, the caster must "hit" the opening with a ranged touch attack, or else the bead strikes the barrier and detonates prematurely.

Creatures that take damage from the *frost nova* must succeed at a Fortitude save or be chilled for 1d4 rounds. A chilled creature moves and attacks at a drastically slowed rate. Chilled creatures can take only a move action or standard action each turn, but not both (nor may they take full-round actions). Additionally, they suffer a –2 penalty to AC, melee attack rolls, melee damage rolls, and Reflex saves. Chilled creatures jump half as far as normal.

Material Component: A few drops of water and a piece of glass, which must be shattered as the spell is cast.

Healing Rain

A shower of positive energy heals allies, damages undead.
Conjuration (Healing)
Level: Hlr 5
Components: V, S
Casting Time: 1 standard action
Range: 20 ft.
Area: All living allies and undead creatures within a 20-ft. radius centered on the character
Duration: Concentration, up to 1 round/level
Saving Throw: Fortitude half (harmless)
Spell Resistance: Yes (harmless)

Description

Positive energy falls from the sky in the form of scintillating rain.

Spell Effect

Healing rain cures 1d4 points of damage per round to nearby living allies.

Like *cure* spells, *healing rain* damages undead in its area rather than cures them.

Healing Ward

Totem's positive energy heals allies, damages undead.
Conjuration (Healing)
Level: Sha 3
Components: V, S
Casting Time: 1 standard action
Range: 0 ft.
Area: All living allies and undead creatures within a 20-ft. radius burst centered on the totem
Duration: 1 round/level
Saving Throw: Fortitude half (harmless)
Spell Resistance: Yes (harmless)

Description

The caster conjures a magical totem and plants it in the ground.

Spell Effect

The totem immediately begins emanating positive energy that spreads out in all directions from the point of totem, curing 1 point of damage per round to nearby living allies, up to a character's maximum hit points.

Like *cure* spells, *healing ward* damages undead in its area rather than cures them.

The totem can be attacked. It has an AC of 7, hardness of 5, and hp 5. If the totem is destroyed, the spell ends.

Immolation

Flames covering caster damage opponents and protect her from cold-based attacks.

Evocation [Fire]
Level: Sha 4, Sor/Wiz 4
Components: V, S, M
Casting Time: 1 standard action
Range: Personal
Target: You
Duration: 1 round/level (D)
Saving Throw: None
Spell Resistance: Yes (see text)

Description

The caster is wreathed in blue and green flames.

Spell Effect

This spell causes a great deal of heat, inflicting 1d6 points of fire damage each round to all creatures within 5 feet. If a creature has spell resistance, it applies to this damage. The flames give light equal to a sunrod (30 feet).

The flames also protect the caster from cold-based attacks. The character takes only half damage from cold-based attacks. If a cold-based attack allows a Reflex save for half damage, the caster takes no damage on a successful save.

Material Component: A bit of phosphorus.

Lightning Shield

Electricity covering caster damages all nearby creatures.

Evocation [Electricity]
Level: Sor/Wiz 4
Components: V, S, M
Casting Time: 1 standard action
Range: Personal
Target: You
Duration: 1 round/level (D)
Saving Throw: None
Spell Resistance: Yes (see text)

Description

This spell wreathes the character in electricity.

Spell Effect

Lightning shield causes 1d6 points of electricity damage +1 per 5 caster levels each round to all creatures within 5 feet. If a creature has spell resistance, it applies to this damage. The electricity arcing around the caster sheds light equal to that of a torch (20 feet).

Material Component: A steel rod.

Mana Burn

Ray of magical energy causes target to lose spells.

Transmutation
Level: Sor/Wiz 2
Components: V, S
Casting Time: 1 standard action
Range: Close (25 ft. + 5 ft./2 levels)
Effect: Ray
Duration: Instantaneous
Saving Throw: Will negates
Spell Resistance: Yes

Description

A ray of magical energy leaps toward the target, leeching from it the energy necessary to cast one or more spells.

Spell Effect

The caster must make a ranged touch attack to hit. If the attack succeeds, the target loses 1d4+1 spell levels or spell slots, starting with his highest available levels. If the victim runs out of higher-level spells to drain, then two 0-level spells can be drained instead one 1st-level spell. If the victim runs out of slots than can be drained with a given roll, then there is no further effect.

For example, a 3rd-level caster causes the loss of 1d4+1 spell levels. On a roll of 3, the caster would cause 4 spell levels to be lost. If the victim has a 4th-level spell remaining, then it is lost. If the victim has no 4th-level spells, then one 3rd-level and one 1st-level spell are lost. If the victim has only 2nd-level spells remaining, two are lost. If the victim has only a 1st-level spell left, that spell is lost and the extra 3 spells levels of the effect are wasted.

Moonglaive

Conjured moonglaive can strike multiple targets.

Conjuration (Creation) [Force]
Level: Hlr 2, Sor/Wiz 1
Components: V, S
Casting Time: 1 standard action
Range: See text
Effect: One moonglaive
Target: Up to 3 creatures, no 2 of which can be more than 15 ft. apart
Duration: Instantaneous
Saving Throw: None
Spell Resistance: Yes

Description

The caster conjures a magical moonglaive and hurls it at a target within range.

Spell Effect

If the caster is not already proficient with the moonglaive, the caster gains proficiency with the weapon for the spell's duration. The caster must succeed at a ranged attack to hit the first target. The moonglaive is composed of force energy, but is otherwise treated as a normal moonglaive.

If the moonglaive strikes its first target, it bounces off and continues to the caster's second target. The caster makes another ranged attack at the same attack bonus, but with a –2 penalty. If the second target is struck, the moonglaive bounces again to a third target. The caster makes a third ranged attack at the original attack bonus, but with a –4 penalty. If any ranged attack fails,

the moonglaive stops bouncing to successive targets. After 3 hits, the moonglaive automatically dissipates.

Rain of Fire

Meteorites deal impact and fire damage to creatures, ignite and batter objects.

Evocation [Fire]
Level: Sor/Wiz 4
Components: V, S, M
Casting Time: 1 standard action
Range: Medium (100 ft. + 10 ft./level)
Area: Cylinder (20-ft. radius, 40 ft. high)
Duration: Instantaneous
Saving Throw: None
Spell Resistance: Yes

Description

Small meteorites rain from the sky, exploding on impact and burning all in their wake.

Spell Effect

This spell deals 3d6 points of impact and 2d6 points of fire damage to creatures in the area of effect.

The rain sets fire to combustibles and damages objects in the area. It can melt metals with a low melting point, such as lead, gold, copper, silver, or bronze.

Material Components: A chunk of sulfur and a chunk of iron.

Rejuvenation

Subject regains 2d8 hit points per round for spell's duration.

Conjuration (Healing)
Level: Hlr 5
Components: V, S
Casting Time: 1 standard action
Range: Touch
Target: Living creature touched
Duration: 1 round/level
Saving Throw: Fortitude negates (harmless)
Spell Resistance: Yes (harmless)

Description

The subject's wounds heal slowly; cuts close up, bruises fade, and broken bones set themselves.

Spell Effect

This spell does not restore severed body parts; ruined organs do not grow back. After the spell is cast, the subject begins regaining 2d8 hit points per round for the duration of the spell, up to its maximum hit points.

Roar

Caster's great roar gives allies morale bonus to attack and damage.

Enchantment (Compulsion) [Mind-Affecting]
Level: Drw 1
Components: V
Casting Time: 1 standard action
Range: 50 ft.
Area: All allies within 50 ft.
Duration: 1 round/level
Saving Throw: None
Spell Resistance: Yes (harmless)

Description

The caster opens his mouth and lets loose with an earth-shaking roar, filling his allies with courage and strength.

Spell Effect

The caster's allies gain a +1 morale bonus to attack and damage rolls.

Druids of the wild in dire bear form may cast this spell.

Second Soul

Returns subject to life, curing all damage and most poisons and diseases.

Conjuration (Healing)
Level: Hlr 9
Components: V, S, M, DF
Casting Time: 10 minutes
Range: Touch
Target: Living creature touched
Duration: Permanent
Saving Throw: None (see text)
Spell Resistance: Yes (harmless)

Description

The caster creates a second link to bind the subject's soul to the world and restore him to life should he die.

Spell Effect

If the subject dies, it is restored to life 2d4 rounds later in the same spot. The subject's soul must be free and willing to return. If the subject's soul is not willing to return, the spell does not work; therefore, subjects who want to return receive no saving throw. The subject loses a level (or 1 Constitution point, if she is 1st level) when raised.

Second soul cures all hit point damage and ability score damage. Normal poisons and normal diseases are cured in the process of raising the subject, but magical diseases and curses are not undone. The condition of the remains is not a factor. The dead creature's equipment or possessions are untouched by this spell.

A creature that has been turned into an undead creature or killed by a death effect cannot be raised by *second soul*. Constructs, elementals, outsiders, and undead creatures also cannot be raised. The spell cannot bring back a creature that has died naturally of old age.

Coming back from the dead is an ordeal. The subject of the spell loses one level when it is raised, just as if it had lost a level to an energy draining creature. This level loss cannot be repaired by any spell. If the subject is 1st level, it loses 1 point of Constitution instead. A character that died with spells prepared has a 50% chance of losing any given spell upon being raised, in addition to losing spells for losing a level. A character with spellcasting capacity (such as a sorcerer) has a 50% chance of losing any given spell, in addition to losing spells for losing a level.

Material Components: A sprinkle of holy water and diamonds worth a total of at least 20,000 gp.

Sentinel

Magical bird allows caster to scry an area.

Divination
Level: Elr 3
Components: V, S, M
Casting Time: 1 standard action
Range: Close (25 ft. + 5 ft./2 levels)
Effect: Magical sensor
Duration: 1 hour/level
Saving Throw: None
Spell Resistance: No

Description

The caster must target a tree. The caster creates a visible, magical sensor in the form of a bird. The caster chooses the form, but the bird is always Diminutive in size.

Spell Effect

The bird remains stationary where it is cast, though it can move its head. The caster may concentrate on any of its sentinels to view through the bird's eyes and hear through the bird's ears from any distance. The bird sees exactly as the caster would see if the caster were present.

The caster must concentrate to use a sentinel. If the caster does not concentrate, the bird remains motionless until the caster again concentrates. The powers of the sentinel cannot be enhanced by other spells or items (though the caster can use magic to improve her own eyesight). The caster is subject to any gaze attack met by the bird. A successful *dispel magic* cast on the caster or the bird ends the spell. With respect to blindness, magical darkness, and other phenomena that affect vision, the bird is considered an independent sensory organ from the caster. (For example, the bird is not blinded if the caster's normal eyes are blinded.)

Sentinels have a Hide bonus of +7, AC 9, and hp 1. If a sentinel is damaged, it is dispelled. Any creature may notice a sentinel, but even if the Spot check succeeds, a DC 20 Survival check is required to notice that the bird seems artificial. Spells such as *detect scrying* can also detect a sentinel.

Material Component: An owl's feather.

Serpent Ward

Totem releases fireballs at targets within 30 feet.

Conjuration [Fire]
Level: Sha 3
Components: V, S
Casting Time: 1 standard action
Range: 0 ft.
Area: One target/round
Duration: 1 round/level
Saving Throw: Reflex half
Spell Resistance: Yes

Description

The caster conjures a magical totem and plants it in the ground.

Spell Effect

Once planted, the totem immediately begins attacking enemy creatures within 30 feet by hurling small, single-target fireballs. It makes 1 ranged touch attack per round for 1 round per caster level or until the totem is destroyed. The caster may change the totem's current target as a free action each round. The totem is treated as having the Precise Shot feat and its attack bonus is equal to the caster's base attack bonus + the caster's Wisdom modifier. The fireballs each deal 1d6 points of fire damage per 3 caster levels (maximum 5d6).

The totem can be attacked. It has an AC of 7, hardness of 5, and hp 5. If the totem is destroyed, the trap is ruined. The totem automatically disappears after 1 round per caster level.

Shadow Meld

Remaining motionless near shadows, the caster becomes invisible.

Illusion (Glamer)
Level: Sor/Wiz 1
Components: V, S
Casting Time: 1 standard action
Range: Personal
Target: You
Duration: 10 minutes/level (D)
Saving Throw: None
Spell Resistance: No

Description

The caster fades into the shadows, becoming nearly invisible to normal sight.

Spell Effect

After casting the spell, if the caster remains motionless on his next round (does not move, takes a move action, or any standard action such as attacking), then at the end of the round he vanishes from sight, even from darkvision. This effect functions only in light no brighter than a torch's. Sunlight, or a spell that simulates light as bright as the sun's, ruins the effect while the caster remains in the light. When the caster moves or takes a move action, or takes any standard action such as attacking, he becomes visible immediately. If the caster then remains motionless for a round, he again becomes invisible after that round.

If the caster is carrying gear, the gear also vanishes. The caster's allies cannot see him, unless they can normally see invisible things or employ magic to do so; the caster, however, can see himself.

Items dropped or put down by the caster become visible; items picked up disappear if tucked into the clothing or pouches worn by the caster. Light, however, never becomes invisible, although a source of light can become so (thus, the effect is that of a light with no visible source). Any part of an item that the caster carries but that extends more than 10 feet from him becomes visible, such as a trailing rope. Of course, the caster is not magically silenced.

Shockwave

A powerful wave of force shakes the ground and damages creatures.

Evocation [Force]
Level: Sha 3, Sor/Wiz 3
Components: V, S, M
Casting Time: 1 standard action
Range: Close (25 ft. + 5 ft./2 levels)
Area: 10 ft. wide to close range (25 ft. + 5 ft./2 levels)
Duration: Instantaneous
Saving Throw: Reflex negates
Spell Resistance: Yes

Description

The caster stomps on the ground or slams a staff or other weapon into the ground, causing it to shake violently.

Spell Effect

The caster releases a powerful shockwave that deals 1d6 points of force damage per caster level (maximum 10d6) to each creature within its area. The wave begins at the caster's feet and extends along the ground. If the damage caused to an interposing barrier shatters or breaks through it, the wave continues beyond the barrier if the spell's range permits; otherwise, it stops at the barrier. If the ground ends, say at the edge of a cliff, then the wave stops at the edge. Creatures that are not in contact with the ground before the spell is cast do not take damage from the shockwave.

Material Component: A piece of a shattered rock.

Starfall

The caster turns starlight into devastating missiles.

Evocation [Force]
Level: Pre 9, Sor/Wiz 9
Components: V, S
Casting Time: 1 standard action
Range: Close (25 ft. + 5 ft./2 levels)
Targets: One creature/round
Duration: Concentration, up to 1 round/level
Saving Throw: Reflex half
Spell Resistance: Yes

Description

The caster calls down starlight that solidifies into a destructive missile of matter and energy. The missiles appear as searing stars from the air above the targets, rocketing down into them with devastating explosive power.

Spell Effect

For each round the caster concentrates, she targets two creature, structures, or objects with a starlight missile that causes 1d6 points of damage per caster level (maximum 10d6); a Reflex save halves the damage. The caster can target different subjects each round or the same subjects over and over. The caster, however, cannot target the same subject with both missiles at the same time in the same round.

Stasis Trap

Totem explodes and dazes creatures.

Conjuration [Sonic]
Level: Sha 1
Components: V, S
Casting Time: 1 standard action
Range: 0 ft.
Area: All creatures within a 20-ft. radius burst centered on the totem
Duration: See text
Saving Throw: Will negates
Spell Resistance: Yes

168

CHAPTER FOUR

Description

The caster conjures a magical totem and plants it in the ground.

Spell Effect

The totem is visible for 1d4 rounds before turning itself invisible. Once invisible, the totem is active. If an enemy creature moves within 10 feet of the totem within 1 round per caster level, it explodes in a shower of sparks. All enemies caught in the area of effect must succeed at a Will save to avoid being dazed for 1d4 rounds. A dazed creature can take no actions, but it defends itself normally.

The totem can be attacked. It has AC 7, hardness 5, and hp 5. If the totem is destroyed, the trap is ruined. The totem automatically disappears after 1 round per caster level.

Storm Hammer

Caster throws a magical hammer that damages and dazes foes.

Conjuration (Creation) [Force]
Level: Sor/Wiz 2
Components: V, S, M, F
Casting Time: 1 standard action
Range: Close (25 ft. + 5 ft./2 levels)
Effect: One force hammer
Duration: See text
Saving Throw: See text
Spell Resistance: Yes

Description

The caster conjures a magical force hammer and tosses it at the target.

Spell Effect

The caster must succeed at a ranged touch attack to hit the target. The hammer deals 2d4 points of force damage, +1d4 points of force damage per 3 caster levels, and dazes the target for 1 round. (It deals 2d4 at 3rd level, 3d4 at 6th, 4d4 at 9th, 5d4 at 12th, 6d4 at 15th, and finally 7d4 at 18th level.) A dazed creature can take no actions, but it defends itself normally. A successful Fortitude saving throw negates the daze effect.

Material Component: A tiny metal hammer.

Thorn Shield

Thorns cover the target and damage attackers.

Transmutation
Level: Drw 3, Sor/Wiz 3
Components: V, S
Casting Time: 1 standard action
Range: Touch
Target: Creature touched
Duration: 1 round/level (D)
Saving Throw: None
Spell Resistance: Yes (see text)

Description

Tiny thorns pop out of the target's skin, armor, and clothing that cause damage to each creature that attacks the target in melee.

Spell Effect

Any creature striking the target with its body or handheld weapons deals normal damage, but at the same time the attacker suffers 1d6 points of damage +1 point per caster level. If a creature has spell resistance, it applies to this damage. Note that reach weapons such as two-handed spears do not endanger their users in this way.

Touch of Life

Caster brings creature briefly back to life.

Conjuration (Healing)
Level: Hlr 9
Components: V, S, M, DF
Casting Time: 1 round
Range: Touch
Target: Dead creature touched
Duration: 1 round/level
Saving Throw: None (see text)
Spell Resistance: Yes (harmless)

Description

The caster temporarily restores life to a deceased creature.

Spell Effect

The caster can raise creatures who have been dead only up to 1 round per caster level. In addition, the subject's soul must be free and willing to return. If the subject's soul is not willing to return, the spell does not work; therefore, subjects who want to return receive no saving throw.

Upon completion of the spell, the creature is immediately restored to full hit points, vigor, and health, with no loss of level (or Constitution point) or prepared spells. Normal poisons and normal diseases are cured in the process of raising the subject, but magical diseases and curses are not undone. While the spell closes mortal wounds and repairs lethal damage of most kinds, the body of the creature to be raised must be whole. Otherwise, missing parts are still missing when the creature is brought back to life. The dead creature's equipment or possessions are untouched by this spell.

The caster can revive someone killed by a death effect or someone who has been turned into an undead creature and then killed again (essentially, an inanimate body). Constructs, elementals, outsiders, and (animated) undead creatures cannot be raised. The spell cannot bring back a creature that has died of old age.

When the spell expires, the subject immediately drops dead as though it had never been raised.

The original death of the creature is used to determine the time limit for casting this spell. For example, if a 17th-level caster raises a creature on the round after that creature died and the creature is slain again 5 rounds later, the 17th-level caster could cast *touch of life* again any time within the next 12 rounds. If the creature survived to the end of the spell's normal duration (17 rounds in this case), then the 17th-level caster could not cast the spell again because it is now beyond the time limit of the corpse.

Casting this spell does not affect in any way the ability of another caster to use *raise dead*, *resurrection*, or *true resurrection* to restore permanent life to the subject.

Material Component: Diamonds worth a total of at least 5,000 gp.

Unholy Frenzy

Target gains the strength and speed of the undead, but also suffers damage.

Necromancy
Level: Ncr 2
Components: V, S
Casting Time: 1 standard action
Range: Close (25 ft. + 5 ft./2 levels)
Target: One creature
Duration: 1 round, +1 round/2 levels
Saving Throw: Fortitude negates (harmless)
Spell Resistance: Yes (harmless)

Description

The caster grants the target the untiring stamina and energy of the undead.

Spell Effect

The transmuted creature moves and acts more quickly than normal. When making a full attack action, the creature may make one extra attack with any weapon he is holding. The attack is made using the creature's full base attack bonus, plus any modifiers appropriate to the situation. (This effect is not cumulative with similar effects, such as that provided by *haste* or a weapon of speed; nor does it actually grant an extra action, so you cannot use it to cast a second spell or otherwise take an extra action in the round.)

There is a price for the stress this spell places on the creature's physiology, however. The subject suffers 1d4 points of damage each round.

Unholy frenzy is countered and dispelled by *slow*.

METZEN·95

"It's all falling apart," Underchief Boraga said, sprawled on the thick furbolg hides that littered the reception hall of Shargha's Stronghold.

"What's falling apart?" yawned Chieftain Shargha. He did not bother looking up from the maps sprawled on his campaign table.

"The world," Boraga said. "It's all about to tip into the Twisting Nether, you just watch."

Shargha gave a noncommittal grunt and reached for another map. Boraga had a strong sword arm and was as fearless as a troll, but he whined whenever he was not in the thick of action. Still, Shargha found the orc's brooding to be strangely comforting. If he was complaining, at least he was not plotting against his superior.

"Think about it. Wherever we go, things are always falling down on our pointed ears." Boraga pulled himself to his feet and started pacing. "From back in the beginning. We rule an entire world only to see it get swallowed up. We just managed to escape here before it did."

The lout speaks as if he was there, rather than something that happened generations ago. In a calm tone, Chieftain Shargha offered a correction. "Actually, we came here first. And then our leaders at the time, the warlocks, screwed things up so badly that we lost that First World."

Boraga was hardly listening. "So we come to Azeroth, and it gets roughed up by undead and demonspawn."

"Again, I think some orcs were involved somewhere in that as well," Shargha said. "Some of the same warlocks as the first time, to be accurate."

"So we escape again, on ships stolen from humans, and come to Kalimdor — to find ourselves in the middle of another huge war against more undead and demons."

"Which," Shargha said, "we won." He looked at a spot on the map, frowned, then reached for a heavy, bound atlas.

"Aye, but what have we won?" the younger orc steamed. "This is a broken land. There are ruins on top of ruins here. The coasts are littered with half-sunken ships. Petty kingdoms rise and fall like clockwork. Everyone with a sword and three followers wants to make himself Warchief. Fields have been scorched to stubble, livestock slaughtered or gone feral, and most of the buildings here burned down at least once."

"Interesting," Shargha remarked, almost to himself. "This map shows some old stronghold at the headwaters of the river, but later atlases don't show it. Do you know what that means?"

"Exactly what I am saying," Boraga snarled. "This place is a wreck, a mess, a pile of debris. Two steps from the Twisted Nether, with the demons banging on the doors."

Shargha sighed and rose from the table, walking to the window. This level of the stronghold was even with the treetops. He saw a vast green carpet spread out to the base of a line of snowcapped peaks. Somewhere among those peaks were headwaters, and by those headwaters a lost city — Titan ruins, if the map notation was correct, filled with secrets and treasure. Yet all Boraga could do was complain that it had been lost in the first place.

A pillar of smoke rose from the forest, off to the right, about two days' ride away by wolfback — and a mighty blaze, given how easily he could make it out. It could be a natural lightning strike or forest fire, or it could be something worse. Invaders, perhaps, or some battle between forces Shargha knew nothing about. Maybe a funeral pyre. Maybe a chimaera carving out a roost. Maybe dwarves with their steam tanks, on their way to this lost stronghold.

Whatever it was, the fact remained that the blaze was two days' ride away. If it was trouble, it would come soon enough. He would send out extra grunts on evening patrol, just in case.

Aloud, the chieftain said, "Look at the world beyond our windows, Boraga. Here's an ancient world, with old treasures lost among ancient vegetation, fallen cities high within the mountains, and more knowledge lost than even the humans had in the days of Lordaeron. It's a world that is starting anew. What do you see when you look out the window?"

"I see a world that is ruined. That which isn't already ruined is burning, and that which isn't already burning isn't worth having." Boraga snorted. "What do you see?"

"I?" Chieftain Shargha said, his lips twisting around his great fangs in a satisfied smile. "Opportunities, my lad. What I see are opportunities."

CHAPTER FIVE:
THE WORLD OF
WARCRAFT

The Third War was a time rife with shock and surprise. Perhaps as startling as the return of demons to Azeroth was the discovery of an entire continent previously unknown to both the Alliance and the Horde.

Separated from the continent of Lordaeron by the swirling seas of the Maelstrom, the wild land of Kalimdor proved to be the Burning Legion's ultimate destination. The Horde had already come to Kalimdor based on insights from their Warchief, Thrall. The Alliance races, their kingdoms ravaged by the demons' undead minions, followed soon after.

Though rugged and untamed, this new land was far from uninhabited. Orcs, humans, Ironforge dwarves, and high elves encountered night elves, tauren, and other races. Night elves and tauren joined with them to defeat the Burning Legion upon the slopes of holy Mount Hyjal.

After the war, the orcs of the Horde founded their new homeland of Durotar, also on the continent's eastern portion. Not far distant, their newfound allies, the massive yet peaceful tauren, established their own home on the vastness of Thunder Bluff in Mulgore. In the north, night elves struggled with their new mortality as they worked to heal their ravaged homeland.

Victory proved bittersweet for the Alliance races. The humans, Ironforge dwarves, and high elves faced a most perilous journey if they wished to return to Lordaeron. Even if they made it safely past the Maelstrom a second time, little awaited most except ruins and devastation.

The Alliance leader, Jaina Proudmoore, and the rest of the Alliance races remained on Kalimdor — there, like the orcs, to build new cities and establish a new future. Recently, fleets under the command of Jaina's father, Grand Admiral Daelin Proudmoore, arrived from [...] Grand Admiral disputed his [...] orcs desired only peace, [...] tween the races. [...] sided with Thrall [...] ng in Grand Admi- [...] the shattering of his [...] tenuous peace was established between the orc nation of Durotar and the Alliance stronghold of Theramore.

A new era has begun in Kalimdor, but only time will tell if it will end, as always, in war.

Affiliations on Kalimdor

Life is far from peaceful on this new continent. The races' initial settlements lay far enough apart that the different groups seldom encountered one another. Yet each has ventured beyond the confines of its villages for exploration, colonization, diplomacy, trade... and conquest. Increasingly volatile encounters between Alliance and Horde may ultimately shatter the truce established in the Third War.

Also, while the demons of the Burning Legion were defeated, the marks of their passing still scar the landscape. The Scourge, once a tool of the Burning Legion, still stalk the living in some areas. Rumors even claim that not all the demons were destroyed in the Third War.

Despite the tension of strained treaties, the constant danger of encroaching evil, and the mystery of a wild land, members of both the Alliance and the Horde are more hopeful now than ever before in recent memory. Hardened veterans of all races feel that their struggle is no longer a battle for domination but a search for a new destiny.

Alliance

The Alliance is formed of distinct races and sub-races, each with their own interests and agendas. Their dedication to one another seems more out of habit than due to any shared ideals. Rifts occur within the ranks: the races often chafe at sharing the confines of Theramore; night elves and high elves barely tolerate one another; no one really accepts half-elves or half-orcs. These seemingly innocuous grudges sometimes threaten to undermine the Alliance's strength in ways that neither the Burning Legion nor the undead Scourge could achieve.

Although the melting pot of Theramore is stressful and chaotic at times, it serves to keep the Alliance together. Having representatives of each Alliance race on hand allows the authorities to deal with conflicts quickly before they become major diplomatic disasters.

Humans

Though multiple races ostensibly make up the Alliance, the humans founded it and consider themselves first among equals. The same holds true for Theramore, their stronghold on Kalimdor. The humans do not flaunt this assumption too loudly to their fellow Alliance members. They understand the racial strife that permeates the city and wish to act as peacemakers. Sadly, they do not understand that this "big sister" attitude makes the other races resent them even more. Tensions can run high among the Alliance races, but so far a shared dedication to the Alliance has won out when different races and organizations clash.

Jaina Proudmoore led the Alliance to victory in the Third War and continues to lead the humans in the time since. She does not rule alone, however; some of the surviving mages and paladins serve as her advisors — those who remained with her after the betrayal by her father Grand Admiral Proudmoore. These veterans turn their minds to the world of politics and give Jaina the benefit of their experience.

Some hope eventually to return to Lordaeron, but the Maelstrom makes sea travel very risky and there is still much to be done on Kalimdor. The continent offers tremendous potential for all of the Alliance, whether on Kalimdor or back on Lordaeron, and only time may say what kind of relationships may be formed with the many races that share the land.

Unfortunately, there's no telling if the Alliance will even have enough time. The truce established in the aftermath of Grand Admiral Proudmoore's attacks is a fragile one.

Ironforge Dwarves

Many tales paint dwarves as gruff, humorless figures with hearts as cold as the stone of their mountain homeland, Khaz Modan. In truth, if

Magic and the Alliance

Those who study arcane magic and who follow the teachings of the Holy Light found their numbers diminished greatly by the Third War. Not enough wizards are available to open formal schools, nor enough priests and paladin warriors to establish a unified church. Those who wish to learn the ways of the arcane or the Light must find someone with the time and desire to teach.

Mages are eager for apprentices. Not only do they desire to pass along their knowledge to a new generation, but those who do not get formal guidance may look for knowledge elsewhere, including in forbidden lore. Beings have turned to demonic power out of ambition before and always to their downfall.

Priests of the Holy Light welcome any who profess a desire to walk the divine path, while paladin warriors scrutinize any aspirants closely. The Knights of the Silver Hand still feel the sting of Prince Arthas's betrayal. The paladin warriors are careful to confirm the worthiness of those who would join them before passing on their wisdom.

dwarves are stern in combat or in counsel, they are so only because of their dedication to the task before them. Under the proper circumstances, dwarves are quick to joke and are often the stout heart that prevents Alliance forces from becoming demoralized.

Ironforge dwarves long lived comfortably with their role in the world: protecting their mountain fortresses and rising to battle in the name of the Alliance when necessary. Then, dwarven excavations unearthed ruins near Khaz Modan that offered evidence of an ancient race called the titans. Pure-hearted and noble beings who helped shape the world in its earliest days, the titans were also eternal enemies of the demons the Burning Legion. The dwarves scrutin every artifact recovered from Uldaman, h to find ways to protect against the Burn gion. Instead, they found something that changed the dwarven race forever.

If dwarven scholars could believe the translation gleaned from a set of iron disks found among the ruins, the titans had created dwarves — crafting the race from living stone! The revelation shook the dwarven people to the foundation of their deepest beliefs. Some refused to believe the translation from the Disks of Uldaman, while others delved eagerly into this long-hidden heritage. When study awakened within the Ironforge dwarves a unique ability to turn their skin to stone for short periods, even the most stubborn among them relented.

When the Burning Legion invaded Azeroth again, many dwarves answered the call to battle. Finding themselves on Kalimdor after the war ended, they were overjoyed to have a whole new continent to explore. The ruins of Uldaman had set the Ironforge dwarves on a journey of discovery to every portion of the known world, exploring the highest mountain peaks and the tangled depths of jungle valleys. Kalimdor was sure to hold ancient cities and tunnel complexes that the titans might have called home.

Dwarves from the Explorer's Guild soon established the immense excavation site of Bael Modan in the Barrens west of the orc lands of Durotar. Additionally, dwarven explorers wander the land, following up on any rumor of titan ruins or artifacts. Dwarven scholars in Theramore gather each piece of information, no matter how small, that their brethren uncover.

Some are willing to take advantage of the dwarves' quest. The marketplaces of Ratchet overflow with crudely forged "artifacts," and individuals of every affiliation have fashioned maps ... "titan ruins" that they happily turn over for a ... dwarves who discover that they have ... demonstrate that they have ... rtime skills.

... ppy to help with ... in hopes of find- ... pes of discovering ... es argue that some ... n buried, but seldom ... itions. Orcs had long

considered dwarves nothing more than servants to humans, but fighting alongside them in the Third War has generated grudging respect for these "stonechildren." The goblins eagerly provide technological devices to assist the dwarves in their pursuits.

New expedition outposts, from single tents to small villages, are established across Kalimdor almost every week. Some become targets for retribution by natives, fragments of the Horde, and other enemies of the dwarves. Still, the dwarves persevere, firm in their belief that even if they discover nothing more about their past, they have opened the frontier to a future that stretches far beyond the old boundaries of Khaz Modan.

High Elves

This proud race suffered a staggering blow to ego and existence in the Third War when the undead Scourge defiled the high elves' home on Lordaeron. The destruction of Quel'Thalas is just the most recent in a legacy of tragedy for the high elves (or the Quel'dorei, as they call themselves), a legacy that began millennia ago when they could not resist the lure of arcane magic. Their cousins, the night elves, call it an addiction, and the term seems to fit. What path high elves choose in life matters not. Those who do not study magic must nonetheless meditate to replenish their spiritual energies each day to function normally.

The handful of high elves who settled in Theramore wish to return to Lordaeron someday, but the pang of loss is still too fresh. Until they gather the strength to brave the Maelstrom, most high elves channel their grief, shame, and addictive desires into hunting down undead that lurk on Kalimdor. Ironically, battling the undead Scourge often requires magical force, which ends up fueling even more the high elves' thirst for arcane power.

Although they feel they can control the urges, the high elves are not proud of this dependence and take pains to keep it secret. They have grown increasingly introverted and distant from the other Alliance races. Humans always considered elves a bit odd, so this behavior strikes them as

177

nothing more than a little irritating at times. Dwarves are more tolerant yet cautious, sensing the desperation in the high elves. Night elves are just shy of antagonistic to their cousins, knowing from their shared history just how far the Quel'dorei may go to feed the magic addiction. This attitude galls the high elves most of all. The elven peoples diverged 10,000 years ago; in the high elves' opinion, it's time to move on. They know that uncontrolled use of the arcane is dangerous, but they have worked for generations to master the arts. Moreover, arcane magic is clearly essential for eradicating enemies such as undead and demons, so where lies the harm?

Given their circumstances and the growing tension toward other races, the Quel'dorei have discussed privately the idea of establishing their own realm on Kalimdor. The north is most appealing, with its more heavily forested areas… and its mystic moon wells, which sate their magic pangs. That the north also falls primarily under night elf control is frustrating, but high elf expeditions — ostensibly tracking down undead — look for promising sites.

Night Elves

The night elves, or Kaldorei, have lived on Kalimdor for thousands upon thousands of years. They were the first to face the Burning Legion, and that memory remained fresh in their minds when the demons recently returned. Talk of memory is no mere hyperbole, for the night elves were immortal — that is, until they sacrificed much of their mystic power to infuse the World Tree with sufficient energy to defeat the demons.

The destruction that remains in the wake of the Third War, the loss of their immortality, and meeting the Alliance races has caused a significant change in the night elves. Forced to contemplate their own mortality and witnessing how other cultures have developed, the night elves have lost some of their lofty views regarding other races. Yet they retain a healthy ambivalence toward their cousins. The high elves' return showed that they never relinquished their dangerous pursuit of arcane magic. They can claim all they want that it's not a danger, that they can control their power, but the Kaldorei cannot

forget what results from dabbling in the arcane. Few night elves would have a problem with slaying their cousins outright, but for the pledge they made to the Alliance. So they settle for watching the high elves carefully… ready to strike at the first evidence that these slaves to the arcane put them in danger.

The Kaldorei have settled in several areas of northern Kalimdor, notably in Darkshore, along the slopes of Mount Hyjal, and in the forests of Ashenvale. The largest night elf city is their capital, Nighthaven, located in the magical forests of the Moonglade. Their lands suffered damage in the recent war, and they work to restore their cities and the wilderness in which they live. They also continue their efforts to cleanse Felwood. This forest was destroyed in the previous war with the Burning Legion, thousands of years ago. Time has not healed the land; it remains cursed, petrified, and patrolled by monstrous creatures and cursed ancients.

Those Kaldorei not involved directly with healing the land have ventured south, curious to visit the Alliance and even understand the Horde better, fascinated by everything from the strange goods they fashion to their odd customs. The night elves have also seen that their courage in the Third War was not an isolated circumstance. Young the Alliance and Horde may be compared to the Kaldorei, but they show great potential.

Half-elves

Half-elves are not new to the Alliance races, but they are seldom welcome. These unloved beings share traits of both parents, but they can seldom pass for either. They claim that babies born of a high elf and a human were once slain upon birth. No records support this charge — at least, none that survived the destruction of Lordaeron — and high elves and humans deny it. Still, such stories give vent to the half-elves' bitterness at being brought into the world unwanted and unloved, shunned by both of their parents' races.

The half-elf's life involves enduring the distrust and rejection from those she would view as kin. Caught between two cultures and welcomed by neither, and with no society of their own, half-elves spend much of their existence just trying to find their place in the world. Most leave their place of birth as soon as they reach maturity and adopt a nomadic lifestyle. They sometimes find a home within the towns of the Horde, although the culture is so different from elf or human culture that it seldom offers a comfortable fit for long.

They push themselves to excel in whatever their chosen field, whether to hope that success will help them fit in or to spite those who consider them inferior. You will not find a more dedicated priest, a more loyal fighter, or a more studious mage than a half-elf.

That a half-elf will ever serve in a high position in the Alliance is virtually impossible, but their desire for acceptance nonetheless drives many to volunteer whenever the Alliance has a need. They always face the chance that great heroism may give them the acceptance they have wanted all their lives.

While half-elves do not have their own culture, they do share common traits — primarily, insecurity and mistrust. They are often exceedingly grateful to anyone who shows them a kind turn or even the hint of friendship. This desperation can make them easy marks for manipulation — which, in turn, can lead to the other extreme, making them overly suspicious of anyone who shows even a slight amount of kindness. Still, half-elves make the most steadfast of companions once they feel certain that others are genuine in their friendship. Given their bias, half-elves prefer fellow half-breeds as companions, sometimes maintaining friendships with other half-elves or half-orcs even when they cannot stand the other individual.

Horde

Once an engine of destruction in the service of the Burning Legion, the Horde has changed significantly since it first burst through the Dark Portal onto the world of Azeroth. The once unstoppable juggernaut now serves as a loose coalition of orcs, tauren, and a handful of other allies dedicated to survival and prosperity rather than conquest.

This is not to say that the Horde lost its will to fight with the Archimonde's destruction. The Horde responded aggressively to Grand Admiral Proudmoore's recent attack on Durotar, and it keeps a wary eye turned to Alliance lands. Still, its focus is on its own expansion. The mighty war drums remain silent for the time being, but dutiful peons keep the skins well oiled. Orc patrols are a common sight, as grunts ferret out quilboar camps that stray too close to Horde towns and flush out harpy nests situated along trade routes. Tauren warriors battle the centaur tribes with increasing regularity, driving away their ancestral enemies with the help of their new allies from beyond the ocean. Should the Horde find itself in need of land or resources, it will encounter little trouble in marshaling the strength to take what is necessary.

The leaders of each race — Thrall of the orcs and Cairne Bloodhoof of the tauren — have worked out a coalition between their races. Thrall serves as warchief to the orcs, with Cairne the chieftain of all the tauren tribes. In theory, both hold the same rank, but in practice Thrall often requests Cairne's counsel in matters of state while the tauren defers to the orc in matters of war.

Orcs

The orcs of Draenor were once known as "the green plague" and "the Bane of Azeroth." Sworn to the service of the Burning Legion, the orcs burst onto the world of Azeroth in a howling flood. Clashes with the human nations fueled their bloodlust. They chased their foes across the sea, where defeat in Lordaeron shocked them to the core. Few offered resistance as they were corralled and sent to internment camps. Divorced from their shamanistic heritage and suffering withdrawal from the demon-inspired bloodrage, most captive orcs entered a fugue state that left them listless and weak-willed. Then Thrall took the mantle of both warchief and spiritual leader. The orcs reconnected with their spiritual heritage and followed Thrall across the seas, braving the danger of the Maelstrom to start a new life on a new continent.

The orcs' return to their shamanistic roots revived a cultural sense of individuality and elicited ardent pledges to rely upon none but themselves. The courage of the orc people in the Third War, ending with Archimonde's defeat at Mount Hyjal, gave them a sense of triumph over the foul demons who had used them as unwitting dupes.

In the aftermath of war, the orcs founded the nation of Durotar. They remain ever vigilant for the Burning Legion's foul influence from within while keeping a watchful eye on their borders. Never again will the last sons and daughters of Draenor allow another to take away their land or their freedom.

Orc society functions much as it always has, although tempered now by a spiritual reawakening and altered by certain changes that Thrall has instituted. Gone is the clan structure and chieftainships of the Horde — all the old chieftains are dead anyway — and now women are viewed as equals, able even to become warriors.

Strength and tenacity determine an orc's lot in life, with the strongest and most dedicated attaining positions of greatness regardless of gender or lineage. While physical strength and martial prowess are prized, strength of wit, character, and spirit are equally important to a well-rounded orc. Life as an orc involves one's strengths and applying them where the Horde needs them most.

Orcs consider weakness a liability that affects the Horde as a whole. They quickly — perhaps overzealously — stamp out "expressions of failure." The truly unmotivated and the inept are saddled with grueling scutwork, and failure to pull one's own weight at this lowest rung of orc society results in exile from the Horde.

The Battle of Mount Hyjal left many orcs with the sense that debts of blood and honor are paid and that future dealings with the humans start with the slate wiped clean — until the Grand Admiral's fleet arrived. Still, with that conflict settled, Thrall believes in Jaina Proudmoore's sincerity enough to discourage outright battle between orc tribes and Alliance forces. Despite such cautions, skirmishes are not uncommon.

Tauren

A tauren tribesman's life is often arduous, but he meets bleak times with a toothy grin and daily veneration of the Earth Mother for his continued existence. Somber past-chants recount the hundreds of mighty tauren tribes that once called Kalimdor home, but the tribes' numbers have dwindled to a handful. Centuries of protracted conflict with centaur clans leave the tauren a pale shadow of their former might, but none begrudge history's capricious path for their misfortune. The tauren endure with the strength of their commitment to tribe, integrity, and the Earth Mother's grace.

Personal honor and pride in one's self are the hallmarks of the tauren. Their history is relatively short compared to Kalimdor's other races. Ancient accounts suggest they were the result of magical experiments that fused titan with beast, but details are lost to the ages. Unlike the dwarves with their frenzy to dig up their past, the tauren are content with the present. For, in truth, the past is always with them in the veneration of their ancestors.

All tauren histories name the centaur clans as their ancestral enemies. No quarter is asked or given on the battlefield, although the peace-loving tauren refrain from slaughtering those unable to defend themselves. The centaur, it should be noted, do not limit themselves in a similar way.

The Horde's timely arrival on Kalimdor revitalized tauren society. The orcs seek answers to questions of spirit, and the tauren are more than willing to share their divine experiences with their new allies. Many tauren feel a great responsibility to lead the orcs along the path of spiritual maturity. Orc youths may even study under tauren spirit singers, treated as younger siblings to the tauren as they walk the path of the prophets.

The tauren position on the Alliance is more complicated. Though they recognize the human-dominated forces as former blood enemies of the orcs, they are not quick to share hatred. Most prefer a cautious approach to the steel-clad strangers from across the sea.

Independent Factions

Some races on Kalimdor swear allegiance to neither the Alliance nor the Horde. Once servants of the Horde, the goblins have proven themselves to be a major independent power on Kalimdor. Though many heed the example set by their parents, half-orcs are fiercely self-reliant and often follow their individual whims to join whatever faction suits them.

Other intelligent races can be found across Kalimdor, from the savage centaur to the powerful dragons. Yet these races still run wild and seemingly want little to do with the new arrivals. Whether they will ally themselves with the Alliance, the Horde, or no particular faction at all remains to be seen.

Goblins

Some questions are debated endlessly by friends over a tankard of ale. A tavern favorite is, "How in the name of the Holy Light did goblins come to be a race of any importance?"

Goblins came to dubious fame in the First and Second Wars for the suicide missions they undertook for the Horde, strapping explosives to themselves and floating behind enemy lines with the aid of an inflated sheep's bladder. In the aftermath of conflict, the goblins established that they had no political orientation. Their only real interest was trade: if you had the coin for their goods, they were your friends. Such neutrality gives them as broad a trading basis as possible for their wares, from magic items to mundane goods to their own mechanical inventions.

Though once nothing but fodder for more taproom banter, goblin inventions have shown their worth in recent years. Whether clockwork "shredders" that allow a single goblin to do as much harvesting as 10 field hands or zeppelin-like "airships" that can ferry troops over otherwise impassable terrain, the goblins' inventions have become legendary. Such technological ingenuity is as central to the goblins' rise among the races as any trading prowess.

The goblins are also legendary for the sheer variety of trade in which they are willing to indulge and for their tenacity in bargaining.

Goblins rarely let an item slip from their shelves for a single copper less than it is worth. Ratchet, on the east coast of Kalimdor, is easily the largest and best known of the goblin trading posts, but it is far from the only one. The industrious goblins have established shacks and minor trading towns across much of Kalimdor in an impressively brief span of time. These outposts may vary in size and location, but all have a similarly impressive array of goods. The outposts get regular supply shipments (or as regular as possible, given the hazards of travel across Kalimdor), all coordinated by the goblin trade princes.

On the whole, the Alliance and the Horde respect the goblins' new power, taking advantage of the trade princes' ability to produce or procure otherwise difficult-to-acquire items. Rumors have emerged of goblins engaging in massive strip mining and deforestation operations to harvest the raw materials, however, which cause the nature-loving night elves and tauren great concern. Since the tales have surfaced, the trade princes have suffered guerilla attacks on their supply trains and sabotage of their factories. The goblins are clever enough to know the list of suspects is a short one, and they appear undaunted by the threat. They have amassed enough wealth to hire additional security for their mercantile concerns.

Yet goblins are not purely mercenary. They are known to form strong bonds with individuals of other races. Their small forms and odd behavior make other races — elves in particular — ill at ease, but goblins do not seem to care much for the impression they make. They judge by deeds, befriending those who treat them as friends and standing apart from those who would offer them abuse.

Even with the malfunctions and explosions that occur (not as frequent as tavern chatter suggests, but far from rare), goblin technology is proving to be of a quality that rivals the dwarves and their firearms. If they possessed physical strength and mystic power to match their inventiveness and cunning, they would be a force of some significance. Of course, the goblins claim that they are already — if not for their frail physical forms, goblins would rule the world.

Then they laugh and say they prefer a challenge and offer to buy the taproom guests the next round.

Half-orcs

During the many battles fought between orcs and humans, half-orcs were usually the unfortunate product of invading orc (and occasionally human) armies. The orc internment after the Second War produced a marked rise in half-orc births. Many were a result of a harsh existence, but some were actually the outcome of surreptitious love between human guards and orc prisoners.

Half-orcs have a marginally easier time finding acceptance than half-elves do. They find themselves in the unwelcome position of needing to prove themselves repeatedly simply because of what they are. Humans offer a grudging tolerance to those who show that they are not victims of base orc urges, while orcs accept the half-breeds who distinguish themselves as superior warriors or shamans.

The road to success for half-orcs in the Alliance is fraught with obstacles. For example, no Alliance laws keep half-orcs from becoming titled knights, but any half-orcs who aspire to this lofty goal must work three times as hard as their human companions — while avoiding being passed over on technicalities that the worst human aspirants would never suffer. Those who persevere can achieve incredible deeds, but such constant striving has broken more than one half-orc's spirit.

Half-orcs are welcomed more easily into orc society, but the fit is still not perfect. By and large, the Horde believes that orc blood, even that which mingles with the "weak" blood of humans, is still fundamentally orc blood. Half-orcs living within the Horde, however, suffer some of the same limitations as in the Alliance, albeit for entirely different reasons. Because so much of orc society involves the application of strength, and because full-blood orcs are typically tougher and stronger, half-orcs must work much harder and much longer to achieve what comes more naturally to most orcs. Those of quick wit are welcomed in other roles, but with the Horde's emphasis on martial prowess, the difficulty in rising to prominence often serves as a great discouragement to the half-orc populace.

The more determined half-orcs are often the most dangerous, for they are willing to do just about anything to garner acceptance — or dominance — among their peers.

Regions of Kalimdor

Much of this large continent remains wild, free of all but the most rudimentary exploration or colonization. This situation offers plenty of room for adventure — whether it's rooting out a Scourge nest from Darkshore, repelling a centaur warband in Desolace, or prowling after a warlock through ruins in the Barrens.

Thieves and brigands have established entire colonies in the middle of nowhere, sending out their thugs for robbery or hire. Demon cults practice outlawed arcane magic with very little to stop them. Monsters emerge from the wilderness to prey upon the weak and unwary. Adventuring in Kalimdor can be dangerous indeed, but it can also be rewarding and fulfilling for those heroes looking for fame, wealth or to vanquish the legacies of evil left behind by the Burning Legion.

History offers a quick overview of a region's past.

Geography explains where the region is located and what it's like physically. See "Wilderness Adventures" in Chapter 3: Writing Adventures of the *DMG* for specifics on the different terrain types listed with the various entries.

Inhabitants describes any significant presence of Alliance, Horde, and/or independent races, as well as creatures of note common to that region. The **Manual of Monsters** sourcebook or the MM have complete information on races or monsters not already listed in this book.

Areas of Interest offers a selection of noteworthy cities and/or locales known to inhabitants of Kalimdor. There are certainly more places to explore than those described here — but that's what your campaign is for, right?

Ashenvale Forest

History

Ashenvale is a vast primordial wilderness long given over to beasts and nature's savage ways. The night elves who settled on Kalimdor after the Cataclysm hunted in the Ashenvale's wilds but never settled within its borders. When the Burning Legion invaded in the Third War, the night elves ceased even hunting in order to battle the demons. The lack of hunting has allowed many creatures once more to live and thrive within the vast woodland, creating danger for all who venture into the forest.

Geography

Terrain Type: Dense to medium temperate forest.

Ashenvale Forest runs in a great arc south of Mount Hyjal, with the Stonetalon Mountains to the southwest and the Barrens directly south. The ruined lands of Azshara lie across a river to the east.

Ashenvale is an old forest, with growth long untouched by any mortal race. The weather is fairly mild, though rain is almost constant. The woods are so old and thickly grown that only trickles of precipitation get through the thick canopy.

The forest has become ever wilder since left to its own devices after the start of the Third War. Any roads through it are overgrown, some even impassable. In contrast, the game trails see increased traffic as beasts living in the shelter of the massive trees grow in number and boldness. Those traveling through Ashenvale will wisely keep their guard up at all times.

Inhabitants

In addition to bears and great cats prowling the dense woodlands, hulking beak-faced wildkin forage throughout Ashenvale. Vicious harpies are known to make massive nests in the tops of the tallest trees. They hunt at dawn and dusk when the light filtering through the canopy throws the forest into a confusion of shifting shadows. Ancients — sentient trees who act as wardens of the forest — roam the Ashenvale as well.

Ashenvale is under the protection of the ancients and the night elf sentinels. Neither has established a community as such within the forest, though, preferring to leave the vast woodlands in its natural state. Travelers through Ashenvale should treat these forces with respect, especially if they hope to reach their destination.

The ancients and night elf sentinels guard Ashenvale zealously with constant patrols. Any who threaten the forest — cutting down live trees, poaching beasts of the forest, and the like — are met with the ancients' powerful attacks and the sentinels' deadly arrows.

The only unified night elf presence dwelling in Ashenvale is a reclusive group of rangers. The Farstriders use the terrain and other inhabitants to train in their specialized skills. They hold a difference of opinion regarding strangers in Ashenvale. Some believe that their duty is to welcome and protect travelers, as long as they show no threat to the forest. Others see any strangers as unwelcome interlopers who must be "escorted" to the southern border. Still, whatever their opinion on Ashenvale, the Farstriders bow to the wishes of the ancients and the sentinels.

There is little reason to try to take the forest, since it has no cities to invade and no treasures to plunder (that anyone knows of), but the rangers and the ancients remain vigilant nonetheless.

logistical difficulties in transporting the gold from the mine and to frequent encounters with beasts of the woods, including outraged Farstriders. Animals have since started using the excavated tunnels for shelter.

Shrine of Aessina: Built ages ago by the night elves, this ancient shrine to the wilderness spirit Aessina lies in the midst of a forest glade in Ashenvale's heart. The shrine is a clear forest pool with a statue of Aessina standing beside it, clothed only in ivy. Dryads are known to visit the shrine to venerate Aessina.

Windshear Pass: Along the southern border of Ashenvale lies the entrance to Windshear Crag. The winding path leads from the wilds of the primordial forest into the stormy canyons of the Stonetalon Mountains, where harpies roost.

Azshara

History

Before the great Sundering, this shattered stretch of coast along Kalimdor's northern border was once part of the night elves' capital of Zin-Azshari. Then came the demons' expulsion from the world. The land was rent asunder and the sea thundered in, making the region into a watery grave and leaving naught but ruins of the once great city. The night elves who survived named this region — once glorious, now nothing but a shattered relic — Azshara, after their queen driven mad by demon influence.

Since that time, this place of rocky islands, jagged cliffs, and coral-choked seas has given birth to many tales. Some night elves suggest that not all of the demons were banished, lurking even now beneath the glittering waters of the Coral Sea and awaiting the time to strike back. Others claim that Queen Azshara was not drowned, but transformed into a hideous aquatic thing who will someday lead her accursed followers to retake the surface world. A few whisper that the Dark Portal that first brought the demons to Azeroth yet remains and rests under the sea waiting for someone to reopen it. Still others assert that the ancient Sundering awakened something that dwelled in the deepest part of the ocean, something that will eventually burst forth

Areas of Interest

Ashenvale boasts no cities; the old forest's inhabitants are primarily beasts, and there are few humanoid settlements. It is devoid of any notable ruins.

Farstrider Camp: Night elf rangers created this outpost from several large trees that were hollowed out and attached by suspension bridges. The night elves maintain regular trade with their people in Nighthaven.

Goldcrease Mine: Orcs mined this site in eastern Ashenvale not long after settling on Kalimdor. They since abandoned it due to the in a tidal wave of destruction. Whatever the truth, night elves agree that the region is cursed.

Geography

Terrain Type: Temperate aquatic (nonflowing water) and rugged hills.

The coastal region of Azshara lies east of Ashenvale Forest and north of Durotar.

A river separates the primordial wood from what land there is. The terrain beyond the river is little more than a strip of green above fragmented cliffs that rise high over a stretch of ivory beach. The waves of the shallow Coral Sea sweep against this beach, and islands — little more than spires of jagged rock — jut from the water. A twisted expanse of reef creates a labyrinth of coral beneath the ocean surface, making sea travel here virtually impossible.

Inhabitants

The night elves consider the place cursed, and most other races find the constant storms unpleasant. There is but a single known habitation in Azshara, the orc trading village of Grim Ulang, its residents telling of creatures flitting about the ruins of Zin-Azshari further along the cliffs and murlocs and naga swimming in the Coral Sea. Bands of undead have appeared along the beach and at the fringes of the Ashenvale Forest. As well, the dark chants of demon cultists have echoed along the cliffs in counterpoint to the thunder of storms. Steady rumors and sightings have led to frequent night elf patrols and an increased martial presence in Grim Ulang.

Areas of Interest

Coral Sea: This shallow sea is home to an abundance of fish and underwater plants that illuminate the brilliant waters, creating an eerily beautiful contrast to the storm clouds that often loom over the area. The labyrinthine coral reef that gives the sea its name makes boating impossible; however, the reef has vast stretches that lie close to the surface, and even some portions that lie exposed. Only the brave (or foolhardy) would attempt travel along the coral, especially since murlocs and naga are known to attack those who venture away from shore.

Grim Ulang: This Horde outpost was established to compete with goblin merchants. It offers goods and weapons for everyone from dwarven explorers to high elves hunting undead.

Ruins of Zin-Azshari: The cataclysm caused most of this ancient city to crumble to the oceans below. A cluster of ruins clings to the eastern cliffs, long shunned by night elves. More recently, treasure hunters and dwarf exploration teams have made tentative forays into the ruins. They have consistently been repelled by ferocious bands of naga who appear to have claimed Zin-Azshari for their own.

The Barrens

History

The vast region now known as the Barrens was once a thriving forest under the protection of the night elves and their kind. Then came the Burning Legion and the great Sundering, which shook

ancient Kalimdor to the bedrock. This forested landscape transformed into a scorched plain is battered now each day by the sun's rays.

Geography

Terrain Type: Hot rugged hills, plains (grassland), some rocky desert and rugged mountains.

The Barrens is a sprawling and arid savannah that stretches between the Stonetalon Mountains to the west and Durotar to the east. The grasslands and mesas of Mulgore rise to the southeast, while the wetlands of Dustwallow Marsh lie to the southwest.

The majority of the region consists of vast plains. Mountains to the west hold in a mass of air heated constantly into swirling winds that rage across the plains. These windstorms stir up dust devils and tear apart anything larger than the small but tenacious scrub trees. Water is more valuable than gold in the Barrens, and the loca-tions of hidden watering holes are among the residents' most closely held secrets. Dry riverbeds and a never-ending spider web of canyons make any journey across the Barrens a dangerous and winding trek.

Inhabitants

Before the upheaval, several large Kaldorei cities stood here. Now, those brave few willing to scrape out a life on the arid plains inevitably run afoul of centaur warbands or quilboar raiding parties. Despite its often uninviting terrain and hostile inhabitants, the Barrens receive a good deal of interest from Alliance and Horde alike, as well as races native to Kalimdor. Trade routes crisscross the landscape leading to and from more inviting regions, most notably the Gold Road that runs north-to-south through the Barrens and beyond, and rumors suggest that precious minerals and ruins await those with the courage to investigate.

Centaur warbands are most often seen in the Barrens' canyons, though they roam as far as the river that forms its eastern border with Durotar. Fearlessly aggressive, the centaur are known for their savagery, especially against tauren and night elves. They are not above attacking trade caravans also, for the goods or just for the sake of violence. Travelers who survive the centaur's battle lust are used as slave labor in the hardscrabble mines the centaur carve into the hard-baked earth.

Displaced from Durotar by orcs, quilboar have built crude villages along the river that separates the orc nation from the Barrens. From there, they strike out across the river to raid settlements or deeper into the Barrens to attack caravans along the Gold Road. The caravan raids have hurt the goblin trade princes' profits, so they have started negotiations to pay the quilboar gold and goods to protect caravans against centaur warbands.

The quilboar have also erected a fortress called Razorfen Downs in the northwestern Barrens. Razorfen is a sprawling mass of giant, twisting thorns and crude mud huts. It serves as the center of quilboar society.

Other dangers include harpies who watch from perches atop mesas in the northern Barrens and large beasts such as lions and thunder lizards — though these creatures tend to avoid the Gold Road.

Native dangers have not stopped the Ironforge dwarves from establishing a stronghold near the titan excavation site of Bael Modan. The centaur have made forays against it, but were repelled decisively each time. Scouts claim that the centaur are amassing other tribes to launch a major attack, but the dwarves are unconcerned. Each day that passes sees Bael Modan grow stronger as the inhabitants build up its defenses and new dwarves and some other Alliance members come to settle.

Areas of Interest

Bael Modan: The largest settlement in the central Barrens is marked by the sturdy stone walls and guard towers blocking the mouth of a cavern into the mountain that the Ironforge dwarves have named Bael Modan — "the red mountain." An encampment just inside the wall offers shelter to Alliance caravans and travelers crossing the Barrens. The stores of food and supplies at Bael Modan are a tempting target to centaur warbands and quilboar raiders, but thus far the dwarves' trusty rifles and mortars have proven more than able to withstand such attacks.

Behind a second wall is the largest dwarven archeological dig in all of Kalimdor. Nearly a thousand dwarves dig around the clock to uncover the most significant set of titan ruins discovered since Uldaman on the continent of Lordaeron. Travelers are welcome in Bael Modan, but not within the titan ruins. Few non-dwarves ever receive such an honor. The Ironforge dwarves are otherwise forthcoming with hospitality, offering a meal and a place to sleep and asking only a good tale in return. Still, dwarven riflemen patrol the streets and keep a close eye on all visitors, fearful of thieves so close to titan artifacts.

Those who visit discover that the dwarves have not forgotten their traditional weapons since the invention of gunpowder. The dwarves of Bael Modan have established a midwinter tournament, with the highest prizes — elaborate bronze helms — given to those most skilled with the axe and the hammer.

The Circle of Dust: In the heart of the Barrens is a deep, semi-circular canyon the centaur call the Circle of Dust. The centaur gather on the rim of the Circle to watch the dust devils roll in off the savannah, believing that the earth writes their destinies in the whirling sand. They also believe that the earth can be appeased with offerings and throw gold and jewels into the dust devils as they collapse into the canyon. The accumulated offerings have proved nearly irresistible to passing orcs and goblins, although most potential thieves are caught by the centaur, who behead the intruders and post their heads around the rim of the Circle of Dust as a warning.

The Field of Giants: In the south Barrens, near the Thousand Needles, spreads an open plain where termites have constructed hundreds of mounds, some towering more than 60 feet tall. The tops of these spires are popular perches for lions that keep watch over the surrounding terrain and prey upon those passing below. The misshapen mud pinnacles take the vague form of giants, hence the name.

Centaur consider this a holy place, with tribes making regular journeys to leave totems upon the field. A popular sport among young tauren involves stealing these centaur offerings and even leaving insulting icons in their place.

The Gold Road: This trade route is named for the trade caravans that travel regularly along the highway from Ratchet in the south all the way to Nighthaven in the north.

Ratchet: Built from equal parts of industry and decadence, the goblin port city of Ratchet sprawls along nearly a mile of coastline where the eastern Barrens poke between Durotar and Dustwallow Marsh to the sea. Ratchet is the pride of the goblins, a trade city where you can find almost anything your heart desires — and if something is not in stock, you can bet the goblins can order it. Ratchet also has regular ferries that traverse the safe though roundabout route to the island stronghold of Theramore to the south. See the "Ratchet, City of the Trade Princes" sidebar for more information.

Shady Rest: This inn is a welcome sight for weary travelers taking the Gold Road. Though no shade can be found here, a day's travel south of Ashenvale, the inn is built next to a deep natural well and is popular for its soft beds, warm meals, cold drinks, and standing garrison that protects against centaur or quilboar raids. Minstrels have immortalized the Shady Rest's proprietor in the chorus of a ballad: *"He'll bring you mead, he'll bring you beer / A grinning face from ear to ear / He's served us all from year to year / We call him Smiling Jim."*

Ratchet, City of the Trade Princes

Ratchet is a city where creatures who were once the butt of jokes now reign supreme. Its streets wander without rhyme or reason through neighborhoods dedicated to one activity: commerce. Ramshackle warehouses stand next to stately stone homes. Fine shops press cheek to jowl with rude huts. Wares of every type imaginable — and some beyond the imagination — are on display in markets and in exclusive boutiques.

Ratchet is run by a corporate group known as the Venture Company, a collection of greedy entrepreneurs who keep both eyes on the bottom line at all times.

Goblins welcome anyone with gold or items of value and a willingness to trade them for their wares and services. Merchants throng the marketplaces each day, selling everything from silks to slaves, and even at night the stores lining the twisting streets and alleys remain open for business. Those with the money can listen to skilled musicians while drinking fine ales and eating food prepared by expert chefs. For those with earthier tastes, the streets along the wharf teem with whorehouses, taprooms, and casinos.

In addition to commerce, Ratchet hosts a series of arenas that sponsor gladiatorial tournaments. These enormously popular tourneys are open to all comers, and winners can reap enormous prizes. The princes of the Golden Circle often hire those who distinguish themselves in the arenas, either as bodyguards or as caravan escorts.

Ratchet is the largest port on Kalimdor, with as many ships bringing cargo in as there are ships heading out for other sites around Kalimdor. In addition to legitimate trade vessels, pirate craft receive amnesty while in the port of Ratchet as long as they can pay the stiff docking fees. This situation makes many merchant captains furious, but they cannot hope to stay in business if they boycott Ratchet. Moreover, the Lawkeepers and hired mercenaries prowling the waterfront are eager to deal with anyone looking to cause trouble.

The skies above Ratchet are almost as busy as the harbor, full of goblin zeppelins, dwarf flying machines, and other aerial contraptions. The aircraft provide merchants and travelers with quick airborne transport to anywhere in Kalimdor — though when the regular cargoes of the trade princes need to be bumped, stiff premiums are charged well above the normally high cost of such a service.

Yeah, But It's a Dry Heat

The central lands of Kalimdor — from Durotar on the east coast through the Barrens and Mulgore and on down to Desolace in the southwest — are a rough place and not just because of the inhabitants. Large areas contain no established civilization and have an arid climate. The heat and lack of water sources can kill as quickly as a fall from Stonetalon Peak. The temperature in Desolace and the Barrens can reach up to 130°F in the summer. Mulgore and Durotar are a little more temperate, but no more merciful to those foolish enough to travel without an adequate water supply and protection from the elements.

In the summer months especially, battling the heat in central Kalimdor presents as much of a challenge as fighting off a centaur warband. Heroes will quickly find themselves in dire straits if they do not take adequate precautions when traveling across the arid landscape. Some basic tips include:

Do not travel when the sun is high. The sun bakes the land throughout the day, but the heat starts to dissipate when the sun is lowering in the western sky. Night ranges from humid in the south near the Dustwallow Marsh to chilly in the dry desert near the Stonetalon and Thousand Needles ranges. Mornings lose any chill quickly, but they are still bearable for a few hours after sunrise. Travel unprotected from late morning through mid-afternoon, though, and you will be subject to the full force of the sun.

Bring more water than you think you need. On average, you should drink 8 quarts of water per day in a hot climate. The heat can leach fluids from your body after just a couple hours — and by the time you feel dried out, dehydration is already well advanced.

Make a DC 15 Fortitude save every 4 hours your character does not ingest water in a hot climate during the day (the DC increases by 2 for every 4 consecutive hours). Failure means heat exhaustion has set in: the character moves at half speed and takes a –6 penalty to Strength and Dexterity. When suffering heat exhaustion, a DC 18 Fortitude save is required each hour. On a failed save, the character falls unconscious from heat stroke.

Finding cover out of the sun allows the character to become merely fatigued after 1 hour (cannot run or charge and suffers a –2 penalty to Strength and Dexterity) and eliminates the need to roll for heat stroke.

Ingesting water after heat exhaustion has begun re-sets the 4-hour timeframe, but does not negate any effects of heat exhaustion or fatigue your character may suffer already.

See "General Guidelines and Glossary" in the *PHB* or "Condition Summary" in Chapter 8 of the *DMG* for specifics on being exhausted, fatigued, and unconscious.

Most visitors, however, do not know that the standing garrison is secretly Quarvel's Raiders, bandits who attack Horde caravans traveling on the Gold Road.

Southsea Freebooters: This small fleet of goblin pirates has no landward home — at least none that the authorities have found — but it is a common sight along the coast of the Barrens and in the free port of Ratchet. These scoundrels are just one of a number of pirates who roam the trade routes from Darkshore to Theramore in search of fortune and plunder.

Tidus Stairs: A half-day's travel north of Ratchet is the coastal fishing village of Tidus. The town is unremarkable except for the set of ancient stone stairs that extend from the beach and vanish beneath the waves. Local legend says that they descend to a Kaldorei city that fell into the ocean after the collapse of the first Well of Eternity. Adults and children of the village dive down as deep as they can manage, but thus far none has found anything but a continuing staircase.

Darkshore

History

After the Sundering, some night elves settled in the continent's northern reaches, on and near Mount Hyjal, including this port at the mountain's northern foot. The night elves left Darkshore in the course of the Third War, moving to the safety of Mount Hyjal and the Moonglade.

A small number of night elves has returned to the cold and desolate beach to revive the port. They dwell in the village of Auberdine and currently use it as a ferry outpost. The remainder of the seaside is left in ruins.

Geography

Terrain Type: Temperate aquatic (nonflowing water), medium forest, and forbidding mountains.

Darkshore covers northwestern Kalimdor. The tainted land of Felwood rises toward Mount Hyjal to the south.

The rocky cliffs, sandy soil, and ever-present sea mist ensure that little worth noting grows in Darkshore. Kelp, seaweed, and rocks litter the beaches, and a few sparse trees dot the landscape away from the beach.

Once a thriving night elf settlement, it is now little more than a desolate beach dotted with ruined buildings. The weather is cold and stormy much of the time, with a wicked wind stirring up the waves. Rain and fog are prevalent for a good part of the year, allowing only the most talented sailors to navigate the dangerous waters. Shipwrecks of the less talented litter the shallower waters and beach.

The night elves currently living in Darkshore have focused their attention on rebuilding Auberdine. Most of the town is made of new buildings, as the night elves cleared away the ruins they could not restore. Many ruins remain outside Auberdine, and harsh winds and salt water continue to corrode the once sturdy buildings. These worn pillars and crumbling structures are not totally abandoned — stories abound that murlocs and naga are slowly taking the ruins for their own.

Inhabitants

The night elves have a limited presence in Darkshore. They spend much of their time keeping the area directly around the port town of Auberdine safe. The night elves subsist mainly on what they can catch in the ocean and what they can get through trade.

When not fighting one another, naga and murlocs that lurk elsewhere in the ruins of Darkshore attack any travelers who look like easy picking.

Furbolgs inhabit a series of caves beneath the port. Uncultured but friendly to night elves in the past, their time in the ruins has turned many of them feral.

Areas of Interest

Auberdine: Auberdine is the sole warm haven amid the desolate land of Darkshore. The oppressive weather and the creatures that lurk in the shadows make much of Darkshore inhospitable, but this thriving trading post is a safe place for heroes to restock and rest. The town has about 200 residents, mostly night elves. Visitors can stop at the Fish Eye Tavern for a hot bite to eat, purchase supplies at Tassik's Tradepost, or, if they have the knack for sailing, rent a skiff at Syran's Boat House. Residents are quite outgoing for night elves and free with advice, whether offering tips on sailing or advising on travel through Darkshore. Auberdine is also one of the very few night elf settlements that will tolerate a high elf's presence.

Auberdine is a small town with little to defend except a safe way of life. The residents' jovial demeanor is but a thin veneer covering a grim determination to protect their homes. There are few armed forces in a military sense, but local scouts and rangers serve as a ready militia and are prepared to defend their quiet hamlet to the death.

Black Fathom Bay: On the northernmost side of Darkshore lies Black Fathom Bay, an area of harsh, salty marshes. It is uninhabited but for the rare trapper and woodsman. A variety of nasty bay-dwelling beasts make the salt marsh their home, stalking one another and feeding upon those who get caught in the thick mud of the banks.

Black Fathom Deeps: This series of ruins and caverns is built into the side of a cliff directly south of Black Fathom Bay. Many dangerous creatures lurk within — including, if tales at the Fish Eye Tavern are to be believed, ghosts of heroes who fell to some nastiness while within the Deeps. Others suggest that this place, once a night elf temple to Elune, is now the headquarters of the vile warlocks known as the Shadow Council!

Darkshore Ruins: These ruins, located south of the Master's Glaive, are ancient, far older than the other portions of Darkshore that have gone to seed. Not even the night elves know who built the extensive underground complex or when. Whatever the ruins' origins, furbolgs now make their home in the crumbling caves.

The Master's Glaive: To the west of Darkshore stands a mysterious monument, a massive adamantine glaive buried in an unmovable boulder called the Old God Skull. The night elves consider this a sacred area, as they believe the mysterious titans, creators of the world, are the only ones who could have wielded the gigantic glaive.

Desolace

History

Legends claim that the centaur are descendents of a dark union between one of the demigod Cenarius's sons and a princess of the chaotic earth elementals. When the first khans were born of their union, it is said that they murdered their father, for shame of their misshapen appearance. They were born filled with rage and savagery and have not calmed in the centuries that followed. The first of their kind, the first khans, gave rise to the five tribes of the centaur. The race swept across Desolace and soon became legendary for its brutality. The diligent night elves held them in check for ages until the Burning Legion rained its destruction upon the world. The night elves left the centaur out of necessity for their own survival during the wars,

allowing the twisted race to assume control of Desolace.

Though fortunate enough not to be scorched into oblivion in the demon wars, Desolace was savaged nonetheless due to the centaur's ceaseless aggression. No longer threatened by night elves, the tribes plagued other plains races — chiefly, the peaceful tauren. This struggle endured for generations, until recently, when the tauren were at last driven from Desolace.

The centaur were never content with controlling Desolace and have followed their tribal khans in a series of clashes with other races throughout southern and central Kalimdor.

Geography

Terrain Type: Hot rugged hills, some rocky desert and rugged mountains.

The mountainous barriers of the Stonetalons lie to the north and the Thousand Needles to the southeast, isolating Desolace from much of the rest of Kalimdor. The grasslands and mesas of Mulgore stand directly east, and the land runs rugged and open to the storm-tossed coast to the west. The winds create waterspouts against the lowland hills along the shore. The western coastline of Desolace is lush in sad contrast to the wasteland of its interior.

Desolace is a gray, rocky wasteland littered with bones. It seems almost under a supernatural curse, its skies always black and stormy, with lightning and high winds a constant throughout the realm.

The surrounding mountains form a significant barrier to travel, a key reason why the centaur have never established more than a sporadic presence elsewhere on Kalimdor.

Inhabitants

Five barbarous centaur tribes dominate the entire region with the strength of overwhelming numbers and unequaled ferocity. Each tribe is led by one of the dreaded khans and is known by a distinctive tribal color — Black, Brown, Green, Red, and Yellow. Members use the color to mark their weapons and their faces. The khans who lead each tribe rarely have contact with each other except in times of war.

There are no other cultures of any note in all of Desolace. The centaur have run them all down in their unceasing lust for conquest. The only animals that can sustain themselves in this arid and violent land are beasts such as lions, raptors, sand serpents, and harpies.

Areas of Interest

Kodo Graveyard: Mighty as the reptilian kodo beasts are, they are not immortal. Those that feel the approach of death make their way through the Thousand Needles to the plains in eastern Desolace, where they eventually perish. No one knows why the kodo beasts come to this particular place, but it is a habit long maintained. The area is filled with bones as well as the sick and the dying. It is far from peaceful, however, as everything from scavenging raptors to mighty lions come to feast upon the aged kodo beasts.

Maraudon: Although each of the five centaur tribes maintains its own stronghold elsewhere in Desolace, this is the region's capitol. A vast gathering of palatial tents surrounded by a palisade, Maraudon acts as a cultural center and meeting place for all centaur. Behind a series of spiked barriers in the center of this mesa stands Terramok, an ancient titan vault. This place is rumored to hold Theradras, former princess of the vile earth elementals and legendary mother of the centaur race. Some even claim that Theradras guards the tomb of her husband, the Keeper of the Grove killed by the very first khans.

The only permanent centaur resident is Krullaran the Prophet. The centaur of Desolace turn to the khans for protection, but they look to Krullaran for guidance. Many believe he communes with the titans and possesses insight to the glorious return that the centaur will someday make to the northern lands.

Opal Ridge: Prisoners captured by the centaur are forced to work deep underground, mining opals in the heart of Desolace. Centaur use the gemstones to adorn their weapons and armor or to trade with the goblins or quilboar for needed supplies. The mine's existence was a secret until recently, when a dwarf escaped and whispered about his captivity. He died before offering any indication of where the mine is, but this mystery has not stopped expeditions from heading out in search — some to liberate the prisoners who remain, others to take control of the mine and its supposedly limitless riches.

Realm of the Harpies: As with most names bestowed by centaur, this area has a clear if unimaginative label. Harpies call this rocky stronghold their own and use it as a staging point to attack the weak and unwary.

Spearhold: The centaur of Red Tribe call this ruined fortress theirs. Standing atop a rounded hill, Spearhold has many buried spears jutting out the base of the walls. Dangerous though the spears can be, enemies should fear the arrows. Some say that Temuejin, the Second Khan, has so great a supply of arrows in his armory that his archers could volley for three days before exhausting their ammunition.

Durotar

History

For many years, Durotar was home to the quilboar. Then Thrall, Warchief of the orcs, brought his race to Kalimdor in search of a new homeland. The quilboar were tenacious but ultimately no match for the unified might of the orc clans. The bristled "boar men" were driven back in a series of decisive orc victories along the northern canyons and ultimately pushed to the most remote regions of Durotar and even into the Barrens. The orcs claim the coastal realm as their own, but the quilboar vow to reclaim it someday.

Geography

Terrain Type: Hot rugged hills, plains (grassland), rugged mountains.

The realm of Durotar — named by Warchief Thrall in honor of his father, Durotan — occupies the east coast of Kalimdor, just across the river from the Barrens. The goblin port of Ratchet stands to the south, with the ruined shores of Azshara some distance to the north.

The region is warm and rocky, but not as arid as the rest of the Barrens. A fair amount of vegetation grows thanks to the warm easterly winds blowing in from over the ocean, but truly fertile soil is rare, making farmland precious. Sagebrush on the plains and thin pine forests at higher elevations combine with rugged hills and canyons to break up the landscape.

Inhabitants

Orcs are by far the major inhabitants of Durotar. Quilboar cluster in the canyons along the northwestern borders and encroach from the Barrens to the west. Centaur warbands make the occasional foray, and furbolgs and undead have been seen in more than one instance. Herd animals

such as deer and goats roam the land, preyed upon by wolves and coyotes.

A number of Horde settlements have been established throughout the region, but much of the land has yet to be tamed. The cities and towns scattered along the frontier are heavily fortified against attacks from quilboar raiders, centaur warbands, rogue furbolgs, and even sudden appearances by undead and the occasional demon. Caravans are common targets, creating a strong market for caravan guards.

The few large cities are distant from one another, with a variety of smaller encampments and villages scattered in between. Given that Durotar is the orcs' new homeland, Horde races and independents are welcome throughout the region. Alliance races risk their lives when they venture into Durotar.

Areas of Interest

Blackblood Gorge: This expanse of jagged canyons and narrow valleys in northern Durotar is the last bastion for the region's quilboar. Cutthroats and thieves also hide in these twisting canyons . Orc hunting parties from Orgrimmar raid the area regularly, both for matters of security and for sport.

Drygulch Ravine: Centaur warbands have assumed control of this canyon in western Durotar. The violent creatures use the many twists and folds within the canyon to hide out from Horde patrols in between their periodic raids.

Orgrimmar: Built into a jagged mountain valley, the city of Orgrimmar (named after Thrall's mentor, Orgrim Doomhammer) is a fortified bastion. With its massive palisade walls and its structures carved into the very sides of the cliffs, Orgrimmar stands as a brutal tribute to orc might and resolve. The city is ruled by the orcs' beloved warchief and shaman leader, Thrall.

Thunder Ridge: This breathtaking gorge is untamed by humanoids as yet. Thunder lizards give the place its name, dominating the landscape for some distance. Tallstriders are also seen hanging out on the fringes with an eye out for an easy lunch.

Dustwallow Marsh

History

Dustwallow Marsh was once a high plain filled with herd animals that thrived on the tall grasses. Then came the great Sundering, and the plain was smashed down into a sundered valley. The water table bled up into the ruined landscape, creating the great marsh that exists today.

Geography

Terrain Type: Temperate to hot watery swamp.

Dustwallow Marsh is located southeast of the Barrens and north of the Thousand Needles. The swamp curls to the east, forming a bay around the island of Theramore.

Dustwallow is a flood plain fed by underground springs and surrounded by the dry savannahs of the Barrens. The marsh is eternally wet, muddy, and hot, unfit for proper settlements and a haven for creatures that crave the wetness and humidity. Narrow banks of slippery mud separate endless stagnant pools and algae-choked channels, making Dustwallow a traveler's nightmare.

The roads that cross the fen are muddy and treacherous, and the surrounding swamp is even more dangerous to traverse. Those who mistake the thick, wandering bogs of the marsh for solid land may fall through, only to have the floating plants close above and trap them in the brackish water. Also, the Dustwallow teems with predators that lurk just beneath the surface of every pool and skulk behind every bush.

In the east, the turgid water of the marsh mixes with salt water from the sea. The rocky form of Theramore Isle lies just beyond in the bay. The marsh is the best way to approach Theramore by land, as jagged rocks outside the bay make sailing directly from the goblin city of Ratchet difficult.

The marsh's southern expanse grows rockier as it approaches the Thousand Needles. The pools are larger and far deeper, with half-submerged rocky outcrops. Many of these rock clusters have

openings that lead into cave systems. The caves are often surprisingly dry and serve as lairs for a variety of beasts. Some conjecture whether the caves are interconnected with the underground river that keeps the swamp submerged or if they might even extend out to the sea.

Inhabitants

The hundreds of shallow pools that comprise the marsh hold creatures from massive plant-eating kodo beasts to ambushing packs of raptors to territorial water-loving murlocs. The saltwater swamp of east Dustwallow is a popular breeding area for the murloc packs.

Indeed, the waters teem with aquatic creatures of all sorts. Humans and murlocs drag nets down the channels to harvest gigantic mudfish, but also pull in everything from alligators to eels. Poisonous snakes hang from the trees, and some of the larger specimens are known to drag the unwary up into the branches.

Of course, these dangers are nothing compared to those of the Dustwallow's southern region. The rocky outcroppings common to this area are ideal lairs for black dragons, and those creatures are so common in the area that it has earned the name "Wyrmbog."

Areas of Interest

Bluefen: This small village stands on the damp border between the Barrens and Dustwallow Marsh. The area is known for a plant that the locals boil to produce distinctive, bright blue dyes. The powdered form of the dye is popular in markets for its supposed use in mystic tattoos. Shamans have displayed powers ranging from increased endurance to the ability to see in the dark, supposedly derived from the indigo tattoos they wear.

Brackenwall: A large and shadowy fen along the western edge of Dustwallow Marsh, Brackenwall has become infamous for the number of explorers who have entered it and never returned. The tauren refuse to go near Brackenwall and blame disappearances on what they call "the hungry mists." The tauren have even erected a series of stone pillars inscribed with protective runes along the border that

Brackenwall shares with their homeland of Mulgore.

The Broken Giant: In the northern reaches of Dustwallow Marsh, dwarven explorers were thrilled to discover the remains of a titan statue, broken off at the knees. Despite months of study, the statue yielded no information to help in the investigation of their titan heritage. This dead end has not stopped other Ironforge dwarves from making a pilgrimage to lay their hands on the statue's 20-foot wide sandals, convinced that it will bring them luck and prosperity.

Dragonmurk: Only a few abandoned huts remain of the tauren outpost that once stood in the deepest and darkest parts of Wyrmbog. The inhabitants either fled or were consumed when Onyxia, an enormous black dragon, claimed the nearby cave system as the home for herself and her many children. Onyxia bore the tauren no specific ill; they just had the bad luck to be in the way. She carries great malevolence toward the Alliance, which she believes is behind the recent disappearance of her father, the ancient black dragon Deathwing. Travelers through the marsh tell tales of unfortunates abducted and tortured by Onyxia and her brood.

Theramore: The main human settlement on Kalimdor is not actually *on* Kalimdor. Theramore is a rocky island east of Dustwallow; the humans' walled city bears the same name as the island. It was originally settled with the sole purpose of survival. Yet the time since the Third War has seen the city prosper, making for a natural progression from mere subsistence to a desire to restore the glory of old. See the "Theramore, Fortress of the Alliance" sidebar for more details.

Witch's Hill: Tauren tell of a murloc witch who lives in a hut on a high hill and speaks nothing but the truth. Those

Theramore, Fortress of the Alliance

This large island is the Alliance's stronghold upon Kalimdor. It was built primarily as a military fortress, but has grown somewhat to serve as a trading port.

Approach from the sea is extremely difficult due to the jagged rocks jutting out of Dustwallow Bay, leaving travelers to journey on foot through the marsh to one of the villages that run ferries out to the island. Fearful of pirates from Ratchet and elsewhere, the cannons of Theramore will fire without warning on any ship approaching the island unannounced.

Inside the thick walls of Theramore, the people have labored hard to recreate a piece of Lordaeron. Graceful towers rise high above clean, cobblestone streets lined with shops and homes. At the center of the city lies the Foothold Citadel, a squat keep housing the chambers of the Alliance Assembly. Though the streets recall the quiet serenity of the Alliance of Lordaeron, the meetings of the Assembly reveal the considerable strain among the city's residents. After years of near-paternal guidance of the humans of Lordaeron, the high elves resent being forced to rely on the hospitality of the younger race since arriving on Kalimdor. As humans hold five of the seven seats on the Alliance Assembly, both the elves (with two seats) and the dwarves (with none) feel underrepresented in the rulership of both Theramore and the Alliance in general. As the dwarves continue to accumulate more evidence of their titan heritage that they want to present to their king in Khaz Modan, their protests that the Alliance does little to return across the sea grow louder and louder.

Despite this internal debate, the Alliance places a high value on law and order in Theramore, and city guards make regular patrols to maintain the peace. When skirmishes break out between high elves and night elves or Alliance veterans decide to settle old debts upon an orc visiting the city, the guards are quick to round up the offenders for a speedy trial at the Foothold Citadel and imprisonment in Ironclad Prison, the dungeons of which are along tunnels dug deep into the rock of the island. Sentences for fighting and disturbing the peace tend to be light (usually only a few days' incarceration), but sentences for more serious violations of the Alliance's code of law, such as high robbery or murder, can be much more severe.

who have braved the swamp's dangers did find the oracle, but it is not the witch. She takes a supplicant's question and repeats it in a surprisingly strong voice — and the hill gives its reply. In truth, it is not a hill at all but a giant turtle that hears only the witch's voice and replies in an unknown tongue. The witch translates the oracle's words for a fee, and its pronouncements are remarkably accurate.

Wyrmbog: The southern reaches of Dustwallow Marsh are called "Wyrmbog" for all of the black drakes and dragon whelps that lurk among the shadowed rocks and slither across the waters to attack anything foolish enough to come near. Alliance and Horde often come into conflict with the dragonkind as they skirt the edges of Wyrmbog on the way to other parts of Kalimdor.

Felwood

History

This lush and vibrant land of woods and meadows was tended by the Kaldorei and protected by the demigod Cenarius. Bubbling streams ran through quiet, grassy meadows, and the summer sun was tempered by the whispering breeze and the cooling rain. The leafy corridors of the forest rang out with the music of songbirds. It was as close to a paradise as the world has ever known. Then the Burning Legion befouled the land. Any trees and creatures that escaped outright destruction became forever cursed in the demons' rampage.

Geography

Terrain Type: Temperate sparse forest and gentle hills.

Felwood lies south of Darkshore, curling around the lower slope of Mount Hyjal to the southeast.

Known to have felt the cursed touch of the Burning Legion, Felwood is an eerie, dark, and haunted region of scattered gloomy woodlands and tainted vales, all of it teeming with evil. The meadows of Felwood retain the sickly, charred look they took on when the demons cursed the land thousands of years ago. Nothing grows there. The mighty ancients that once guarded the land now roam blindly, their limbs twisted and their

bark hides bleeding fell poisons. The once tranquil rivers and streams now boil with poison and noxious gasses.

Felwood is a dismal and dangerous land to all who enter. Most cross into Felwood only out of necessity, for it lies directly along the road to Hyjal Summit. Armed travelers are usually safe if they pass along the main road by day, but they have no guarantee of safety if they leave the trail or if they venture into Felwood after nightfall.

The night elves feel constant shame that they failed to protect this noble land. All their efforts to restore health to the woods and meadows through divine magic have failed. Despite the lingering curse of 10,000 years, the night elves refuse to cease in their efforts to lift it.

Some think that the key to healing the blighted land lies with Illidan, brother to the night elf hero Malfurion Stormrage. Illidan was known to have consumed the artifact called the Skull of Gul'dan, which originally blighted the forest. Only powerful divine magic can likely save the land, however.

Inhabitants

Felwood has no village, no people of its own. The land is a cursed relic, a danger to all within its bounds. Even creatures united in evil are not safe from the depredations of one another. Explosions and flashes of arcane brilliance erupt throughout Felwood as druids clash with the warlocks they have come to destroy. The ground shakes from the footsteps of accursed ancients who prowl in search of victims. Twisted furbolgs and satyrs range through Felwood in bloodthirsty packs, and savage beasts lie in wait for the unwary.

Felwood is home to many beasts, with bears, wolves, and panthers the most numerous. As herbivores refuse to eat the cursed vegetation, the carnivores have turned to feeding on each other. Combined with the great curse, this development has created in each creature a brutal rage — a rage that the beasts turn on one another and any who dare to enter their territory.

Cursed furbolgs roam the forest, looking for an end to their torment. They are hardy enough to survive drinking the cursed waters of Bloodvenom

Falls, but the water only increases their madness. Cursed ancients lurk near night elf ruins and will attack anyone they see. They are stronger than their healthy counterparts, empowered by evil. The ancients hold a special grudge against the night elves who abandoned them and will unleash special savagery upon anyone remotely resembling an elf. Satyrs dwell by tainted moon wells, their dark magics twisting Felwood's curse ever deeper into the land. Rumors circulate that the shadowy satyrs work as scouts and assassins for the Shadow Council in Jaedenar.

The undead Scourge and what demons survived the Third War have also made a home in Felwood. These recent arrivals have stirred the other residents into turmoil, making the region even more violent than before.

Druids of the wild make forays into Felwood with the aid of elven rangers, hunting down the greatest evil they can find and attempting healing magic upon the land. High elves and paladin warriors have likewise come to Felwood to cleanse it of undead and root out the reclusive Shadow Council.

Areas of Interest

Felwood is home to no cities to speak of; the night elves fled the area thousands of years ago, and no one has found the ambition to settle in the cursed forest since.

Bloodvenom Falls: Once a shimmering waterfall fed by pure springs, these falls now spew putrid water. Venomous poisons pump out of a cursed earth, spilling over a rocky edge into a pool of sinister jade. The night elves claim that drinking the waters will kill you, and being doused by the waters burns like acid — if you're lucky, that is. Rumors suggest that the vile water twists those it touches, birthing evil creatures to wreak havoc upon the countryside.

Jaedenar: Though no habitable villages are found in Felwood, the Shadow Council and its warlock agents have taken up residence in a series of ancient night elf ruins somewhere within the cursed region. They have named this place Jaedenar, after the great demon Kil'jaeden. The Shadow Council purportedly seeks to spread the region's corruption and evil to the rest of

Ashenvale Forest, thereby finishing the Legion's dire plans for Kalimdor's destruction.

Petrified Forest: This expanse at the southern end of Felwood consists of trees and ancients turned to stone. The stone corpses of the sentient trees have looks of terror forever etched upon their granite faces, and they are frozen in poses that suggest they were caught in some nightmarish explosion.

Timbermaw Hold: This ancient furbolg fortress is located near Felwood's eastern border. It is a vast and rambling place, rumored to run deep into the slopes of Mount Hyjal. No one knows for sure how big it is, since the furbolgs abandoned it in ages past. Undead and satyrs may now wander the shadowed corridors… along with whatever cursed furbolgs still roam the depths. Wise travelers would bypass the site entirely if it were not the only passage through to Winterspring and Hyjal Summit.

Hyjal Summit

History

The Kaldorei have long held this great mountain sacred. When the first Well of Eternity was destroyed in the first demonic invasion, the resulting implosion triggered a cataclysm that made the world shudder. Mount Hyjal endured, however, and the night elves emerged to rebuild their society — though without arcane magic this time.

One of the fleeing night elves — Illidan Stormrage, brother to the mighty druid Malfurion Stormrage — had taken a portion of water from the Well of Eternity. Illidan could not bear to live without the Well's magic. After the cataclysm, he poured this water into a lake at the peak of Mount Hyjal, creating a second Well of Eternity. The night elves were outraged at this act, for it was the first Well's energies that originally brought the demons to Azeroth. Illidan was imprisoned, and Malfurion met with three great dragons to create the World Tree, Nordrassil.

The World Tree grew over the Well to obscure and protect it. In the centuries that followed, the night elves were a constant presence, nurturing and protecting the World Tree that stood in the valley between the twin peaks of Mount Hyjal. The Burning Legion targeted the Tree in the Battle of Mount Hyjal, but, infused with the combined power of Azeroth's mortal races, it blasted the demon lord Archimonde and freed the world of the demon menace.

Geography

Terrain Type: Temperate rugged and forbidding mountains.

Hyjal Summit rises high above northern Kalimdor, surrounded by Winterspring, the Moonglade, and Felwood.

The mountain's twin peaks are the highest points on Kalimdor and home to Nordrassil, the massive World Tree. The climb to the peak takes travelers past everything from dense forests at the foot to rocky meadows with sparse growth as the grade gets s t e e p e r . Nordrassil's sheer enormity strikes awe into any who have the rare honor of approaching it. The root system spreads over the entirety of Hyjal's peak, and its vast, charred branches seem to touch the sky. Damaged in the recent war, it now heals itself at a rapid rate.

Although the World Tree rests upon a high mountain peak, its magic keeps the weather pleasant and warm year round — until this past year, when Hyjal saw its first winter. Otherwise, the air remains warm and crisp and the sky is always a dark blue peppered with a blanket of stars. The night elves hope that the regenerating tree will begin to regulate the weather again soon.

Inhabitants

Few elves live at the peak of Mount Hyjal, but the mountain and the World Tree shelter the night elves in the forests and shores at the foot of the mountain.

The forests and rocky mountain slopes harbor many dangerous beasts. With the magic of the Well of Eternity and the World Tree saturating the air and infusing the groundwater, the creatures of the forests are stronger and smarter than those anywhere else on Kalimdor.

Deadly black tigers and bears prowl the forests, as do powerful stags. These creatures do not fear fights; they even seek them if the prey looks weak enough. Even smarter and deadlier beasts inhabit the forests. Hippogryphs and chimaera are a common enough sight among the forested peaks of the Summit. Hippogryphs, magical beasts that look like a stag crossed with a raven, patrol the skies and attack anyone they deem a threat to the forests. Although friendly to night elves, they do not show kindness to strangers or to those they consider a menace. Wild dire wolves also lurk on the mountain slopes. They have no natural enemy and are fearless even when met with several armed hunters.

The forests on Hyjal are also known to be home to the occasional treant and stray ancient. These sentient, motile trees protect the night elves' towns and the surrounding forests.

Areas of Interest

Eternity Bridge: This ornately worked ivory bridge arcs from the south shore of the Well to the massive roots of Nordrassil. The bridge is wide and strong, but dangerous beasts occasionally attack travelers as they cross.

The Well of Eternity: The glowing, swirling pool was once a sizable lake. It extends around Nordrassil, creating a layer of protection around the Tree. Its mystic power is so potent that none who attempt to drink from it — or, foolishly, swim in it — can hope to survive, assuming that the ambassadors would let anyone get close enough to make the attempt.

The World Tree: The key point of interest on Hyjal is Nordrassil, the World Tree. It stands thousands of feet high, and its vast canopy almost blocks out the sky. Although the tree suffered much damage in the last war, it is healing itself. It did not flower or grow leaves this past year, but the druids hope that this coming year it will begin to grow again.

The Moonglade

History

The Moonglade was the druids' home for thousands of years. When the Burning Legion ran rampant over the land in ancient times, the Moonglade remained untouched. The night elf druids went into deep meditation in the secure caves of the Barrow Dens, sending their minds into the plane of the Emerald Dream. The remaining night elves built the town of Nighthaven.

During the Third War, the Moonglade again remained the safe haven of the elves. Although battles were fought there, the land was not befouled. Most of the night elves' population remains in the Moonglade, surrounded by the old forest trees and the ancients, preferring solitude over communion with other races.

Geography

Terrain Type: Medium to dense temperate forest and alpine meadows.

The Moonglade ranges east of Felwood, just north of Winterspring Grove along the lower slope of Mount Hyjal.

The Moonglade is a magical, sylvan forest draped in perpetual night. The moon stays high within the ebon sky, illuminating the woodland below with a silvery glow. The land never suffers the extremes of weather, enduring in an endless warm summer eve.

Considered holy to the night elves, the Moonglade is home to the night elf race and its powerful druids of the wild. Indeed, the druids had long rested in meditation under the glade, until the return of the Burning Legion awakened them. They remain awake, vowing to protect nature and heal the fractured continent from its war wounds.

Inhabitants

The sacred forest of the night elves is home to many beasts both dangerous and friendly. The Kaldorei themselves live in cautious harmony with the wildlife, such as the black tigers and the bears that prowl and hunt in the woods. The elves often capture and tame the proud saber cats to use as mounts, but encountering one in the wild is dangerous.

Less harmony is enjoyed with the forest's more dangerous denizens. Satyrs — cursed, deranged night elves — also lurk here and plague the night elves' solitude frequently. Some furbolgs, driven feral by drinking the foul waters of Felwood, will attack travelers as well. Fierce dire wolves and hippogryphs have also been reported in the area.

In addition to these animals are the ancients: sentient trees that act as protectors of the forest. Treants, the smaller tree-men cousins to the ancients, roam the Moonglade. These beings act as fierce protectors of the forest. They do not hesitate to unleash their might upon any who

would damage trees or otherwise harm nature. Many ancients live in the forest near Nighthaven. These sentient trees once had the vital task of channeling forces of the land to sustain the night elves' immortality They now aid in the elves' warrior training and help protect their village.

The Keepers of the Grove, powerful druids said to be the direct offspring of the demigod Cenarius, roam the Moonglade as ever-vigilant protectors. The night elves send their own patrols out, though they focus primarily on defending Nighthaven and the Barrow Dens.

Areas of Interest

The vast forests and vales of the Moonglade are sparsely populated. The sole settlement of any size is the night elves' capital, Nighthaven.

Barrow Dens: The northeastern corner of the Moonglade holds the Barrow Dens. This area is sacred to the druids and is also formerly home to the late demigod Cenarius. The Barrow Dens are an ancient underground fortress, with passages and caves containing the living and working chambers for the druids of the wild. The dome in the center of the hill holds Cenarius' Lair, now a shrine to the valiant demigod.

Moon Wells: Enchanted pools throughout the

Moonglade give the night elves their spiritual power and feed the World Tree that stands atop Hyjal Summit. The shimmering waters within give off a blue light, causing the moon wells to glow slightly in the night. They are scattered throughout the forest, often near giant standing stones covered in ancient runes.

Nighthaven: This city holds the largest concentration of night elves anywhere on Kalimdor. Massive trees, ancients, and many forest beasts fill the surrounding woods. Nighthaven has survived for centuries despite demon and undead attacks, and the night elves protect their home fiercely.

They are very cautious of whom they let enter the village. High elves are not allowed under any circumstances, and anyone smelling of arcane power is likewise turned away. Those allowed entry find Nighthaven hospitable, though a subdued and even eerie place. Night elves run the inns, taverns, and shops, and their way of life is rooted in nature. This spiritual heritage manifests in many small ways that foreigners may find unsettling — from how the buildings are constructed to mesh with the surrounding woods to a wildness that seems to lurk just beneath a quiet demeanor.

While visitors may come and go as they please for the most part, they are never allowed near moon wells. In addition, any high elves seen near a moon well are attacked on sight.

Mulgore

History

This rich plain was once used by the night elves as prime hunting grounds. When the Great Sundering shattered the world, mountains pierced the earth and the night elves fled north. The mighty tauren made their home upon the low valleys and high plateaus after the night elves left. In time, the ash of upheaval disappeared and the once fertile grasslands returned.

The aggressive centaur claim the right to the fertile grasslands and have warred constantly against the tauren for supremacy of the land, but the tauren's mesa strongholds have so far proved impregnable.

Geography

Terrain Type: Temperate rugged hills, plains (grassland), some rugged mountains.

Mulgore is a landlocked region, with Desolace to the west and the Barrens to the east, the Stonetalon Mountains to the north and the Thousand Needles to the south.

Mulgore is the ancient homeland of the tauren, who live on the windswept mesas and roam the grassy valleys. Below the mesa's ridgeline are the vast emerald plains, which hold an abundance of life including prairie wolves, young kodo beasts, and tallstriders.

Inhabitants

The centaur horde mercilessly hounds the tauren throughout Mulgore. The tepee-like tents and crude hide huts that comprise tauren towns stand in stark contrast to the turning windmills and pulley structures that keep the tauren grainmills operating. Large, ornately carved totems dot every street and stand above every major structure.

Toward the eastern border, quilboar displaced from Durotar have started creating dens with thorned hedgerow barriers. For now, it is a small concern for the tauren, but if the bristly "boar men" encroach too far, there will be a price to pay. At present, the tauren are far more interested in what the centaur are up to.

Mulgore is filled with a variety of antelopes, rabbits, and wild boar, making it the ideal place for game hunting. A tauren pastime involves hunting these animals to improve one's combat skills. The tauren rarely eat their prey, preferring to graze on the wheat and grass that grow wild in the valley.

Areas of Interest

Dalsh-Beran: The tauren do not build cities like other races do. Instead, they build many smaller communities that trade on the barter system. With the growing presence of other settlements, the tauren leaders established the

settlement of Dalsh-Beran near the Barrens and let the Horde construct one building where they can reside and conduct business. All races are welcome to trade here, but those not of the Horde are discouraged from wandering around town, especially at night. Dalsh-Beran has grown from a small trading outpost to a large fortified city, capable of maintaining the trade routes passing north to south and to the east through the Barrens.

Grassmount: This trio of grassy hills is a favorite encampment of the tauren. A series of tombs surround the Grassmount, monuments to tauren who have fallen in battle against the centaur. Among these monuments is the tomb of the legendary Lazur Hornblade, whose spirit is said to protect all who camp at Grassmount.

Lake Stonebull: Mulgore is home to the only major source of water in western Kalimdor. The lake is named after the mighty tauren hero who fell battling the Burning Legion. Water fills the lake from underground rivers stretching as far north as the Ashenvale Forest.

Monolith Glen: The most fascinating area in Mulgore, and some say in all of central Kalimdor, is the mysterious Monolith Glen. This small

Thunder Bluff: Thunder Bluff is the single largest gathering of tauren. Built atop a near-impenetrable mesa deep in the south of Mulgore, this collection of tents and thatched huts serves as the tauren's central home.

The tauren learned long ago they could build no wall that would hold back attackers. Having no real ranged weapons, they could at least defend from behind a wall. So, surrounding the tauren dwellings is a wall made of great logs and granite boulders that twists in winding corridors from inside to outside. This circuitous defense ring is designed to utilize the tauren's most vicious attack. As raiders try to enter through the corridors, the tauren block the entrances with their bodies and smash their foes with massive logs resting on their shoulders. To this date, Thunder Bluff has never been sacked.

The Por-ah Stone

Shamans have interpreted wall paintings in a network of caves outside of Thunder Bluff, paintings that speak of the ancient tauren artifact called the Por-ah Stone. The paintings suggest the Stone can be used to communicate with the elder tauren of days before the Sundering. Many chieftains have argued whether they should search out the Por-ah Stone. Some say the elders could use the Stone to guide the tauren better in the old ways, restoring the tribes to their former glory. Others proclaim it to be the work of arcane magic — which might therefore destroy the tribes. With no tribal decision made yet, the Por-ah Stone remains undiscovered. Whatever its true function, it would likely fetch a high price if found, even if sold by someone other than the tauren.

grove of upright obsidian black stones was set by the night elves aeons ago. The massive stones are covered in ancient Kaldorei runes and are avoided by the local centaur and the tauren. No one knows why the night elves chose this spot to be hallowed ground, and research has so far not uncovered any clues.

Redrock Mesa: This training ground is found along Mulgore's northern border, in the foothills of the Stonetalon Mountains. It is used to train young tauren in hunting skills and combat to make them prominent warriors within tauren society.

Stonetalon Mountains

History

The Stonetalon Mountains were once a low set of hills giving a gentle view to the ocean waves in the west. The Sundering that tore apart the world drove great sandstone cliffs and mountain peaks high in the air. Water from the eastern coast poured into the newly created chasms and gorges. With the aid of erosion from the Blackwolf River, the Stonetalon Mountains have expanded into a vast network of canyons and cliff openings that invites adventurers and beasts alike to explore the virgin lands.

Geography

Terrain Type: Temperate rugged and forbidding mountains.

The Stonetalons rise in central Kalimdor, south of Ashenvale Forest and north of Desolace. The mountain range feeds into the bleak expanse of the Barrens to the east.

The atmosphere of the Stonetalon Mountains can best be described as extreme. At the lower elevations it is windy, hot, and dry. It is a harsh place where food cannot grow and flash floods are commonplace in the early summer months. Moisture from the ocean builds up into huge rain clouds, but the towering peaks are too high for the clouds to pass inland. They crash against the mountains' western side and pour massive sheets of water upon the slopes to run through narrow canyons and back into the ocean or into a valley to dry up in a marshy sink. When the weather turns to rain, the ground grows slick and gray. Walking on a slope or a cliff in the rain is treacherous — water seeps through the sandstone and threatens to send even careful travelers plummeting to their deaths.

Oftentimes, when the clouds expel all their moisture, hot winds push them farther up the slope, surrounding the Stonetalon Peak in a shroud of thundering mist.

An immediate feature any visitor notices — aside from the sheer cliffs and deep crevasses — is the constantly blowing wind. Sometimes a gentle breeze carries fresh air in from the ocean and other times a violent gale stirs up vicious dust devils or brings a storm in from the western mountains.

Inhabitants

The rugged mountains are home to many wild beasts and only a few civilized habitations. Hippogryphs roost near Mirkfallon Lake in cave complexes high on the slopes. Their nests are defended by large bramble hedgerows, making access nearly impossible without flying. Other creatures found throughout the mountains are striders, hyenas, kobolds, swoops, crag panthers, and even rock elementals and the rare sabertooth cat.

Further up the Stonetalon Peak, on its eastern side, are the chaotic lands of the wyverns and drakes. These ancient "flying lizards" have long been rivals for supremacy of the skies. Every once in a while, when other races threaten to interfere, the two will set aside their differences long enough to deal with the interlopers.

Agents of the goblin-run Venture Company have also been sighted in the area, searching for potential tracts to deforest and streams of precious ore to plunder with their mining machines.

The Ill Winds of Stonetalon

The winds whip through the Stonetalon Mountains with great force, slowing travelers' progress and throwing up clouds of grit and dust that can confuse the best sense of direction. Small and lightly built individuals have even been flung off a mountainside by a particularly forceful gust.

The wind in the Stonetalons seldom drops below moderate even on a calm day and can change from a steady breeze to a brutal windstorm without warning. To simulate these conditions, roll on Table 5–1: Stonetalon Wind Effects every 4 hours that the characters are in the region.

Table 5–1: Stonetalon Wind Effects

d20	Wind Force	Wind Speed	Ranged Attacks Normal/Siege	Creature Size*	Wind Effect on Creatures	Fort Save DC
1–2	Light	0–10 mph	—/—	Any	None	—
3–9	Moderate	11–20 mph	—/—	Tiny or smaller	2x movement cost	—
				Small or larger	None	
10–14	Strong	21–30 mph	–2/—	Tiny or smaller	Knocked down	10
				Small or larger	2x movement cost	
15–18	Severe	31–50 mph	–4/—	Tiny	Blown away	15
				Small	Knocked down	
				Medium	Checked	
				Large or larger	2x movement cost	
19	Windstorm	51–74 mph	Impossible/–4	Small or smaller	Blown away	18
				Medium	Knocked down	
				Large or Huge	Checked	
				Gargantuan /Colossal	2x movement cost	
20	Hurricane	75–174 mph	Impossible/–8	Medium or smaller	Blown away	20
				Large	Knocked down	
				Huge	Checked	
				Gargantuan / Colossal	2x movement cost	

* Flying or airborne creatures are treated as one size category smaller than their actual size; thus, an airborne Gargantuan dragon is treated as Huge for the purposes of wind effects.

Double Movement Cost: Creatures must spend double the normal cost to move against the force of the wind. So, each square of movement counts as 2 squares, and each diagonal move counts as 3 squares.

Checked: Creatures are unable to move forward against the force of the wind. Flying creatures are blown back 1d6 x 5 feet.

Knocked Down: Creatures are knocked prone by the force of the wind. Flying creatures are blown back 1d6 x 10 feet.

Blown Away: Creatures on the ground are knocked prone and rolled 1d4 x 10 feet, taking 1d4 points of nonlethal damage per 10 feet. Flying creatures are blown back 2d6 x 10 feet and take 2d6 points of nonlethal damage due to battering and buffeting.

These rules build upon wind effects covered in "Weather" of Chapter 3: Writing Adventures in the *DMG*. The steep mountain terrain makes movement more treacherous than normal, so additional factors apply to the wind forces than those listed in the *DMG*. In addition to the details in Table 5–1, apply the following factors depending on the wind speed:

Strong Wind: Grit, sand, and stone are flung about, obscuring all sight, including darkvision, beyond 60 feet. Balance checks suffer a –2 penalty due to the force of the wind.

Severe Wind: The air grows thick with gritty particles, obscuring all sight, including darkvision, beyond 30 feet. Climb checks suffer a –2 penalty and Balance checks a –4 penalty.

Windstorm: A roiling, howling wind overwhelms the character. The effect is identical to the *fog cloud* spell — except for being dispersed by wind, of course — and lasts the duration of the windstorm. Traveling through a windstorm requires a DC 20 Survival check every hour to avoid getting lost. Climb checks suffer a –4 penalty and Balance checks suffer a –20 penalty due to the strength of the wind.

Hurricane-Force Wind: In addition to the visibility effects and danger of getting lost as described in a windstorm, a DC 15 Survival check is required for each hour the character is exposed to hurricane-force winds. On a failure, the character grows fatigued from the constant battering. He can neither run nor charge and takes a –2 penalty to both Strength and Dexterity. The character recovers from fatigue after 8 hours of complete rest. If a character fails two Survival checks in a row, he becomes exhausted. He moves at half normal speed and takes a –6 penalty to both Strength and Dexterity. After 1 hour of rest, the exhausted character becomes fatigued. Climb checks are at a –8 penalty for those who want to struggle against the violent wind.

Areas of Interest

Mirkfallon Lake: This lake, high in the Stonetalon range, is home to the tallest waterfall in Kalimdor. Aside from the breathtaking falls, one can also find the legendary hippogryphs, which migrate here from the cooler north.

Stonetalon Peak: The highest point in the mountain range, this peak was actually made hollow with numerous eruptions in the great Sundering. The caves have become home to several wayward beasts, which gain entrance through an opening to the south. The Horde knows of their leader Thrall's passage through the legendary caves, but he explored only one of the many twisting routes of empty lava tubes that fill Stonetalon Peak.

Valley of the Bloodfurys: This canyon stronghold is the home of the infamous and hated harpy brood. The canyon walls are lined with giant harpy nests and guano. Few living creatures have survived an encounter with the harpies, as food is hard to come by in the mountains. Treasure is abundant thanks to the number of dead that litter the valley floor. Some adventurers have bragged that they crept in to gather treasure and left before the harpies ever noticed. For those who listen closely to such tales, one theme is common: stealth.

Windshear Crag: This cut in the mountains leads from the southern border of Ashenvale into the stormy canyons of the Stonetalons.

Tanaris Desert

History

The Tanaris Desert has been an endless sea of sand for aeons. Nozdormu, the great dragon of time, was said to make this land his home since time immemorial, thriving in the solitude of oppressive heat and miles of sand.

Geography

Terrain Type: Hot sandy desert and some rocky desert.

The Tanaris Desert covers a vast expanse of southern Kalimdor, just south of the Thousand Needles.

It is a blazing hot expanse of rolling sand dunes under a cloudless sky. The southern region is more mountainous, with large cavern networks —some extending deep beneath the surface.

A vast realm, the Tanaris Desert holds many secrets. The land is mostly desert, with many huge creatures such as kodo beasts, sand worms, and tallstriders roaming about looking for food. Below the ground are gigantic tunnel networks. They remain largely unexplored, for few have the fortitude to venture into such a harsh landscape. Still, rumors tell of all manner of creatures that hide within the tunnels and slaughter trespassers without hesitation.

Inhabitants

Although the sea of dunes does not look as if it would support a variety of wildlife, kodo beasts, tallstriders, lions, and massive birds of prey are quite common. Drakes and the occasional dragon are also seen soaring on the thermals that swirl over the great desert.

Areas of Interest

The Abyssal Sands: This endless dune sea is said to be home to the sand-dwelling silithid. The creatures reportedly live in hive tunnels just beneath the surface, waiting for the unwary traveler.

The Caverns of Time: Relics of past ages lie half-buried in the sands near the entrance to this vast cave system. The bronze drakes of the mighty dragon Nozdormu patrol the borders, making sure that no mortals enter the sacred grounds at the caverns' entrance. Those who somehow slip past the drake guardians and enter the caverns have never returned quite the same — tales describe how some appear as old men, while others are reduced to infancy by the caverns' strange energies.

Gadgetzar: The neutral trading outpost of Gadgetzar — goblin owned and operated, of course — is the only spot of civilization in the entire desert. Explorers can find most gear that they need here, as well as a place to escape from the blistering sun and other dangers of the desert.

Northrock: The northernmost point in the Tanaris Desert, Northrock is home to a large population of kodo beasts that feed upon the shrub grasses poking up in the area. Their presence brings many tallstriders and lions hoping to nab a straggler in the herd.

Uldum: Fragments of notes unearthed from Bael Modan suggest that a great titan city lies deep within the rocky expanse of the southern desert. So far, dwarven expeditions have yet to track down the location of Uldum, but they are confident that it's only a matter of time.

The Thousand Needles

History

Before the great Cataclysm, the region of the Thousand Needles was a river canyon, the spires of sandstone shaped from the years of rushing water. The water flowed to the sea from a large lake to the east, fed by an underground tributary. Then came the demons and the destruction that threw the entire world into upheaval. The canyon was thrust above the water table; the eastern lake dried into a vast salt flat and the Thousand Needles became a sandy gorge.

Geography

Terrain Type: Hot rocky desert and rugged mountains.

The Thousand Needles rise south of Dustwallow Marsh and serve as a channel to Desolace to the west or the Tanaris Desert to the south.

The long canyon stands as a natural divide between central and southern Kalimdor. The realm gets its name from the dozens of giant, cylindrical columns of sandstone that rise from the bottom of the canyon in a forest of sandstone. Bridges have been constructed atop many of the spires, connecting pathways across the canyon from one side of the surrounding mountains to the other.

To the east of the Thousand Needles, the canyon opens out into a large, dry lakebed. This dried-out salt flat is actually below sea level. At its center stands an alkaline lake with ten times the salt of any ocean.

Inhabitants

The sere region is so hot, dry, and salty that few creatures venture here. Lizards, scorpions, vultures, and birds of prey are not uncommon and neither are centaur warbands. A contingent of goblins mines for oil in the Scorched Basin.

The spire bridges allow travelers to traverse the canyon without running into the barbaric centaur who patrol the canyon floor. The bridges are not entirely safe, however, as birds of prey will attack the unwary. Larger birds have even sabotaged the bridges from time to time.

Areas of Interest

There is very little of interest in this land, unless you have a passion for salt or sandstone… or oil.

The Scorched Basin: Thanks to goblin prospecting, the large salt flat is actually a rich source of oil. The goblins have ventured to the basin in great numbers to collect and refine the "black gold." The otherwise amiable goblins are not very hospitable in this region and maintain guards to ensure no one steals their claim.

Winterspring Valley

History

Thousands of years ago, this valley upon the slopes of Mount Hyjal served as a place for the

night elves to start anew in the wake of the Sundering. A realm of perpetual winter, the valley has long been involved in a struggle between malevolent blue dragons and the fearsome white frostsaber cats.

Geography

Terrain Type: Cold medium forest and rugged mountains.

Winterspring Valley is above the Moonglade and is the last stop along the road that winds up to Hyjal Peak.

The valley is separated from the Moonglade, lower on the mountain slope, by a thick, white cloud bank. Winterspring is a cold realm consistently covered with snow and frost. Once above the clouds, the air is crisp and clean and the sun shines often when the snow is not falling. The trees of Winterspring were bent and twisted into odd positions during the climactic Battle of Mount Hyjal. Many of the World Tree's massive roots are also exposed here, towering overhead like massive oak archways.

Inhabitants

This otherwise cold and serene place shakes with the periodic conflict between the forces of the sorcerer-dragon Cobaltann and the night elves who strive to drive them from the slopes of Mount Hyjal. Snow cats, bears, and other creatures of the wild are seen here on occasion, but only rarely due to the high altitude.

Areas of Interest

Caverns of Mazthoril: Within these caverns lies the true stronghold of the blue dragons, the forces of Cobaltann. Guarding this stronghold is an entire legion of dragonspawn sworn to protect Mazthoril. Night elf forces — including those rare few who can tame the feral frostsaber cats — often clash with the dragonspawn legion, using blade and fang in an attempt to rid themselves of the malevolent dragons.

Darkwhisper Gorge: This treacherous cavern lies along Winterspring Valley's southern slope. Poisonous green vapors bubble out of acid pools deep within the bottom of this gorge. Malevolent sounds echo from a cave at the furthest end of the

gorge, leading some night elves to believe that demons may have taken refuge in the toxic depths.

Everlook: This town is the last point of civilization before reaching Hyjal Summit. It is run by goblins as a trading post and is officially neutral to all races and factions. Even so, pilgrims allowed to venture up to the World Tree stop here, but otherwise this is the highest that merchants and explorers may venture without the night elves' permission. Everlook would offer a commanding view of Kalimdor, if it were not at such a high altitude that clouds constantly shroud the mountain's lower flanks.

Frostsaber Rock: This site is home to a great pride of sabertooth cats, ruled by the gargantuan female named Shy'Rotam.

The Rest of the World

Traveling about Kalimdor is difficult enough. Traveling anywhere other than Kalimdor is often fatal.

The raging seas of the Maelstrom remain the primary obstacle for those who would journey back to Lordaeron. A yawning whirlpool that draws in the entire central ocean, the Maelstrom nearly destroyed the Horde and Alliance fleets as they attempted the first treacherous passage west to Kalimdor. Many ships were lost, pulled down into the watery void. No concerted effort to brave the Maelstrom again has arisen. A handful of ships have ventured from Kalimdor away from the Maelstrom — to the north, west, and south. None have yet returned.

Despite the danger of the journey, and even knowing the truth about the old lands, some heroes consider themselves sufficiently skilled and more than adequately armed to confront any danger they might encounter. The ships that made the attempt can be counted on the fingers of one hand, and those who watch them leave say that they carry a full load of over-confidence and declare them lost forever. Yet given the overall safe passage of the Horde and Alliance fleets — and with the recent arrival of Grand Admiral Proudmoore's fleet, the trip is certainly possible, no matter the risks. Many people of Kalimdor now discuss the lands beyond in more than just idle tones.

Lordaeron

When Jaina Proudmoore led Alliance forces across the sea to Kalimdor, she reluctantly left behind a land falling to the undead Scourge. Prince Arthas, heir to the throne of Lordaeron, had succumbed to the Lich King's power and killed his father, King Terenas, to shatter the kingdom. Weakened by the plague released by the Cult of the Damned, the peoples of Lordaeron could offer little resistance as dread lords summoned a rain of green fire and unleashed the monstrous Burning Legion upon the land.

While the defeat of Archimonde at the World Tree marked the end of the Burning Legion's invasion, its minions in Lordaeron remain. The death knight Arthas rules all of what once comprised the human lands from his court in Lordaeron, and the Cult of the Damned continues to raise the corpses of humanoid and beast alike to add to the ranks of Arthas's undead army. The once-proud capital of the Alliance lies in ruins haunted by shades and gargoyles.

What once was a beautiful and vibrant realm is now a shattered land. Mighty forests were reduced to ash and charred stumps that reach from one horizon to the next. The blight spread by the influence of the undead has consumed many crops and fields, making food scarce. Wailing spirits surround seams of gold and iron, ripping the minerals from the earth for the use of the necromancers and their acolytes. Consumed by their ancient lust for magic and with their Sunwell lost, certain high elves of Quel'Thalas have even turned to drawing upon the dark power of the Burning Legion.

Life itself seems to have no place in Lordaeron. Any who survived have fled to the south. The dwarves of Khaz Modan give refuge to some, helping them to defend high mountain valleys where they can harvest the food and timber they need in these dark times. Their numbers are small and the ranks of the undead are legion, but they struggle to survive nonetheless. They keep hope alive with stories passing among the people of a small band of human and elven warriors striking back at the undead. Nobody knows if these stories of a "New Alliance" are true, but as skeletons and acolytes are reported protecting crypts and necropolises in greater numbers, the people dream of a brighter future.

Still, late at night, when they're unable to sleep for fear that the shadows themselves might attack, the people of Lordaeron huddle close to their campfires and wonder what happened to Jaina Proudmoore and the ships that set out across the sea. They wonder if they survived the journey across the dangers of the Maelstrom. Mostly, they wonder if they're ever coming back.

Northrend

If a land can be more naturally inhospitable than Kalimdor, it's Northrend. This frozen tundra serves as the Lich King's stronghold, as well as the site where Prince Arthas fell to the influence of evil. More than a thousand Alliance soldiers made the journey north to cleanse the land of the Scourge. Few returned before Arthas stranded his men by burning their ships. Those that did return tell stories of a barren, unforgiving land where the cold wind howls through trees bare of leaves. The rocky hills and canyons are haunted by bloodthirsty wendigo, while blue dragons make predatory circles in the sky overhead.

Northrend is also the longtime home of the ice trolls, who have lived there since they were driven out of civilized lands thousands of years ago. Vile, evil creatures who practice voodoo against their enemies, they are hated even by their forest-living of the south. Living in isolated camps and strongholds across Northrend, the ice trolls hunt the giant frost wolves, taking joy in ripping apart their prey and consuming the meat raw.

Yet the greatest evil in Northrend is the undead. When Prince Arthas seemed to be on the verge of destroying the Cult of the Damned, they lured the prince to Northrend. There, he was tempted to ever more extreme courses of action, drawing him ever further from the Holy Light and into the corrupting embrace of the Lich King. At last, weakened by his hatred of the evil the undead were spreading, Arthas drew Frostmourne and his soul was lost to the cursed blade. He was transformed to the greatest of the Lich King's death knights and gathered to him an undead host that journeyed south to Lordaeron on a quest of destruction.

Even the ice trolls know to avoid the necromancers and their undead minions as they still wander the land, waiting for their dreadlords and death knights to summon them forth.

Stormwind

After two wars and a journey through the Dark Portal, the Alliance finally reclaimed the lands of Stormwind, conquered by the Horde in the First War. This land was spared the greatest depredations that Lordaeron suffered in the Third War, but it would be some time before it recovered the glories it enjoyed before the Horde first rampaged through the Dark Portal.

As the Burning Legion ravaged Lordaeron, small groups of peasants and commoners fled south to Stormwind. Aside from the rebuilt settlements lay evidence of the constant warring of recent years. Hard-edged debris of wartime fortresses stand softened by wind and rain. Grapevines entwine abandoned siege machines, and battlefields are carpeted in wildflowers. Wolves stalk herds of wild pigs around the stumps produced by decades of harvesting and among the saplings that now grow to take their place.

Even as the humans rebuilt, much of Stormwind reverted to wilderness, closer to the world's natural state than in a thousand years. The tribes of forest trolls and the ogre lords emerge to stake claims on the wild lands, resulting in rising clashes between all races.

The Universe Beyond

The **Warcraft** universe is both simple and vast. Unlike the standard *PHB* world, Azeroth has no distinct Astral, Ethereal, Inner, Outer, Positive, or Negative planes — just a measureless nothingness known as the Great Dark Beyond. An infinite number of worlds spin within this space, and it is impossible to say whether they are scattered across the universe or superimposed upon each other.

Each plane specific to the universe of **Warcraft** is described below, including relevant traits. See "Adventuring on Other Planes" in Chapter 5: Running a Campaign in the *DMG* for more details.

Creatures of the Planes

Many beings roam the Twisting Nether, the Elemental Plane, and the Emerald Dream. Ethereal beings such as the phase spider and the invisible stalker make their home in the Nether, elementals of each variety dwell in the Elemental Plane, and most of the creatures stalking the Emerald Dream are dire animals. The intelligent inhabitants of each plane — the demons, the elementals, the dragon Ysera (and her brood, the green dragonflight) — are even more formidable. These creatures will all be covered in greater detail in **Manual of Monsters**.

Twisting Nether

The worlds of the universe are orderly, bound by physical law, comprehensible. The Twisting Nether is everything the worlds are not. It is a stream of pure chaos that surrounds the worlds and binds them together.

The Twisting Nether does not co-exist with the worlds in any physical sense. It is a completely different state of being, one that is fundamentally incompatible with the universe as most creatures know it. You cannot look from the Nether into a world and vice versa; it is much easier to move between the Nether and a world. A *shadow walk* spell will take you through the Nether as you move from place to place, and you can reach the Twisting Nether and its inhabitants with just about any planar travel or communications spell.

Entering the Twisting Nether brings you to a realm of pure, lunatic thought. Most of the Twisting Nether is protean, never appearing the same for more than a few seconds. Colors change, it grows dark and light from moment to moment, sparkles and strange sounds emit and then vanish. One moment you are suspended in nothingness, the next you are standing at the bottom of a deep canyon of purple rocks. Your next shift may be to a tiny rock suspended in a starry night, and you have no way of knowing whether the change will occur in seconds or days.

The Nether is an intensely magical environment, and some speculate that it is the true source of all arcane magic.

The Twisting Nether has the following traits:

• *Subjective directional gravity.* Movement is controlled by the will, and you can travel in any direction simply by deciding to do so. Though limited to regular movement speeds, you can sprint as long as you wish without growing tired. The Twisting Nether does not restrict you from simply appearing wherever you want within it (this is known as point-to-point movement). Merely existing within the Nether strains the mind of non-native creatures, though, and ignoring traditional physical laws is even more painful. Attempting "impossible" actions such as point-to-point movement requires a DC 35 Will save.

On a failure, the non-native creature remains where it is and suffers 1d6+3 points of temporary ability damage to Wisdom. Creatures native to the Twisting Nether, such as demons, may move point-to-point at will without any handicap.

• *Infinite size.* There are no known borders to the Twisting Nether.

• *Highly morphic.* Little shifts occur all the time in the Twisting Nether, and many changes are caused by the landscape adjusting itself to fit the thoughts of those within it. Worry about war, and the landscape may become a battlefield populated with undead soldiers. If you are lonely, your lost love may step out of a nearby cottage.

The solidity, detail, and potential danger these images possess depend on how well a creature can control its thoughts. Each non-native creature must make a DC 15 Will save each hour while within the Twisting Nether. If the save is a success, the images that the creature's mind triggers are benign or easily ignored. If the save is failed, then the images that appear are realistic and frightening.

Strong-minded individuals may consciously influence the Twisting Nether. If a creature succeeded at its most recent hourly Will save, it may take a full-round action to control the immediate environment. Roll 1d20 + character level or HD. A result of 20 or greater means that the creature may determine the nature of the surrounding environment up to a radius equal to 20 feet + character level or HD.

The changes made may be subtle or drastic. One can create an image of a dog wandering around the area sniffing others and licking any hand that is presented or place oneself and those nearby at the top of a windswept mountain. A creature cannot create any knowledge that it does not already have. If a character creates a well-appointed library, for instance, the only information in the books is information he already knows.

If more than one creature succeeds at an environment manipulation check, the one with the highest result controls the environment. This control persists until another creature makes a successful environment manipulation check.

The forces of the Twisting Nether steadily erode any attempt at a static environment. If a character creates a cozy chalet with a roaring fire on the hearth, he should not be surprised if a few moments later the fire poker has morphed into a duck. A harmful environment created requires all those within the area to make a DC 15 Will save to avoid being harmed by it, as with the hourly check.

• *Timeless.* Age, hunger, thirst, poison, and natural healing do not function in the Twisting Nether, though they resume functioning when the traveler leaves the plane.

• *Mildly chaos-aligned.*

• *Enhanced magic.* Magic is extremely powerful here. Any spell cast while in the Nether is treated as if it has the Extend Spell feat applied to it. Illusion spells can be cast as free actions and are treated as if they have the Extend Spell, Quicken Spell, Silent Spell, and Still Spell feats applied to them. This benefit does not require the expenditure of higher spell slots, as is normal with such metamagic feats.

The Elemental Plane

The Elemental Plane is a mystery to Azeroth's denizens. It is the home of all elementals — air, earth, fire, water — that were removed from Azeroth long ago by the titans. The elementals have grown attached to their adopted home in the millennia that passed since. They can be called back to Azeroth for short periods of time, but most are eager to return to their world when the spell that summoned them ends.

Communicating with elementals is difficult, and they have provided little information about the nature of their realm. Scholars believe that the Elemental Plane takes the form of a single world suspended in nothingness, and that each kind of elemental has claimed a portion of the world. Apparently, the surface of the realm is divided almost equally between deep ocean and a gigantic continent dotted with active volcanoes. If the lava flows, earthquakes, windstorms, and tsunami are as common as the scholars predict, then the Elemental Plane is a very dangerous place to visit.

The Elemental Plane has the following traits.

• *Divinely morphic*. Elemental beings can alter the plane with a thought (it is considered a standard action). Ordinary creatures find the world as easy to alter as the Material Plane of Azeroth — affected by spells and physical effort normally. Also, the landscape shifts on its own from time to time. Most of these effects are not directly harmful to those present, no matter how distressing the surroundings may seem. If a lake of fire appears, you normally stand safely on rocks within it. The environment is quite real, however, and can cause significant of harm if you plunge heedlessly into the lake.

• *Specific elemental dominance*. No one element dominates over the others in the plane as a whole. Yet each region of a given element — air, earth, fire, water — is treated as if it possesses the dominance trait for that element.

• *Enhanced magic*. Spells and spell-like abilities that use, manipulate, or create the four elemental types — air, earth, fire, water — are treated as if the Empower Spell and Enlarge Spell metamagic feats are applied them, but without requiring the expenditure of higher-level slots to cast.

The Emerald Dream

The Emerald Dream is the primal heart of Azeroth. It is a wild plane of mighty trees and powerful animals — a memory of what the world would have been like if the humans and elves and other intelligent races had never existed. It is a wondrous place, but it is also savage and deadly.

The Emerald Dream can be visited in dreams or in the flesh. Some creatures cannot help but dream of the plane and find themselves there without any preparation or conscious intent. These creatures are usually welcomed by the realm's inhabitants and interact with these inhabitants in ways that prove to be prophetic. These dreams are likely intended to steer the world in a particular course, but nobody knows who is sending them.

Other creatures intentionally use dreams to reach the Emerald Dream, such as with the druid of the wild's hibernation special ability. Any spell that involves the use of dreams to gain information or to move between worlds contacts the Emerald Dream instead of the Twisting Nether.

Dream journeys have advantages and disadvantages. They are relatively safe, and creatures that visit the primal plane in dreams will likely be welcomed — or, at worst, ignored. Bringing any physical item back from a dream journey is impossible, however. The creature arrives in the Emerald Dream with dream versions of its usual clothing and gear, but returns empty-handed to the Material Plane.

It is possible (albeit unlikely) to die from the events of a dream journey. If a creature gets "killed" in the Emerald Dream, make a DC 10 Fortitude save to avoid death in the physical world.

One can also use spells such as *gate* to visit the Emerald Dream physically. Venturing to the Dream in this fashion can be dangerous. The traveler is treated as an interloper; any creature encountered within the Dream has an attitude of Unfriendly and becomes Hostile if threatened in any way. If a creature within the Emerald Dream is harmed, all the creatures with the plane become Hostile to whomever harmed it. (See the "Influencing NPC Attitudes" sidebar in Chapter 4: Skills of the *PHB*.)

Travelers who make physical journeys into the Emerald Dream can bring things back with them when they return. Death is no dream in this case, however: if you die physically in the Emerald Dream, you die for real.

The Emerald Dream is under the protection of the green dragon Ysera, one of the last of the five great dragons. She pays little attention to matters outside her plane, but is not to be crossed within it.

The Emerald Dream has the following traits.

• *Divinely morphic*. Mighty Ysera may shape the plane's traits with a thought, but all other creatures must use spells or physical effort to make any change, just as on Azeroth.

• *Mildly good-aligned*.

They stood in Ramox's tent, the three human adventurers and the tauren who made up the adventuring party. Standing apart was the night elf hired as their scout. Brother Sebast's great treasure, a greenish sphere of pure crystal, pulsed at the center of the tent.

The night elf looked over the party as the other four leaned forward to discern the forms that swam within the crystal's jade depths. The sphere itself belonged to Brother Sebast, their nominal leader. Ramox was an old veteran of the Alliance who claimed to have fought at the fall of Dalaran. Jergen, the other warrior, was little more than a child, unblooded and eager for combat. Stormhoof, the tauren, was dark and moody, questioning everything. Yet all furrowed their brows, trying to unlock the vision within the sphere.

"There," the night elf said, looking back into the sphere. "You can see into the heart of the elven encampment in Ashenvale itself. Clear as day."

"It just looks like a forest," Ramox muttered into his beard. He was unimpressed by the vision.

"Such are the ways of the elves," Brother Sebast countered. "They twist and warp the trees to their own desires, as they do all things."

Jergen snorted and shot the scout a sidelong glance. The night elf grimaced at Sebast's words, but said, "You can see that the northern flank is but lightly guarded in comparison to the rest of the encampment. We could swing around, crossing upstream of their steading, and descend on them from that direction."

"Aye," Brother Sebast responded. "That would be the be best way to assault. We could come directly from the west, but I think we would be hung up along that river. The bridges look easily guarded and held against even an army. Not to mention things like murlocs hanging about in the wet places. On the other hand, a few people could slip down for a raid and be gone before the night elves even knew we were there." He added, almost to himself, "Perhaps find a bit of magic as well, while we're at it."

"I don't like it," Stormhoof said, his broad back brushing the inside of the tent. "It seems too easy. How does she know all this, anyway?"

"Suspicion is a poisonous thing among allies," the night elf said. The huge tauren glowered at her in return. With a shrug, she continued. "I have my own reasons to dislike these particular night elves. Let it suffice that what I say is truth and that my advice is sound. It would delight me to no end to see you raid against Ashenvale. Let it go at that."

"What are those things along the north? They look like big trees," Jergen asked, waving a finger over the orb.

"They are called ancients," the night elf replied, casting a glance with her good eye at each of the adventurers. Brother Sebast nodded sagely. Ramox looked bored, Stormhoof suspicious, Jergen eager for plunder. Seeing no sign of recognition of the name, the night elf continued. "They are weathered trees, millennia old, held in high regard by my former people. You will often find them near our campsites."

"Odd that they would leave these ancient trees far from any protection," the tauren huffed. "Look, their guard towers are all to the south and west."

The scout shrugged again. "These trees have survived for aeons with little need for protection. But there, look in the sphere. You'll see the roots of that one entangle a mine opening. From beneath its roots the night elves take their treasure."

"And we will take it from them!" Jergen said with a laugh.

Ramox allowed himself a grin. "It seems straightforward enough. It's not our fault they forget to protect a flank."

"But is it safe?" Stormhoof said. "Tell me it is safe, elf. Swear on the deities you venerate!"

"Of course what you plan is the wisest action against my former people," responded the night elf. The crystal ball's green light illuminated the scar that snaked over the empty socket of her left eye.

The tauren snorted. Ramox said calmly, "Swear by your gods. Reassure him."

"Of course Elune the Moon Goddess has given me her blessing," Oakwidow lied. She offered the assembled adventurers a mad grin. "And what sort of god would allow her followers to suffer?"

CHAPTER SIX: CAMPAIGNING

One of the greatest qualities of the world of **Warcraft** is its rich and vibrant history, shaped not just by epic-scale battles but by individual soldiers in those battles. Though the *Warcraft* computer games focus primarily on the larger battles in Azeroth's history, the **Warcraft RPG** gives you a chance to tell stories that focus on smaller groups — yet groups that are no less important to the course of history. While war is always a possibility, heroism can occur far from the battlefield. You take on the roles of heroes whose actions will shape the future for the Alliance, the Horde, and the entire world.

Running a Warcraft Campaign

While all but torn apart by decades of brutal warfare, not everything on Azeroth revolves around combat. Still, "peace" is a word unfamiliar to many. The various nations of the world are constantly embroiled with political intrigue, betrayals, and treachery. A **Warcraft RPG** campaign should have plenty of combat as well as complex machinations. It should convey a sense of turbulence and high drama, excitement and impending doom. After all, wars can, and have, begun from the slightest of slights in a king's throne room!

The time following the war with the Burning Legion represents a significant turning point in history. The world lies in ruins. The Alliance of Lordaeron was fragmented, and the undead have overtaken Lordaeron itself. The Horde is free of its ancient bond to the demons of the Burning Legion, but it has lost all it once fought to conquer. The night elves sacrificed their immortality and work to heal their ravaged homeland.

Though so much is lost, the future opens wide with possibilities.

Later sections in this chapter will address themes that you may want to touch on in specific campaigns. When planning a **Warcraft RPG** campaign, however, considering your campaign goals as a whole is a good first step.

Every adventure in your campaign is the next chapter of a grand tale in the epic *Warcraft* tradition. You do not need to know every chapter before you begin telling the story — usually, the story feels less interesting if you do, and you cannot respond as well to unforeseen actions taken by the heroes in your campaign. Nor must every adventure be a crucial moment in the larger plot. Sometimes an adventure that can be completed in a single gaming session can give heroes a sense of accomplishment that allows them to refocus on larger goals.

Yet initially deciding upon an overarching plot for your campaign can give it a structure that makes it consistent and memorable. This overarching plot may also help inspire ideas for individual adventures while making certain that the larger course of the campaign stays on track. Most importantly, it helps you to place your heroes at the center of the action.

Following are some general campaign types that you can tailor to create your campaign:

Campaign Types

• **Diplomacy:** A tenuous peace lies between the races and factions on Kalimdor. The Alliance, the Horde, and the night elves banded together to defeat the Burning Legion and have since spread to different parts of Kalimdor. The scars from generations of warfare do not heal quickly, though, and whether the orcs and humans can avoid a new war remains to be seen. Night elves have even older conflicts with high elves over the nature of magic — philosophical differences that almost destroyed the world in the era that led to the War of the Ancients. Even the unaligned races such as furbolgs and murlocs live defined by the conflicts between them.

What Kalimdor needs are peacemakers.

Diplomacy campaigns can take heroes across the land on missions to negotiate new treaties or enforce standing ones. With opportunities for heroes to succeed with a quick mind and a clever tongue as readily as fast reflexes and a sharp sword, diplomacy campaigns give heroes of all sorts chances to shine. High intrigue, encounters with some of the most powerful people in the land, and a constant battle with the threat of war are the hallmarks of a diplomacy campaign.

Some ideas for a diplomacy campaign might include arranging for night elves to accept high elf wizards who want to study the ways of "uncorrupted magic"; keeping the peace between neighboring human and orc villages; and heroes of any faction trying to get an unaffiliated group (such as centaur or quilboar) to join them.

In contrast, a campaign of a darker bent could focus on a group of heroes dedicated to *sparking* a war rather than preventing one.

• **Dungeoneering:** Caves and ancient ruins dot Kalimdor's landscape, from the Barrow Deeps beneath Mount Hyjal to the titan excavations at Bael Modan. The collapse of the Well of Eternity shattered the ancient cities of the Kaldorei, and the locations of their remains are lost to history — their secrets awaiting discovery by intrepid explorers and adventurers.

The discovery and exploration of ruins and dungeons is a classic staple of fantasy campaigns.

Campaigns that string together a number of dungeoneering adventures might be part of a quest, or heroes may be seeking out ancient treasures to gather wealth for themselves or their faction. When designing adventures for a dungeoneering campaign set in **Warcraft**, however, remember the world's rich history. Plundering a tomb will almost certainly have consequences, and the sealing away of an underground complex was almost certainly done for a reason.

In a dungeoneering campaign, the Alliance might send a group of heroes to accompany a dwarven explorer entering titan ruins. The night elves will need heroes willing to return to the Barrow Dens and make certain that demons from the Burning Legion are not hiding in the caves. A dungeoneering campaign might even take heroes to a number of ancient burial grounds on a quest for the tomb of a Kaldorei hero.

- **Espionage:** The Alliance and the Horde may have a truce, but that does not require them to trust one another. Both train and employ spies to ensure a constant stream of information about the opposition. The night elves remain concerned about the "demon-corrupted" magic their high elf cousins employ and pay for information on their brethren as well as all the other newcomers to Kalimdor.

An espionage campaign can throw heroes far behind enemy lines with little support and with secrets — their true identities, their true masters, and their true missions — that they must protect at all costs. At the same time, they often work covertly to discover highly protected information. GMs who want to keep the level of tension high in their adventures and heroes who relish the thrill of working undercover will enjoy espionage campaigns.

A hotbed of espionage on Kalimdor is the newly founded goblin city of Ratchet, one of the few places where members of all races and factions interact freely. Yet espionage campaigns could involve a group of orcs sent by the Horde to spy on Theramore, Alliance scouts sent to report on the tauren homelands in Mulgore, or heroes sent by a group of high elves to watch over the activities of the druids.

- **Exploration:** The Alliance and the Horde have established colonies on a new continent about which they know little. The orcs have allied themselves with the nomadic tauren, and their journeys with the tauren could take them far from their new homes in Durotar. The Alliance has established the central fortress of Theramore, which serves as a base for Ironforge dwarf expeditions looking for the secrets of their heritage. After the destruction wrought by the Burning Legion, the night elves must explore their own homelands to find what dangers might yet remain.

An exploration campaign forever points heroes toward the frontier, taking them on a never-ending tour of the unknown. The heroes may have a specific goal in mind, or they may journey into lands never before traveled. For GMs, exploration campaigns offer the opportunity to fill the blanks on the map of Kalimdor with excitement and adventure.

Possible frameworks for an exploration campaign include a search for titan ruins and artifacts, mapping a new trade route between distant cities, or the journey home for a group of escaped prisoners.

- **Horror:** Kalimdor holds the promise of a bright future for the Alliance and the Horde, but that future is thrown in sharp relief by the darkness that lurks throughout the land. Undead, satyrs, and corrupted ancients wander the Felwood's blasted forests. Demons and their mortal minions hide in shadows, plotting revenge against the world that humbled them. Deep inside the earth, creatures that have hidden from sunlight for thousands of years wait for adventurers foolish enough to come to them.

A horror campaign takes heroes to the darkest corners of Kalimdor and pits them against the most fearsome of monsters. Survival is a possibility in a horror campaign, but never a certainty. Heroes can be stalwart champions of good sent to combat the darkness or those of more dubious morality who run the risk of being consumed by the very evil they hope to destroy. Horror campaigns require GMs who can balance their game in the narrow gray shadows between hope and despair and heroes who are as eager to confront their own mortality as they are monsters and demons.

Though Felwood is the obvious setting for a horror campaign, other horror campaigns might involve monster hunting in the murky depths of Dustwallow Marsh, rooting out any members of the Cult of the Damned that might be hiding among the Alliance or the Horde, or heroes captured by demons plotting once again to strike out at Kalimdor.

- **Mercenaries:** Though most of Kalimdor has sworn allegiance to one faction or another, some look out only for themselves. Some were once part of the Horde, while others belonged to the Alliance. At times, they are gathered together into armies; other times, they are small groups hired for unique and particularly dangerous tasks.

They work for anyone with the gold to meet their price. They are mercenaries.

A mercenary campaign means that heroes leave behind all the benefits of being part of a faction in exchange for a chance to seek their own destiny. Of course, their choice of destiny is sometimes determined by their search for someone to pay them for their skills. Those who choose the life of a mercenary, however, do so for the constant excitement of battle and journeys to strange new places. As their employers are the sort who hire others to do difficult jobs — and in turn, their companions are the type whose loyalty can be purchased — trust (or the lack thereof) is often a theme in mercenary campaigns. If your heroes enjoy being buffeted by the winds of fate and are willing to trade what they believe in for a sack of gold, a mercenary campaign allows GMs to use potential employers to pull heroes into adventure.

A mercenary campaign might have heroes hired by an Alliance soldier who needs help to rescue his kidnapped family, or it may have mercenaries paid to journey into Felwood to recover night elf artifacts. Though the call for mercenaries to join armies has fallen silent in the current peace on Kalimdor, mercenaries who gather in Ratchet have no trouble finding work ranging from protecting wealthy nobles to joining bandit gangs.

• **The Quest: Warcraft** is full of quests, from the journey Malfurion Stormrage took to find the demigod Cenarius during the War of the Ancients, to Prince Arthas' ill-fated search for Frostmourne. Kalimdor is a new land full of ancient mysteries and magic. The Ironforge dwarves search for titan ruins and artifacts, and the night elves seek anything that will help to cleanse their land of the Burning Legion's taint. Kalimdor offers a land with legends and artifacts that can be investigated by heroes of any affiliation for any purpose.

On a quest, the heroes are dedicated to a difficult and far-off goal. Their goal can be a person, a place, or an object, but reaching it cannot be easy. The obstacles that lie on their path should seem insurmountable and quite possibly fatal. Yet the reward should be worthy of the risk: a good quest will empower the heroes at its conclusion, and a great quest may allow them to save the world. Quest campaigns are good for GMs who enjoy challenging their heroes and for heroes who are determined to overcome those challenges.

Possible goals for quests on Kalimdor might be a legendary titan city not yet fallen into ruins, an artifact that could heal those infected with the Scourge, and a long-lost druid of the wild wandering far from the lands of the night elves.

• **Settlement:** Outside of a few very limited places on Kalimdor, nearly everything lies in the wilderness or in ruins. The night elves work to rebuild a homeland pillaged by the Alliance, the Horde, and the Burning Legion. While the Horde travels with the tauren, the orcs will likely begin building villages along the paths of their wanderings as they spread out from Durotar. The Alliance has claimed Theramore, but soon the island will not be large enough for the Alliance's growing population.

Kalimdor remains a wild and dangerous land, and a settlement campaign can be built around heroes carving out areas of safety and civilization. Elements of exploration might be included while they locate the proper area, along with elements of diplomacy if there are already local inhabitants. Finally, even after a settlement is complete, the battle remains to maintain it against everything from bandits and raiders to natural disasters. Settlement campaigns are perfect for heroes who like to play the role of jack-of-all-trades and find a sense of accomplishment in everything from battle to working with their hands.

Any number of areas on Kalimdor would be perfect for a settlement campaign. Among them are the Alliance's and the Horde's attempts to settle Dustwallow Marsh and the incredibly difficult task the night elves face in reclaiming Felwood Forest. Goblin trade princes might hire a group of heroes to build new trading posts in the wilderness — a job that could take them anywhere on Kalimdor.

• **Survival:** When the Well of Eternity collapsed, so did elven civilization. The night elves and high elves alike needed centuries to rebuild their homes and culture on two continents… just in time for the Burning Legion to return and destroy everything anew. In the aftermath of war and cataclysm — or even when simply stranded in a foreign shore, as the Alliance and the Horde were upon their arrival in Kalimdor — survival takes precedence over everything else.

A survival campaign has much in common with an exploration campaign, as heroes find themselves in faraway and possibly hostile territory. In a survival situation, though, heroes are cut off from any support and find themselves forced to be entirely self-reliant. GMs define the situation in a survival campaign, and the heroes must decide how they proceed. Will they attempt to build their own village and await rescue? Will they venture to travel home? How will they get the weapons, food, and shelter they need to survive? Heroes in a survival campaign must be willing to roleplay their answers to these questions, though GMs should be certain that continued survival provides the appropriate sense of accomplishment.

A shipwreck might launch a survival campaign with a group of Alliance heroes stranded in Darkshore, far from Theramore. Orcs of the Horde might hire the services of a goblin zeppelin to scout southern Kalimdor, only to have it crash in the Tanaris Desert. Members of either faction might be exploring in the Stonetalon Mountains and find themselves trapped in the passes by a furious windstorm or sudden avalanche.

• **Trade:** As culture spreads across Kalimdor, merchants and caravans lead the way. Bringing food, cloth, wine, and other trade goods to markets from the smallest village to the grand bazaar of Ratchet, merchants can only connect distant places by traveling the leagues between them. On Kalimdor, the goblin trade princes maintain a network of trading posts that gives them dominance over trade — even if some of their merchants are driven crazy from the isolation while they wait for customers. Yet as the Alliance and the Horde become better established on Kalimdor, their merchants and traders will travel the routes pioneered by the goblins.

In a trade campaign, heroes can play the part of merchants leading a caravan or of guards hired to protect a caravan while it travels across Kalimdor. In some ways, a trade campaign is much like an exploration campaign with higher stakes—a merchant caravan carries goods that make it an almost irresistible target to bandits and thieves.

A trade campaign could be built around the efforts of the Alliance to establish trade with their allies among the night elves in Moonglade. As trade is a new concept to a race more accustomed to pillaging whatever is needed, a Horde campaign in which the orcs attempt to establish trade with anyone at all could be quite an adventure. Of course, as even goblin caravans fall under attack, the goblin trade princes always need heroes who would defend their cargos.

• **War:** The battles among the Kaldorei that brought the world to the edge of ruin, the wars between the Alliance and the Horde, the invasion of the Burning Legion — wars mark the largest milestones in **Warcraft** history. The *Warcraft* computer games tell the story of many of these battles. Though the time of the **Warcraft RPG** is an era in which a semblance of peace has emerged for the first time in generations, war may once again wash over the land in a bloody tide.

A war campaign can place heroes anywhere from the commander's tent to the front lines of a massive battlefield. While it can provide for more combat than any other sort of campaign, GMs should think carefully before launching a war campaign in the **Warcraft** world. As shown in the computer games, wars tend to reshape the world. Without considering the political and even geographical repercussions of a war, a war campaign can simply become a series of meaningless battles rather than an epic cast in the **Warcraft** form.

On Kalimdor, the grudges from two generations of warfare kindle the possibility that war might once again ignite between the Alliance and the Horde. The night elves' mistrust of high elf magic could become a campaign that would pit one race against the other. Smaller, more regional war campaigns might explore the battles between tauren and centaur or the struggles of the goblins to claim the oilfields of the Thousand Needles.

Combining Campaign Types

Once you have established the shape of your campaign, you likewise establish the heroes' expectations — potentially leading to a campaign lacking in surprise and wonder. Incorporating elements of another campaign type can help to reinvigorate a flagging campaign or at the very least provide a refreshing change of pace.

A diplomacy campaign might involve some espionage adventures, or the heroes of a trade campaign might suddenly be stranded far from home and find themselves in a survival adventure. In the midst of a war, a group of soldiers might be sent on a quest to recover a crucial magical artifact or explorers might stumble into a land of horror adventure.

Sometimes, these changes involve only a few adventures, after which your campaign can return to its planned course. If you find that you and your heroes are enjoying the new flavor of the campaign, however, you may choose to change the shape of your campaign permanently. The **Warcraft RPG** is a *game* first and foremost, and you should take whatever steps are necessary to ensure that everyone continues to have fun.

Affiliation

Every player in a **Warcraft RPG** campaign must make a choice as to her character's affiliation (see Chapter Three, "Affiliation"). All characters in the same party must belong to the same affiliation and undertake adventures and missions that further their allegiance. An Alliance campaign will necessarily be different than a Horde campaign in feel and focus. The Alliance, excepting the night elves, lives in virtual exile on Kalimdor while still looking east to the past. The Horde looks to the past in a very different fashion, drawing upon shamanistic traditions to strengthen its newly established homelands on Kalimdor. Taking these differences into account for a **Warcraft RPG** campaign is important. The players should feel as if their characters are part of a larger organization and

world, even if they do not consistently undertake adventures that further their affiliation's goals.

Before you begin a **Warcraft RPG** campaign, the GM and players must decide whether it will be focused on the Alliance or the Horde. This should be a group choice. The GM may have a great adventure idea for a Horde campaign, but don't force the players into it if they want to be part of the Alliance. (At this early stage, adapting an idea to fit either affiliation should not be difficult.)

Remember, while each race has its "default" affiliation, heroes can belong to any faction. Tauren and orcs can be in the Alliance; humans, dwarves, elves, and half-elves can be in the Horde. These individuals are exceptions, but heroes are exceptions by default. This option may open doors to create a unique, dynamic history for such a character. After all, the player must decide *why* the character left his own side. Some suggestions are listed below:

• Reared from infancy by members of the new affiliation to which he now belongs.

• His values mesh more completely with the new affiliation.

• Saved from certain death or a terrible calamity by members of the new affiliation.

• Befriended by members of the new affiliation.

• Witnessed members of his old affiliation perform a horrible atrocity.

• Disgusted with the leadership of his old affiliation.

• Magically altered or controlled.

• Is really a double agent, pretending to belong to the new affiliation, while still reporting to his old faction.*

* A double agent must be handled with care. The situation can make for interesting roleplaying, but it can cause friction among players if it is not dealt with well — for instance, if the other players do not know of the agent's true affiliation and have their heroes betrayed or even killed as a result of that character's actions.

Outside the realm of Alliance or Horde, factions exist that threaten both. Such factions include the remnants of the Burning Legion and

Mixed Parties: Game Killer or Fun Challenge?

Seasoned GMs know that players will inevitably want to have a party with Alliance *and* Horde heroes. Having all characters be part of the same affiliation is always best. Still, if you have a veteran group of players, you can look upon a mixed-affiliation group as an enjoyable challenge.

The Alliance and the Horde fought on the same side at the end of the last war. The PCs could be soldiers who met on the battlefield in that fateful time. Each still believes in his affiliation, but none can deny the bond that was formed between them in that epic battle. Or perhaps the heroes are eager young adventurers who share a desire for wealth that overshadows any political affiliations.

An even more challenging scenario would have the characters be staunch followers of their affiliations but finding themselves forced to unite against a common threat. Undead still roam the land, and both humans and orcs hate the Burning Legion. Given the choice of killing an undead or a human, an orc will usually choose the undead, and a human would most likely do the same if the tables were turned. At the least, the orc and human may agree to destroy the undead before laying into one another. That common cause could be all that's needed to develop a new relationship.

Having the heroes develop from rivals to respected traveling companions makes for just as rewarding a game as those games in which the characters start out as good friends.

the Scourge, as well as the native inhabitants of Kalimdor such as quilboar, harpies, centaur, and trolls. These creatures (and their cultures) provide adventure hooks for campaigns of several varieties. Additionally, the opposing affiliation can provide numerous sources of conflict, as Alliance and Horde members clash over old wrongs.

Remember also that while the heroes in a **Warcraft RPG** campaign are members of a strong affiliation in a grim and vibrant world, they are still people. The same goals that have motivated adventurers since the dawn of time — greed, excitement, discovery, the drive to better themselves — will motivate the characters in your campaign.

Table 6–1: General Adventure Hooks offers possible story hooks for a **Warcraft RPG** campaign.

Table 6–1: General Adventure Hooks

• The local graveyard has been ransacked. The common folk fear an invasion of undead.

• Goblins have developed a new technological weapon of great power, called The Reaper. They offer to sell this device to the highest bidder.

• A powerful satyr has taken control of a pack of dire wolves, and they ravage the countryside.

• A human archmage claims to have inherited Medivh's power and become the next Guardian of Tirisfal. Unknown to others (and even to the archmage), he is actually under demonic influence.

• A black dragon, along with its brood of black drakes, takes up residence near a local settlement, declares itself ruler of the town, and demands tribute. The townsfolk need someone to slay these vile beasts! Plus, tales claim that powerful magic items can be crafted from the dragon's remains.

• A mighty demon has stolen Archimonde's sword. It plans to use the weapon's power to control an army of Infernals, Doomguard, and fel stalkers.

The Alliance

An Alliance campaign has a distinct feel. It includes elements of dangerous volatility, despair, and suspicion combined with a feeling of new beginnings, exploration, and hope. An Alliance campaign involves a great deal of exploration, discovery, rebuilding, and, if the players wish, internal peace keeping and shadow games due to strained race relations.

Aside from the night elves, the Alliance races are living in virtual exile in Kalimdor and have yet to establish a true home for themselves on this rugged continent. The high elves grow alienated from their allies and draw distrust from the night elves. The night elves must, in turn, adjust to their new, diminished stature. Ironforge dwarves range across the land, searching eagerly for titan ruins. The humans struggle to establish their new realm and keep Theramore from exploding due to interracial tensions. As if internal strife was not enough, tensions with the Horde make everyone uneasy, and demonspawn and undead still lurk in the wilderness.

Many opportunities for heroic acts await in an Alliance campaign. One way to generate adventure ideas for Alliance heroes is to consider the interests and motivations of each of the different races that make it up.

Humans have their hands full with promoting strained peace with the other races and with the Horde. The loss of the Kirin Tor has reduced the humans' access to magical learning, and they may need to send out heroes in search of potent artifacts (of course, just this sort of quest got Arthas into so much trouble).

Ironforge dwarves feed a racial obsession with their supposed titanic ancestry. They happily work with or offer handsome rewards to heroes who discover titan ruins, particularly ruins with lots of juicy, incomprehensible writings scrawled onto their walls. Adventurers explore Kalimdor for just such a purpose. Also, the dwarves are the inventors and technicians of the Alliance and constantly create and modify technological wonders. In an Alliance campaign, adventures may focus around inventing (and field testing) new dwarven gadgets.

High elves grow alienated from their allies, thanks to the harrowing of their homeland Quel'Thalas and the destruction of the source of their arcane power, the Sunwell. A great deal of friction exists with the night elves, although this tension has not yet boiled over into serious violence. Heroes may find themselves caught up in attempts to ease relations between these factions or may be forced to choose sides. The high elves' addiction to arcane magic makes them highly suspect to night elves. Certain high elves may attempt to overcome or cure this taint, the addiction may grow worse for some, or demons may tempt others to terrible acts.

Night elves have changed the most since the days before the Third War. They retain their racial homeland, but they have lost something far more profound. The night elves' immortality is gone, sacrificed to defeat the Burning Legion. Alliance adventures may focus on the night elves' adjustment to their weakened state. Naïve night elves could make foolish mistakes or attempt acts that are no longer possible. Perhaps some rogue night elves seek dark methods to rekindle their lost immortality… though this path leads to the same magic addiction that high elves suffer — or, worse, to being transformed into a satyr. The night elves' homeland has been ravaged; satyrs, warlocks, corrupted ancients, and demons must be purged from the land. The sentinel ranks were decimated during the war, but the night elf high command has some thoughts on to how to initiate new members. They may even be open to the idea of sentinels from other races.

Demons and their lackeys remain at large, and they pose a constant (though much decreased) threat to civilization. They may target high elves as new pawns to replace the orcs, or they may strike at night elves for revenge. Without a doubt, the power demons offer draws many into their fold, and no one stands truly above suspicion.

Alliance Campaign Emphasis

Tension is high, especially between the elven races. Thus, an Alliance campaign may focus on political machinations and intrigue, as the races vie with one another for power and influence. Heroes may take an active roll in this game of smiles, either at the behest of a patron or of their own accord.

An Alliance campaign may focus on exploration and discovery, as heroes range out of Theramore to find suitable sites for new cities or even a new kingdom of their own. Some factions within Theramore may believe that it is not yet time to give up hope on the shattered nations across the sea and may send experienced heroes back to Lordaeron. As well, the Ironforge dwarves are interested in discovering any titan ruins and would pay much to any explorer who located such a find.

An Alliance campaign may focus on rooting out the lingering pockets of demonic and undead influence. The night elves may request aid to help cleanse the Felwood of demonic taint, requiring battle with corrupted ancients, rogue warlocks, and the demented satyrs lurking in the dark tangles.

Table 6–2: Alliance Campaign Hooks offers possible story hooks for an Alliance-oriented campaign.

The Horde

A Horde campaign focuses on re-establishment and reawakening. The orcs have left their barbaric, demon-worshipping ways, but they cannot return to their home world of Draenor. For years they lived a violent life on Azeroth. Now that they have come to Kalimdor and rekindled their shamanistic mysticism, they have found both a new land to call their own and new ideals in which to believe. Further, though hatred of humans, high elves, and dwarves lingers, it is blunted by the allied efforts against a foe many times greater than any of them.

Some orcs have forsaken Thrall's shamanism and still worship the demons. These dark spellcasters, primarily remnants of the Black Rock and Dragonmaw clans, remain on Lordaeron and parts of Khaz Modan. These remnants could certainly reorganize and follow the Horde to Kalimdor. Members of the Horde may seek out

Table 6–2: Alliance Campaign Hooks

- Jaina Proudmoore survives an assassination attempt, but the forces behind it must be rooted out and destroyed.

- A lifeboat washes up on Theramore with a high elf who was part of one of the rare ventures to sail back to Lordaeron. He claims that the ship was sucked into the dread Maelstrom and babbles of the terrible, eldritch horrors that dwelled within… and of a force rising from the depths.

- Dwarves hear reports of a great titan ruin deep within the Tanaris Desert. The party must escort a group of excavators to the site and protect them while they complete the survey process.

- No word has come for some time from the remote night elf village of Moonheart. An exploratory party discovers the inhabitants still alive… but twisted into corrupt and bloodthirsty satyrs.

- A group of night elves believes that the high elves' arcane addiction can be overcome by feeding their tainted brethren a potion created from a certain mushroom, said to grow only in the Caves of Deep Night. The night elves hire the heroes to help gather the fungus and ultimately release the brewed potion into Theramore's water supply.

- A night elf priestess claims to have a vision showing her that the night elves must defeat the Horde and drive the orcs from Kalimdor.

- Extremist night elves seek to sabotage an attempt by humans and/or high elves to establish a new center of magical study.

- A group of powerful and desperate members of the Alliance hires the heroes to sail back to Lordaeron, in hopes of reclaiming their lost land and riches.

- An ancient rooted close to Felwood Forest is driven mad by the evil energies that seethe beneath the ground. The ancient goes on a rampage, crashing through the forest and devouring every tree in its path.

and destroy these warlocks, and likewise the warlocks may wish to crush or conquer the Horde.

Orc society has changed much under Thrall's leadership, but it remains militaristic and focuses heavily on honor. Including these elements in a Horde campaign is important. Orc heroes may feel compelled to undertake an adventure based on the honor of completing it or the shame in failing to attempt it. Player characters in a Horde campaign may be drawn into the military structure and become an elite, mobile unit within the Horde armies. In such a case, they may even rise to positions of command.

simple as invading a quilboar cavern and laying waste to everything in sight or as complex as planning an elaborate assault against a centaur stronghold while fighting off harpies or bands of Alliance malcontents.

The Burning Legion suffered defeat in the Third War, but it was not destroyed. Groups of demons seek to regain their control over the orcs. Many members of the Horde still feel a terrible rage toward the demons for holding them in thrall for those many years. Militant orcs may be driven to hunt down the demons and crush them in acts of bloodthirsty vengeance.

In a kind of spiritual synergy, the tauren gave up much of their old nomadic ways at the same time the orcs appeared on Kalimdor. The gentle tauren have established their own homeland in Mulgore, but they still face the legacy of long conflict with the savage centaur.

The new tauren homeland and the orc nation of Durotar are each barely a year old. Ancestral enemies of the tauren — including centaur, harpies, quilboar, and others lurking within mountain caves and hidden places in the fields and plains — must be eliminated if true peace will ever be realized. These beasts provide numerous story ideas in a Horde campaign: something as

Stressing the tension with the Alliance is also important. Individuals on both sides still desire to ride out and smash each other, and sometimes they even make a move to do so. A chance encounter with a band of Alliance heroes may end with a glance and a cold shoulder or result in drawn blades and spilled blood.

Horde Campaign Emphasis

The focus and feel of a Horde campaign is necessarily different from an Alliance campaign. A Horde campaign will likely focus heavily on the orcs' return to their lost shamanistic culture and may include adventures wherein heroes help the orcs in rekindling their ancestral shamanism. Many members of the Horde feel an explosive rage toward the Burning Legion for playing the orcs as fools for all those many years. These orcs may strike out into the wilds to hunt down and destroy the remaining demons in acts of bloody vengeance.

Homeless and adrift for too long, the Horde races will do their best to hold onto their new life — from rooting out dangerous creatures to striking at the centaur khans.

Table 6–3: Horde Campaign Hooks offers possible story hooks for a Horde-oriented campaign.

Independent

In many traditional fantasy settings, the heroes have no or a very loose allegiance structure, and this same paradigm could be used in a **Warcraft RPG** campaign. Running a campaign in which the heroes are far removed from both the Alliance and the Horde and have nothing to do with either affiliation is possible. This option has advantages and drawbacks. One benefit is that neutral heroes often act as mercenaries, free agents, and impartial parties. They can thus undertake adventures for both the Horde and the Alliance, and they have more freedom to follow their own whims and desires. An unbiased faction is also required at times, such as in a border dispute between the Alliance and the Horde.

Think carefully before you allow players to choose an independent campaign. Much of the roleplaying fun comes from dealing with those within a given faction. A game lacking that element may lose much of its flavor. Plus, the heroes encounter fewer opportunities within the game to gain notoriety, wealth, and influence. Also remember that whether the heroes belong to an affiliation or not, the Horde and the Alliance still exist and will still affect both the campaign world and (probably) the heroes' lives.

Independent Campaign Emphasis

Independent heroes have more freedom when deciding where they want to go and what they want to do. With no lord ordering you about, life is a lot more open. Independent heroes can often

Table 6–3: Horde Campaign Hooks

• A pit lord has entered into a pact with a sect of disgruntled orcs. Using his blood as a catalyst, the demon has transformed these warriors into fel orcs, who now rampage across Durotar.

• Bands of Alliance warriors have attacked towns along the Durotar border. The Alliance high command does not condone these attacks — but claims it does not have the troops to stop them. A band of loyal Horde heroes must defeat these raiders.

• Centaur warbands appear with increasing frequency, attacking settlements in Mulgore and Durotar and leaving destruction in their wake. The towns must be defended and the khans defeated.

• A group of warlocks sends a message to the Horde demanding that the Horde give up their newfound shamanism and re-embrace demon worship, or it will unleash the Burning Legion onto Azeroth yet again.

• The spirits are concerned about something, but none can determine exactly what. Eventually, it is discovered that a powerful archmage has found a way to manipulate the spirits directly — perhaps even to destroy them.

• An orc warlock steals a clutch of wyvern eggs. He seeks to use his demonic magic on the unborn wyverns to make them mightier and tougher and loyal to him alone.

• A kodo beast swallows something and becomes extremely sick. It seems stronger and heartier after it recovers, perhaps even more intelligent, and bears an aura of magic. The true shock comes when the beast speaks, requesting choice fodder.

• The ghosts of Grom Hellscream and Mannoroth appear and wage ceaseless battle throughout Ashenvale Forest.

enter lands controlled by either Alliance or Horde and can hire out their services to either faction.

Still, neutrality is dangerous. An unaffiliated hero's list of allies is thin, and few places offer solace.

Other Affiliations

The Alliance and the Horde are not the only affiliations on Kalimdor. Many others exist, though often composed of rather unsavory individuals. These affiliations include the Scourge, the Burning Legion, centaur, quilboar, murlocs, and trolls, among others.

The GM may allow heroes to belong to one of these affiliations. The PCs need not necessarily be evil — many of the native humanoids are neutral in their approach and just want to be left alone. Still, others are clearly antagonistic toward Alliance and Horde alike. Affiliating with such groups can force a hero to make a difficult decision — does he attack innocents and risk the wrath of the Alliance and Horde, or does he abandon his affiliation? Regardless of such a quandary, belonging to one of these alternate affiliations will almost certainly make the hero an enemy of both the Alliance and the Horde.

See "The Enemy," below, for more on these other groups.

Affiliations and Setting

The world of **Warcraft** may be a setting unlike any you have ever played. The great wars are already fought. Now, the Game Master and players take over the war-torn world, a world that has suffered three generations of friction and conflict between races. The races are looking at a hard-won, yet still-shaky peacetime. They hope to take advantage of the peace in order to reestablish homelands and heal the wounded land. Many simply want to repair and get on with their lives. The races may never again have what they lost in the war with the undead, but they can at least strive for a brighter future.

This is not to say that the continent of Kalimdor is a world free of strife. The war is over and longtime rivals have agreed upon peace, but grudges — and malevolent forces — remain.

One partnership cannot erase the enmities three generations of warfare created between Alliance and Horde. Night elves and high elves carry grievances going back thousands of years that make any conflict between Alliance and Horde seem like petty bickering.

The issue of magic and its use is a contentious topic for all. Humans and high elves have long histories of using arcane magic, which has led to doom more times than not. Still, its power cannot be denied, and the two races are confident — some say foolhardy — that they can harness it for good. Night elves and tauren look askance at arcane magic, preferring the divine magic of nature and earth. Orcs have recently shed their demon ties and likewise pursue divine magic over arcane. While a tainted thing, many cannot ignore arcane magic's powerful allure. Divine magic is much safer, but not as appreciated by those who hunger for power.

Alliance and Horde Conflicts

The leaders of the Alliance and Horde have finally established peace after years of war. Yet more than words spoken by a leader to reverse a racial hatred encouraged over generations will be needed. The leaders claim there is peace among their citizens, but forcing the armies to unite for one (however pivotal) battle cannot heal the damage done by previous wars. The Alliance fought the Horde for two generations. Even before they understood who the real enemy was in the last war, Alliance and Horde clashed on the battlefield. The leader of the humans, Jaina Proudmoore, and the leader of the orcs, Warchief Thrall, work to bolster their tentative peace agreement borne out of respect for each other, but their soldiers and citizens plot, sabotage, and fight.

Both the humans and the orcs have built new homes on Kalimdor. While the orcs are settling comfortably in Durotar, most of the human population is crammed on the rocky island of Theramore. The orcs are at home with their allies the tauren and live in an area much like their old home world of Draenor. The humans, however, long to spread their influence beyond the cramped confines of their island and the dangerous Dustwallow on the nearby mainland. They also maintain an uneasy alliance with the brooding high elves who share their city. As the humans mourn the loss of Lordaeron, they resent the orcs their happiness with their new lives.

Although separated by water and the Barrens, humans and orcs still meet frequently. The goblin trading port of Ratchet is popular with both groups, but it lies far from a safe place for anyone. Humans have established scattered settlements on the mainland of Kalimdor, and explorers and settlers push ever further inland. Few travel near Durotar unless accompanied by a comfortable number of allies. Orcs at some watch posts think the best policy is "strike first, loot the corpse later" whenever they see a traveling human. The orc leaders know that this prejudice still lives within the ranks. Thrall desires to stamp out such behavior, but not all of his people share the same tolerant attitude. With the Burning Legion defeated, many orcs long to restart the war and obliterate the humans for the last time.

These brewing conflicts can give a GM many paths on which to set his campaign. Even though the Alliance and the Horde both recognize the truce, members often choose to let emotions rule when it comes to the old racial hatred. These issues will almost always crop up in a campaign. Your players should decide where their heroes' loyalties lie, whether they have grudges from the war and if they're likely to ignore peace in favor of revenge for an old slight.

High Elves vs. Night Elves

While the Horde and Alliance struggle with their claims of peace, the Alliance faces another problem within its own peoples. The antipathy between night elves and high elves outdates the formation of the Alliance itself. Thousands of years ago, the elves were a single people, but the high elves' addiction to arcane magic caused a split — and started the first war with the Burning Legion, which led to the creation of the Maelstrom and the destruction of the ancient Kaldorei cities and much of Kalimdor. These grudges do not go away quickly, especially among those long-lived such as the elves. The anger is not solely on the side of the night elves, as the high elves resent being banished from their homeland by their sanctimonious brethren 10,000 years ago.

Jaina Proudmoore did not expect the intense animosity and occasional skirmishes between the elven peoples when she allied with them. She now struggles to rule the city of Theramore, which houses the remaining population of the high elves and hosts many night elf merchants and ambassadors. Dealings between the elves remain within the bounds of civility, but often just barely. Meetings between night elf ambassadors and the Assembly of Theramore have ended in sharp words and halted treaties more often than not because of this lingering conflict. Arguments and even scuffles occur in the streets with surprising frequency. If the Alliance ever broke, night elves would feel no remorse for ridding the world of their magic-hungry brethren, and high elves might see an opportunity to reclaim their heritage.

Healing Old Wounds

The night elves' and the high elves' animosity for each other weakens the Alliance considerably. This situation offers the opportunity for a quest to try and repair this rift and make the Alliance stronger.

While many night elves are old enough to remember the shattering of the first Well of Eternity, most elves of both races were born after the high elves' banishment. These younger elves do not live with the overwhelming prejudice that the older elves do. While some high elves do harbor hatred of those that exiled them, a faction does wish for reconciliation.

The GM could have the heroes be recruited by this faction, hired as guards to help a high elf envoy journey to Nighthaven. The mission will require more than muscle power; it may also demand that the heroes apply their skills as mediators. Reconciliation between the elves will be exceedingly difficult, but the rewards for the Alliance as a whole (and the heroes individually) may be tremendous.

Campaigns based around the hostility between the races of elves can be epic, magic-filled battles. High elves have something to prove: mainly, that they can master the magic everyone else claims is dangerous. Night elves simply want to stop cleaning up the mess left by arcane magic, as they are still healing their forests and protecting them against further damage.

Loyalty and Betrayal

The history of **Warcraft** includes many tales of heroes who betray their race. The powerful human paladin warrior Arthas betrayed his Holy Light teachings and his people by slaughtering the town of Stratholme and losing his soul to the blade Frostmourne. Illidan betrayed the wishes of his race and created another magical Well of Eternity after the destruction of the first one — and recently took the skull of Gul'dan and became one of the demonkind himself. The orc shaman Ner'zhul betrayed his race to seek power with the Burning Legion, eventually becoming the Lich King.

Betrayal for the promise of great power constitutes a common theme in **Warcraft**. The histories do not tell whether tauren, goblins, or dwarves have betrayed their people, but that does not mean it has not happened (or could yet).

For instance, discovery of their titan creators fills the Ironforge dwarves with a lust for exploration into their past. This is a great opportunity for heroes, as they could gain notoriety and wealth by helping in the effort. If all goes well, those they aid could become legends within their race, responsible for uncovering the dwarves' lost history.

Yet what if the dwarves who the PCs help are overcome with the fever of discovery? Such individuals may steal knowledge or relics from their fellow dwarves or pursue dark studies in the misguided hope that the ends justify the means. Is the possible salvation of one's race or the defeat of a powerful enemy worth the risk? Arthas thought so when he took Frostmourne to kill Mal'ganis and defeat the Scourge… only to fall from the paladin warrior's path and become a death knight. Illidan took the Skull of Gul'dan to

defeat the demon Tichondrius… only to be transformed into a demonic entity himself.

In **Warcraft**, noble goals executed through betrayal go horribly wrong more often than not. Still, that's not to say that *this time*, it just *might* work.

More Rivalries

The rivalries in **Warcraft** do not stop with the Alliance versus Horde and night elf versus high elf enmities. The other races do not necessarily live in peace with the other inhabitants of the continent either.

Half-elves resent pretty much every other race. Pariahs from birth, these self-exiled people taste their first rejection from their parents and their parents' peoples. After that, they assume all other races will feel the same, which often leaves them to lead bitter and suspicious lives.

Night elves are not alone in their mistrust of the high elves' obsession with arcane magic. Ironforge dwarves also treat the power-mad elves warily and keep their distance.

The goblins feel a bit of rivalry with the Ironforge dwarves, as they are jealous of the dwarves' skill with gunpowder. A few more ambitious goblins plan a reconnaissance mission to discover some of the dwarves' secrets. Such an affront, if discovered, could turn mere rivals into enemies.

The Role of Magic in Warcraft

Magic is the source of many of the problems facing the races of Kalimdor today. Dabbling in arcane magic inevitably leads to tragedy. Several of the races have wisely turned instead to the practice of divine magic to meet their needs.

Still, there's no arguing that victory against the Burning Legion relied upon the use of magic. When the various affiliations' spellcasters united, wielding both arcane and divine magic, the power was sufficient to drive back the forces of the Scourge and the Burning Legion.

No one disputes the claim that arcane magic is powerful. Many worry that it is *too* powerful. The use of arcane magic has brought the Burning Legion to the world more than once, and arcane magic corrupted the formerly peaceful orc shamans. Its allure was the force behind the split of the elven races. Arcane magic is tainted, destructive power that some believe guarantees doom to its wielder. A more dangerous tool cannot be found on Kalimdor, and yet many races still attempt to control it.

Divine magic, by contrast, is a purer force. The magic of the shamans and druids comes from nature, the elements, or faith. These practitioners become healers or druids of the wild, praising the natural force that runs through them and manifests in miracles.

Night elves are devotees of the natural arts, having shunned the arcane taint long ago. Their druids are powerful, spiritual leaders, admired by their society. Orcs are returning to their older ways, having purged the arcane taint from their spirits. Their shamans are now leaders in the society and try to focus the orc warriors away from their violent pasts to a more devout existence.

High elves are the least likely to devote considerable time to divine magic. They see it as a weaker path than the clear power offered by the arcane. Of course, the divine path does not addict one as does the arcane… an addiction that can color opinions of other schools of magic.

The Enemy

The Third War is over, but many of the enemies of both Alliance and Horde are very much alive and well, if hiding in the shadows. Many bide their time in silence and darkness, waiting for the right opportunity to unleash their vicious plans.

Hidden throughout the broken, war torn land are sinister death and demon cults, vengeful demons, and implacable undead. Then there are the more prosaic, though no less dangerous threats in the form of centaur, harpies, and quilboar.

Demon Cults

During the reign of the Burning Legion, mortals from great lords to lowly peasants who followed demonic ways received power unlike any they had known before. Although this power was ripped away, they are determined to get it back. Many of these power hungry mortals gather secretly to practice the forbidden arts of demonology and to summon demons from the Twisting Nether. They seek to usher in a new era of power at the hands of the Burning Legion.

While cultists follow a unified agenda to regain their power, a great deal of distrust lingers between the races. As such, demon cults seldom include members from more than one race.

Demon cultists obsess over gaining magic or political power of any kind. They infiltrate communities and political structures to deceive key individuals in an attempt to gain wealth for their fellow cult members, to position themselves in places of authority, or even to eliminate a threat that comes too close to learning the presence of a cult. Cult members in public are polite, well dressed, and very difficult to find, sometimes being high members of tribal councils or governing bodies. Primarily businessmen, traders, merchants, smugglers, and clerks comprise a cult's ranks; soldiers are uncommon but not unknown in their ranks. Cult members carry on normal lives separate from one another in the towns and cities in which they live. They hold their meetings in the wilderness just beyond civilization, in dark glades and deep caves where the screams of their victims — offerings to the demon lords, test subjects for new warlock magic, or unfortunates who tumbled upon their secret — cannot be heard.

Each cultist bears an identifying mark hidden on his body that indicates his status and the cult to which he belongs. For instance, the Marapor cultists who reside along the coast region of Desolace have a brand in the shape of a six-sided star hidden under the hair on their scalp. Underblade cultists in the far reaches of the Ashenvale Forest have a small tattoo of a dripping dagger inked onto the heel of the right foot.

Other cultists have various marks and signs on their bodies.

One of the greater challenges when dealing with demon cults involves not how to destroy them, but how to *find* them. Not only do they take great pains to blend in with the populace, but cult members practice a ruthless and deadly system for keeping fellow cultists' tongues silent about their dark activities. Once a person joins a cult, she cannot leave except on pain of death (or worse). This creates a system based on respect steeped heavily in fear.

A powerful warlock stands at the head of each cult. This figure, skilled in summoning magic and able to communicate with the demons trapped in the Nether, is rarely found without the protection of cult members, a fel stalker, or some other kind of fodder he can dispose of to kill those who oppose him… or to buy him enough time to escape. Even without such servants, a warlock poses a dangerous threat. Yet the rest of the cult must never be forgotten, for even if the warlock is slain, the cult simply hides until a new warlock emerges to lead it.

Demon cultists are rarely trained warriors. Stealth and terror are their primary weapons. They do not exist to fight, but to act as the means by which the great demon hosts will someday return to Azeroth. That does not mean they don't indulge in violence, however — just in the controlled (and depraved) application of it: torture, poison, assassination, and other silent deaths.

The Shadow Council

Tales have spread that the Shadow Council — established before the Second War by the orc warlock Gul'dan — is finding its legs once again. Unlike the other cults that dabble in demonology, the Shadow Council consists of dark soldiers who train solely for the ultimate battle. They hold no meetings or petty sacrifices. Instead, they open their bodies to the demons of the Twisting Nether.

These possessed worshippers triple in strength, and their bodies become warped and deformed with glowing red eyes. No race is immune to the group's temptation. Orc and human, troll and high elf have all fallen to the desire… and the Council's ranks are growing.

The Burning Legion

The decaying bones from the fiery host of the Burning Legion litter Kalimdor. Jaina Proudmoore, Malfurion Stormrage, Thrall, and many other legendary heroes risked their lives to hold back the demons and save the world.

Some demons survived the last battle at the Well of Eternity, and now the menace continues to lurk in the forgotten caves of the Stonetalon Mountains or in the dark woods of the Ashenvale. These demons are planning, building, and biding their time until the conquest can begin again.

In addition to those demons brought from the Twisting Nether during the war, mortal demon cults are in the process of contacting — and bringing over — dreadlords. These mighty demons send their call out when they appear, summoning any demonic minions, from banshees to gargoyles and more, who await them. Heroes should learn quickly that renewed demonic activity means a dreadlord is nearby.

With the Burning Legion only a shadow of its former strength, a definite sense of ruthless revenge infuses the demons' attacks. Theirs is a slow, methodical conquest of towns, hamlets, and sometimes even large cities. Already, small areas have fallen to the demons — helped in large part by demon cults. If this process continues unchecked, the Burning Legion will ravage the world of Azeroth for the fourth — and possibly final — time.

Although dispersed across Kalimdor, the Legion functions as a cohesive entity, able to launch small-scale assaults simultaneously in different parts of the continent. Many sages and shamans suspect a leader has risen from the ranks to organize the demons, but to date they have not discovered this source. Some wonder if Sargeras himself has been reborn somewhere in the Twisting Nether.

The Burning Legion works toward a shared goal, but it operates in small groups. Each group is isolated from the others for protection, though they communicate via the Twisting Nether. Some of the groups include warlocks who spend all their waking moments researching ways to generate a permanent gateway to the Nether — vital if the Legion will regain the strength it needs to destroy Azeroth. Others are made up of fel stalkers, Infernals, and Doomguard, used as shock troops and terror weapons.

The Undead Scourge

In the wake of the Battle of Mount Hyjal, the Scourge left pockets of undead roaming the land looking for flesh to devour. The undead also consist of maddened revenants desiring to strengthen their elemental bond at any destructive cost. Ghosts also roam the countryside in sorrowful wails, seeking physical contact — but a ghostly embrace only proves deadly to the living.

These scattered undead display little organization and usually attack caravans, frontier homes, and isolated outposts. Their motivation is sustenance and self-preservation, and they have very little fear of a second death to get it.

Undead often rally around a necromancer for safety and guidance. A necromancer gives the undead a higher degree of tactical sophistication. Upon the necromancer's death, any surviving ghouls and abominations run amok, killing anything in their path, or flee to another necromancer to plead for acceptance. There are instances of one undead group attacking another as rival necromancers wage war over scraps of territory.

As in the days of the Legion, fresh soldiers are always needed to maintain undead numbers, so necromancers carve out a central location near cemeteries, forcing towns across Kalimdor to guard their burial grounds — or worse yet, place them within city walls for protection. This development has enraged the townsfolk, for not only do the cemeteries take up valuable farmland, they also carry the potential of disease. Disposing of the undead is an occupation that pays well in many parts of Kalimdor.

Rogue Liches

The Scourge no longer answers to the Burning Legion in the wake of the Battle of Mount Hyjal. They walk Kalimdor with no intention of raising an army as before, however. Even a single undead draws attention; putting together a large group will surely get the local populace upset. Instead, these liches harbor a single, driving goal: revenge. They seek out those who helped bring about their downfall, first destroying all that they hold dear and then bringing ultimate retribution upon the target.

The Carcass of Durross Malfactin

A hideous abomination called the Carcass of Durross Malfactin is the result of a necromancer's experiment gone horribly wrong. The necromancer tried to instill a small amount of sentience in the corpse of a human knight named Durross Malfactin so that it could lead larger groups of the mutated corpses. Tiny as it was, the abomination's intelligence proved enough to surprise the necromancer: the Carcass killed the old mage as he slept. It is said to roam the Barrens in search of bodies to sew onto its already gargantuan corpse.

Other Races and Mundane Creatures

Beyond the races of Alliance and Horde, beyond the corrupt Burning Legion and insidious Scourge, other beings roam the land of Kalimdor. Some, such as the furbolgs, quilboar, and vultures, work simply for self-preservation. Others, such as centaur and satyrs, carry the mantle of ancient feuds. Though they may not threaten global destruction, these sorts offer dangers of their own.

Some races encountered may bear aggressions toward the heroes, whether due to a grudge at being forced from their native lands or to simple hatred of anything different from themselves. The most common of these races are the centaur, satyrs, and harpies. The centaur tribes are long-time enemies of the tauren and happily carry that enmity over to orcs. Satyrs are corrupt night elves who despise their uncorrupted cousins. Harpies just plain hate everyone.

Though these beings are certainly hostile, only a foolish hero thinks such hostility means they are stupid. Centaur, satyrs, and harpies can act in a surprisingly well-organized fashion — centaur and satyrs are even known to work together. Satyrs especially love woodland ambushes, and harpies build amazingly defended nests high on the mountain slopes.

Other races — notably furbolgs and quilboar — are less aggressive, though no less dangerous. Furbolgs and quilboar are more appropriately highly intelligent animals than they are fully sentient humanoids. They care about their fledgling newborn and build encampments for protection, but neither race demonstrates a solid organization or political motivation. They typically choose to flee rather than confront threats, but they will not hesitate to protect their own or to lash out if driven to anger.

Then there are the dragons. Kalimdor is host to five different breeds: black, blue, bronze, green, and red. Each breed has a different personality and alignment. Dragons do not concern themselves often with the day-to-day happenings on Kalimdor and so are rarely seen. Only in times of severe stress do they emerge to help keep a balance, as in the case of the Third War. Since then, the dragons have retreated to heal their wounded and to monitor the ebb and flow of magic, alert for the time that the Burning Legion appears again. Dragons are highly intelligent and should always be treated with caution and respect.

Warcraft and d20

Manual of Monsters includes **Warcraft**-specific versions of monsters common to **Warcraft**, but you can also use the MM. Just bear in mind a few adjustments:

• Gnolls are known for their habits as raiding marauders or hired soldiers. Though they have average intelligence, they are easily duped by promises of food or treasure.

• Golems can be found in stone, flesh, or iron types and typically guard mystical dwellings. Recent reports tell of golems roaming the countryside as if independent of any masters. Some sages suspect a hybrid form of arcane magic is causing this phenomenon.

• Wildkin (owlbears in the MM) are forthright and not unusually aggressive. These bird-faced humanoids with coarse, shaggy hair are considered an abomination by most, but actually find favor with night elves. Wildkin possess a high intelligence and often understand good reasoning.

• Kobolds are little humanoids afraid to venture into the light for fear of their own shadows. Still, they fight ferociously to the death once backed into a corner.

COMING NEXT FOR

THE ROLEPLAYING GAME

September 2003

Manual of Monsters™

Here Be Dragons… and Demons… and Zombies!

From the merciless Burning Legion to the five draconic broods, from the undead Scourge to the savage centaur, the world of Azeroth is rife with malevolent creatures. **Manual of Monsters** takes the many monsters and allies from the hugely popular series of *Warcraft*® real-time strategy computer games and translates them for **Dungeons & Dragons® Warcraft® the Roleplaying Game.**

A hardcover monster sourcebook for players and GMs of revised 3rd Edition rules

Retail Price: $29.95 U.S.

UPCOMING BOOKS FOR

WARCRAFT®
THE ROLEPLAYING GAME

November 2003

Alliance and Horde Compendium™

Individual heroes skirmish and mighty armies clash in this core sourcebook for **Dungeons & Dragons® Warcraft® the Roleplaying Game**. You'll find more new races, prestige classes, spells, and equipment to take up arms against the enemy. Also included is material from Blizzard's new *Warcraft® III: The Frozen Throne™* RTS expansion and mass combat rules drawn from Malhavoc Press's **Cry Havoc™** by Skip Williams!

A character sourcebook for players and GMs of revised 3rd-Edition rules

$24.95 U.S.

February 2004

Magic & Mayhem™

Sorcerers and wizards truck with demons while tinkers and engineers build mighty engines of battle in this sourcebook for **Dungeons & Dragons® Warcraft® the Roleplaying Game**, based on the popular series of *Warcraft®* real-time strategy computer games. **Magic & Mayhem** offers a wealth of spells, magic items, feats and technology. Hardcover.

A hardcover sourcebook of magic and fantasy technology for players and GMs of revised 3rd-Edition rules

$29.99 U.S.

April 2004

Lands of Azeroth™

Travel beyond the wastelands of Southern Kalimdor; visit the ghost-haunted remnants of the human nation of Lordaeron; journey to the Ironforge dwarves' thriving homeland; take the war to the enemy in Northrend; explore the wonders and horrors beneath the Maelstrom. This campaign setting sourcebook presents the entirety of Azeroth — the World of *Warcraft* — as well as an up-to-date history of events from the world's birth to its current tumultuous state. Hardcover.

A hardcover campaign setting book for players and GMs of 3rd-Edition rules

$34.99 U.S.

WORLD OF WARCRAFT

For generations, mighty
warriors have heeded your
command and battled for control
of Azeroth. Now it's your turn. Descend
into the World of Warcraft™ and join thousands
of adventurers in an online world of myth,
magic and legendary chaos.

Your definition of epic adventure is about to be shattered...

COMING SOON

Icecrow

Azjo

NORT

MAEL

Nighthaven

Mount Hyjal

Orgrimmar

DUROTAR

Thunder Bluff

MULGORE

The Tanaris Desert

The Un'Goro
Crater

Kazan

KALIMDOR